# HISTORY'S
# GREATEST
# LIES

Text © 2009 Fair Winds Press

First published in the USA in 2009 by
Fair Winds Press, a member of
Quayside Publishing Group
100 Cummings Center
Suite 406-L
Beverly, MA 01915-6101
www.fairwindspress.com

13 12 11 10 09        2 3 4 5

ISBN-13: 978-1-59233-336-3
ISBN-10: 1-59233-336-2

Library of Congress Cataloging-in-Publication Data

Weir, William, 1928-
    History's greatest lies : the startling truths behind world events our
history books got wrong / William Weir.
          p. cm.
    Includes bibliographical references and index.
    ISBN-13: 978-1-59233-336-3
    ISBN-10: 1-59233-336-2
1.  History—Errors, inventions, etc.  I. Title.
    D10.W317 2008
    001.9'5—dc22

                                        2008032088


Cover and book design: Peter Long
Book layout: Sheila Hart Design, Inc.
The cover image courtesy of The Art Archive / Museo Capitolino Rome /
        Alfredo Dagli Orti: Nero, 37-68 AD, Fifth Roman emperor,
        marble bust
Inside cover image: The Fire of Rome, 18 July 64 AD (oil on canvas),
        Robert, Hubert (1733-1808): Unafraid to get his hands dirty,
        Nero helped fight the fire, search for the missing, transport the
        homeless, and in one case, rescue a family from a burning building.

Printed and bound in Singapore

Contributing writers: William Weir (Introduction, Paul Revere,
    The Earp Gang, The Philippine Insurrection, John Dillinger);
    Kevin Dwyer (The Goths, Jesse James, Afghanistan); Juré Fiorillo
    (Emperor Nero, The Galileo Affair, The Legend of Lasseter);
    Edwin Kiester (Robert the Bruce, Hernán Cortés); Ed Wright
    (Ramesses II, The Bastille, The Protocols of the Elders of Zion)

# HISTORY'S GREATEST LIES

## THE STARTLING TRUTHS BEHIND WORLD EVENTS OUR HISTORY BOOKS GOT WRONG

### WILLIAM WEIR

FAIR WINDS
PRESS
BEVERLY, MASSACHUSETTS

# CONTENTS

# INTRODUCTION

HISTORY LIES? WELL, MAYBE SOMETIMES IT EXAGGERATES, or oversimplifies. But you do find some whoppers, such as the second Ramesses' tale of how he single-handedly routed the Hittites at Kadesh— a battle in which he was actually lucky to escape with his life.

And there are some really evil lies, like the so-called *Protocols of the Elders of Zion*—an invention of the tsarist secret police to distract the Russian public from the tsar's incompetence and provoke them into killing Jews. The *Protocols* have had a remarkably long life. They have been used to justify the Holocaust and are still taught as fact in some Middle Eastern schools today.

This book is a sampling of historical lies and myths—the evil and the innocent, those aimed to glorify the teller, and those used to demonize his opponents. Most of us learned these untruths when we were in primary school, so this is a somewhat belated effort to set the record straight by debunking these falsehoods. We reveal the characters involved and their motivations, and detail the legacies spawned by these falsehoods.

## SCAPEGOATS AND THEIR BENEFICIARIES

The reason for the *Protocols* is obvious. The origin of most other lies is more complicated. Take the Pinocchio-nosed gentleman on our cover—Emperor Nero.

Nero didn't fiddle while Rome burned because, among other reasons, the fiddle would not be invented for another 1,500 years. But that fiddling tale is probably the most famous of historical lies, which is why it kicks off our survey. Actually, Nero was out of town when the fire started, and when he returned, he did everything possible to stop the disaster, and he even heroically rescued many of its victims.

## NERO DIDN'T FIDDLE WHILE ROME BURNED BECAUSE, AMONG OTHER REASONS, THE FIDDLE WOULD NOT BE INVENTED FOR ANOTHER 1,500 YEARS. BUT THAT FIDDLING TALE IS PROBABLY THE MOST FAMOUS OF HISTORICAL LIES.

Aside from that, though, Nero was not a nice guy. He was an egomaniac who believed he was a supremely gifted musician, singer, actor, and chariot racer among other things. He murdered his brother and his mother and executed his first wife so he could marry another woman. He so completely neglected the affairs of state that historians rate him the worst of all Roman emperors—and for that title, the field is crowded and the competition keen.

Because Nero was so bad, the story went around that he had not only done nothing about the fire, but that he had started it. Nero countered that story by declaring that the Christians—a despised minority—had started the fire, thereby anticipating the ploy used by the Protocols authors by many centuries.

Actually, attempting to create a scapegoat is a fairly common source of historical lies. Hitler had his Jewish scapegoats; Stalin blamed the kulaks, small independent Russian farmers, for the Soviet Union's economic problems. After Stalin had killed most of them, he needed another scapegoat, so he turned to the military. After a series of show trials in 1937 and 1938, Stalin executed 3 of the army's 5 marshals, 13 of the 15 army commanders, 110 of the 195 division commanders, and 186 of the 406 brigadier generals. That's one reason Hitler's legions were able to get as far into Russia as they did.

Somewhat similar to these lies, told to create scapegoats, is the story about how the French revolutionaries took the Bastille, that horrible dungeon filled with the miserable victims of a tyrannical monarchy. Actually, considering the state of most prisons in the eighteenth century, the Bastille was one of the more pleasant—a resort compared to the Old Newgate Prison of the American Revolution, a dark, dank former copper mine where Tories were confined. And at the time the Bastille was stormed, it contained only seven prisoners.

The opposite of scapegoat stories are those lies aimed to make the undeserving look good, such as the account by Ramesses II of the Battle of Kadesh. The FBI's report of the death of bank robber John Dillinger falls into this category, too. The evidence indicates that instead of "public enemy number one," agent Melvin Purvis' men killed a pimp named Jimmy Lawrence who resembled Dillinger. The report greatly boosted public confidence in the FBI and ensured that J. Edgar Hoover would keep his job for a couple of generations.

## COMPLICATED HEROES AND KILLERS

Henry Wadsworth Longfellow was a poet, not a historian, and he wrote his poem about Paul Revere's midnight ride in 1860 to inspire his fellow citizens to do something about the crisis that was threatening the country—a civil war. The last stanza reads:

> For, borne on the night wind of the past,
> Through all our history to the last,
> In the hour of darkness and peril and need,
> The people will waken and listen to hear,
> The hurrying hoof-beats of that steed,
> And the midnight message of Paul Revere.

Paul Revere was a hero, but he wasn't a lone hero. His ride was effective only because of the ancient institution of the militia and the recent network of committees set up by the Sons of Liberty.

People want heroes, and sometimes they find them in unlikely places. Jesse James, a robber and a multiple murderer, came to be revered by Confederate sympathizers as a modern Robin Hood simply because he was a former guerrilla and pretended to be continuing the war against the Yankees.

Others honored him because he robbed banks and railroads, neither of which were popular with rural people. Did he give to the poor? Sure, if by the poor you mean himself and his gang. James' fame was spread by paperback books and movies.

Perhaps the biggest cause of history's lies is over-simplification. Hernán Cortés was brave, chivalrous, ruthless, and faithless—a complicated human being, but not like his lieutenant, Pedro de Alvarado, someone who liked to kill. Cortés killed only when it would give him an advantage. He tried to stop the killing by his Indian allies after the fall of Tenochtitlán.

Galileo Galilei's troubles were not so much about theology as the conflict of an abrasive scientist and an overly sensitive pope. And the tall tales about the so-called Philippine Insurrection resulted from a rather insular and naïve nation being pitched into an exotic and utterly unprecedented situation.

This book aims to eliminate some of the biggest misconceptions about historical events, explain how those misconceptions were born, and at the same time tell some fascinating stories.

# THE FIRST LIE WE LEARNED IN SCHOOL

THE GREAT FIRE OF ROME
BROKE OUT IN JULY 64 A.D.
AND RAGED FOR NINE DAYS.
WHEN IT WAS OVER, HUNDREDS
WERE DEAD AND 70 PERCENT OF
THE CITY WAS RAZED. UNDER
EMPEROR NERO'S DIRECTION,
THE CITY WAS BUILT ANEW.

# DID EMPEROR NERO FIDDLE AS ROME BURNED?

## (64 A.D.)

IN THE SUMMER OF 64 A.D., THE EMPEROR NERO LEFT ROME for his palace in the seaside village of Anzio. Summers in Rome were unbearably hot; the city was overpopulated, dirty, and offered scant shade from the unmerciful sun. Located just thirty-five miles from Rome, Anzio was like another country—quiet, peaceful, and picturesque. The cool breeze from the nearby sea provided welcome relief from the summer heat.

On July 19, Nero and his inner circle were enjoying the scenery at Anzio when a messenger arrived on horseback to report that a fire had broken out in Rome. The emperor waved his hand dismissively and returned to his leisure. The news was of little importance. Small fires were constantly erupting in the city, especially during the summer months. Nero trusted that the police forces in the city would isolate the fire and extinguish it before it could spread.

In truth, Rome was engulfed in fire. Efforts to extinguish it only served to increase its ferocity. The conflagration began in the Circus Maximus, the beloved stadium where the emperor hosted glorious chariot races and public sports. Much of the Circus had been built with low quality wood; the July heat turned the brittle benches and railings into kindling.

The hot winds quickly carried the flames toward the shops and warehouses surrounding the Circus. Fed by the highly combustible trinkets, clothing, and other inventory stored inside, the fire grew in intensity and moved over the hills of the Palatine, the revered quarter where Rome's founders Romulus and Remus were said to have been rescued by a she-wolf.

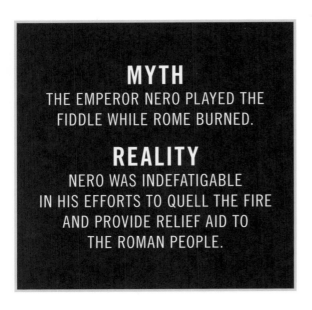

Rome was a class-conscious city, but the fire did not discriminate. From the Palatine, the flames made their way toward the fashionable Esquiline district, where it reduced many of the estates of the patrician class to ashes.

The chaos was greatest in Suburra, Rome's poorest and most densely populated district. Suburra's squalid, rickety tenement buildings and makeshift shelters provided more fuel for the fire. Everywhere, people were running, screaming, and crying. In the pandemonium, many were trampled to death. Some committed suicide by jumping into the fire. The brave dashed into burning buildings to save their loved ones. People carried their prized possessions on their backs as they fled.

Rome was a city of immigrants, and the foreigners struggled to communicate with one another. A cacophony of wailing women, crying babies, squealing animals, and voices shouting in a dozen different languages rang out in the streets.

The deafening sound of buildings crashing to the ground only added to the terrible babble. Half a century earlier, Augustus Caesar had decreed that buildings should not exceed 70 feet. Rome had been smaller and more compact during his reign. Since then, there had been a constant influx of foreigners—Greeks, Arabs, Levantines, Africans, and Asians—and Augustus's decree had been long forgotten.

As the population swelled to more than a million, greedy patrician landowners erected seven- and eight-story buildings to house the newcomers. The buildings were eyesores; they were too tall, poorly constructed, and lacked basic amenities like running water. Their close proximity was stifling, and fire traveled quickly from one structure to another. These ramshackle buildings could not withstand the fire that raged through Rome; every few minutes, another fell.

## OFFERING AID AMID THE ASHES

Back in Anzio, a second and then a third messenger arrived with terrible news: All of Rome was burning. Realizing the enormity of the situation, Nero gathered a contingent of guards and, along with his prefect Tigellinus and secretary

Epaphroditus, set off on horseback for Rome. They traveled throughout the night, stopping only briefly for the men and horses to quench their thirsts.

The party rode into what was left of Rome. Nero was astounded by the devastation. The air was thick and black with smoke. It stung the men's eyes and filled their lungs. Hot embers drifted in the wind, landing on the men and spooking the horses. Stung by the embers and disoriented by the smoke, the horses whinnied and stood firm, refusing to enter the city any further.

Everywhere there was destruction; buildings had been reduced to rubble, and the sickening smell of burning flesh wafted through the streets. Thieves plundered the abandoned shops and residences. Nero was heartsick but determined to take control of the situation. He ordered his men to put out the fires. Coughing and rubbing their eyes, the men made their way through the city.

Speckled with soot, the emperor's famous bronze hair appeared black; in the thick smoke he was virtually unrecognizable. Nero dashed from street to street, assisting the injured, offering aid, and even entering a burning building to help rescue a family. A man who did not recognize the emperor was so grateful for his help that he offered him a reward of gold coins. Nero declined the reward and revealed his identity to the startled man.

## EVERYWHERE, PEOPLE WERE RUNNING, SCREAMING, AND CRYING. IN THE PANDEMONIUM, MANY WERE TRAMPLED TO DEATH. SOME COMMITTED SUICIDE BY JUMPING INTO THE FIRE.

Day after day, unescorted by his guards, Nero returned to the decimated districts. He joined the searches for the missing, transported the newly homeless out of the city, and provided food and shelter. He opened up his imperial gardens on the other side of city to the refugees. He reassured the people—his people—that he would take care of them, and he promised to rebuild Rome.

Nero had long desired to build the city anew, but the senate, whose members owned and leased the tenements and buildings that crowded Rome, had prevented him from doing so. The wealthy landlords feared the construction would cost them money; the emperor might expect them to finance part of the project. Many were also superstitious about replacing structures that had been built by their ancestors. Now, at last, the emperor had the chance to reshape

Rome into a beautiful, cosmopolitan metropolis. He cried for Rome, but he also realized the fire presented him with a golden opportunity. Rome, like a Phoenix, would rise again, only better than before.

## RUMORS SPREAD AS ROME IS REBUILT

Nero and his court took up residence in his pavilion across the Tiber River. It was there that Tigellinus, his closest advisor, suggested that the emperor compose a song to memorialize the sad occasion. The idea of creating a tragic masterpiece appealed to Nero's vanity.

Lyre in hand, Nero stood on his terrace and gazed down at the rubble that was Rome. He plucked at the strings of the lyre and improvised a funeral dirge

UNAFRAID TO GET HIS HANDS DIRTY, NERO HELPED FIGHT THE FIRE, SEARCH FOR THE MISSING, TRANSPORT THE HOMELESS, AND IN ONE CASE, RESCUE A FAMILY FROM A BURNING BUILDING.

The Fire of Rome, 18 July 64 AD (oil on canvas), Robert, Hubert (1733-1808)

for the city. Nero's heart was heavy, and after a few minutes he set down the lyre and returned inside. He had been on the terrace for a short time, but it was long enough for the people below to hear him sing. Soon, an ugly rumor spread that the emperor had set the fire so that he might have a dramatic backdrop for his singing.

The fire lasted for nine days and razed 70 percent of the city. Four of the fourteen Roman districts survived intact. Hundreds of people died. Most of the city's beloved monuments had been destroyed, including the House of Passage, erected by Nero's uncle Caligula, the shrine to Romulus, the altar dedicated to Hercules, and the ancient palace of King Numa.

The fire had also ravaged the imperial palace. Nero was distraught over the loss of his treasured art collection—paintings, statues, and books from around the world that his agents had purchased or pilfered on his behalf. Members of Nero's inner circle suspected that he, an avowed aesthete and self-proclaimed virtuoso performer, was more upset over the loss of his collection than the devastation of the city.

The emperor devoted himself to drawing up plans for a new Rome. Construction on the new city commenced as soon as the rubble and debris were cleared away. Nero, like Augustus before him, imposed height restrictions on the new buildings and undertook safety measures to protect the city against fire. He enlarged the streets and added numerous courtyards, provided water reservoirs, and reimbursed homeowners for the huge cost of the porticoes he asked them to install in front of each house. Expedient builders received awards.

During the construction, Nero housed the refugees in the Pantheon and other public buildings that had survived the fire. Temporary shelters erected in the emperor's private garden provided additional lodging. Wine, food, and clothing, brought in from nearby towns, were distributed to the refugees. But homeless and restless, the refugees soon became disgruntled and directed their anger at the emperor. They whispered that it was Nero himself who had set the fire. Some people speculated that the theatrical emperor had wanted to sing to the accompaniment of fire. They recounted and embellished the story of Nero standing on the terrace and singing as Rome burned in the distance.

Others attributed Nero's alleged arson to his desire to rebuild Rome. It was no secret that the senate had vetoed his plans for renovating the city. The rumormongers insisted that the emperor had his men burn Rome to the ground so that he could erect his dream city, Neropolis. The rumors spread like the wild fire that had inspired them.

## A MYTH IS BORN

The image of Nero playing the fiddle while Rome burned has been etched into the popular imagination. In truth, the story is an anachronism, because the violin was not invented until the sixteenth century. Additionally, Nero's valiant actions during the Great Fire were well documented. Claims that the emperor ignited the conflagration are wholly unsupported. Contemporary historians speculate that the fiddling story was misinterpreted over time, stemming from Roman opinion that Nero, a dedicated performer, "fiddled away" his time on frivolous pursuits such as acting and singing.

Much of what we know about the Great Fire comes from the ancient Roman historians Tacitus and Suetonius, and their writings exhibit a clear bias against Nero. Tacitus was just nine years old when the fire broke out; his memories of the incident were likely colored over time. Suetonius was born several years after the fire. Both historians' accounts of the catastrophic event are based almost entirely on secondhand information and reflect public opinion of Nero at that time. Fierce critics of the emperor, the men downplayed his good deeds, accusing him of arson and callously singing while his city burned. Nero's enduring bad reputation can be traced back to this early negative press.

There are reliable accounts of Nero singing and plucking at the strings of a lyre while taking a break from fighting the fire. Such accounts continue to eclipse those of the emperor's heroic efforts to quell the flame and comfort the populace.

## THE CRIMES OF THE CAESAR

People who doubted that the emperor was capable of setting the fire were quickly reminded by his critics of his ignoble past. Just a few years earlier, the man who now plied them with wine had engaged in a horrific campaign of deceit and murder.

He'd stolen the throne from his stepbrother, Britannicus, who later died under mysterious circumstances. Most Romans—including Nero's own mother— believed that the emperor had poisoned the young man. Nero also banished his

first wife, Octavia, levied unfounded charges of adultery against her, and finally sentenced her to death so that he could marry the beautiful Poppaea Sabina.

Most egregious of all was the murder of his mother, Agrippina.

The daughter of the great Roman hero Germanicus, Agrippina possessed a regal bearing, angular beauty, and ruthless ambition. As members of the imperial family, she and her siblings were raised in the palace. Surrounded by the constant intrigues of the court, Agrippina mastered the art of manipulation. She had many admirers, but her incestuous relationship with her brother Caligula scandalized the court. To mitigate the damage, her uncle, the Emperor Tiberius, married her off to Gnaeus Domitius Ahenobarbus, a wealthy, dishonest man from a distinguished Roman family. The newlyweds loathed each other and spent most of their married life apart. Nero was conceived during a brief and rare reconciliation.

After Tiberius' death in 37 A.D., Caligula became emperor. His debauchery knew no bounds. He engaged in sexual affairs with men, women, and family members. He decreed that emperors were exempt from incest laws and then

NERO HAD LONG DESIRED TO RENOVATE ROME. A RUMOR SPREAD THROUGH THE DEVASTATED CITY THAT THE EMPEROR HIMSELF HAD SET THE FIRE IN AN ATTEMPT TO CIRCUMVENT THE SENATE, WHICH CONSISTENTLY VETOED HIS PLANS TO MODERNIZE ROME.

Nero (AD 37-68) holding a golden lute with Rome in flames, from 'Quo Vadis' by Henryk Sienkiewicz, published 1897 (oil on canvas), Pyle, Howard (1853-1911)

# THE MAN BEHIND THE MYTH

Born Lucius Domitius Aheno-barbus on December 15, AD 37, the boy called Nero harbored a life-long love for music and theater that bordered on obsession. He was expressive, theatrical, and exuberant, much to his mother Agrippina's chagrin. An emperor was expected to be solemn and reserved, but Nero's bonhomie was irrepressible.

Nero was just sixteen when he became the Roman emperor. His youth, compassion, and generosity quickly endeared him to the masses. According to an ancient Roman saying, the public is easily placated with *panem et circensus*—bread and circuses. Nero took the adage to heart, spending great sums of money on banquets, concerts, circuses, and sporting events for the public. This overt attention to the proletariat alienated and angered the senate. Their disapproval mattered little to the young emperor—the public adored him, and he was intoxicated with his great popularity.

The first five years of his reign represented an unprecedented period of peace and harmony in Rome. Nero's advisors, the Praetorian Prefect Afranius Burrus and statesman and philosopher Lucius Annaeus Seneca, encouraged the young ruler to embrace a policy of clemency and forgo

the brutal treason trials and executions that had previously been the norm at the palace. Nero was content to follow their advice. In reality, he cared little for politics and fancied himself an artist.

While Burrus and Seneca tended to the affairs of the state, the emperor read and wrote poetry, studied the Greek tragedies, and took singing lessons. Agrippina's efforts to redirect Nero's attention were in vain. To the horror of the imperial court, Nero took to the stage, entertaining the masses with his singing and by performing in classical Greek plays. Although his behavior scandalized the upper classes, the rest of the public was initially thrilled by Nero's performances.

Roman audiences were notoriously demanding and vocal with their praise and their criticism. Fearing the crowd's response, the emperor's counselors secretly filled the audience with paid applauders. Spurred on by the applause and the constant flattery of his subjects, Nero routinely remained on stage for hours, treating the crowd to numerous encores.

Eventually, the public tired of the emperor's marathon performances. Nero played to a captive audience—literally. While he was onstage, the doors to the theater were kept

locked. No one was permitted to leave. Desperate to be excused, one man pretended to die, regaining consciousness only after he was carried outside the theater.

## Victims and Vices

Burrus and Seneca had their hands full with the theatrical emperor. For amusement, the emperor and his motley band of friends made late night raids on the city. With Nero incognito, they made catcalls at the women and started fistfights with the men. One victim fought back, leaving the emperor with a black eye. Later, he committed suicide when he learned his opponent's true identity.

Nero's advisors did their best to rein in the young emperor. Hoping to redirect his energies, they even arranged for him to take a mistress, a quiet freedwoman named Acte.

The peace and harmony that had marked the beginning of Nero's reign began to erode. He ordered the executions of his mother and his wife. In 62 AD, Burrus died of an illness and was replaced by Sophonius Tigellinus, a corrupt, exceedingly cruel Sicilian whose affair with Agrippina a decade earlier had led the Emperor Caligula to banish him from Rome.

Nero was particularly susceptible to his new advisor's

influence. Tigellinus persuaded the emperor to resurrect the infamous treason trials. Nero had already crossed the rubicon when he had Agrippina murdered, and now he eagerly ordered dozens of officials to commit suicide. He became drunk on power. Fearing for his own safety, Seneca begged to be permitted to retire, citing his advanced age and alleged health problems. Nero begrudgingly replaced him with the senator Faenius Rufus.

Without Burrus and Seneca by his side to advocate clemency and restraint, Nero descended into tyranny. He had countless people sentenced to death on trumped up charges. He spent exorbitant amounts of money decorating his palace and entertaining his friends. He abandoned his duties as emperor in order to become a stage actor. By 68 A.D., Nero was oblivious to the needs of the empire. Informed of an uprising, the delusional emperor believed he could win the hostile troops over with his singing.

promptly married his sister Julia. Caligula's love for Julia did not diminish his lust for Agrippina, who had taken the horse trader Tigellinus as a lover. In a fit of jealousy, Caligula banished them both from Rome. Snatched from his mother's arms, two-year-old Nero was sent to live with an aunt. A year later the boy's father, Domitius, died.

In 49 A.D. Caligula was assassinated, and his uncle Claudius ascended the throne. He recalled his niece Agrippina to Rome and reunited her with Nero. Agrippina waged a successful campaign to seduce Claudius and discredit his wife, Messalina. Incest, though frowned upon, was pervasive in the royal family. After orchestrating Messalina's murder, Agrippina ingratiated herself into Claudius' affairs, marrying the emperor and convincing him to adopt Nero and name him his successor over his biological son, the dim-witted, epileptic Britannicus.

Politically ambitious, Agrippina used her cunning and sexual prowess to gain the throne for her only son. She was ruthless in her quest for power, murdering anyone she perceived as a rival. Her efforts paid off: Nero ascended to the throne when he was just sixteen years old. Agrippina saw herself and Nero as co-rulers of the Roman Empire. Coins issued during the beginning of Nero's reign bear the images of the emperor *and* his mother.

## AGRIPPINA DEMANDED ABSOLUTE OBEDIENCE FROM HER SON, AND WHEN NERO BEGAN TO EXERT HIS INDEPENDENCE, SHE BECAME ENRAGED. SHE CONSPIRED AGAINST HIM AND HATCHED A PLOT TO HAVE HIM ASSASSINATED.

However, once Nero settled into his role as emperor he began to resent Agrippina's interference in governmental matters. He eschewed her advice; she wanted him to rule with an iron fist and advocated sentencing traitors, criminals, and rivals to death. Nero favored clemency and chose to banish, rather than execute, the most serious offenders.

Agrippina demanded absolute obedience from her son, and when Nero began to exert his independence, she became enraged. Her love for him slowly turned into hate. She conspired against him and hatched a plot to have him assassinated. Agrippina openly threatened to have him killed and replace him on the throne with Britannicus. During dinner one evening, Britannicus fell writhing to the floor. He died several hours later. Nero insisted that his stepbrother had suffered a fatal epileptic fit, but Agrippina and others suspected Britannicus had been poisoned. Not long afterward, Nero sent assassins to Agrippina's summer home in a preemptive strike.

Long accustomed to the blood lust of the imperial family, Rome was nevertheless shocked by the news of Agrippina's murder. Publicly, people acknowledged that Agrippina had been a negative influence on the city. Privately, they whispered that the emperor was a lowly parricide, an abomination. They agreed that a man who murdered his own mother was capable of anything.

## CHRISTIAN SCAPEGOATS

It was inevitable that the rumors blaming him for the fire would reach the emperor. Nero had an almost pathological need for popularity, and the rumors deeply upset him. He wondered whether the fire had been an accident or an act of arson. And if the fire had been set deliberately, who were the culprits?

It was Tigellinus who suggested that the Christians, a strange sect that believed in one god and preached equality for all men, were responsible. In Rome, many people complained that the sect had refused to help put out the fire.

Led by Paul of Tarsus, the Christians counted mostly slaves, foreigners, and lower class freedman as their members. The sect was highly critical of the emperor and of Rome, which it viewed as a second Babylon. Members of the sect routinely disseminated anti-Roman texts and propaganda throughout the city. The Romans, like the Greeks, were pagans, believing in many gods—gods that the Christians, who prayed to a single god, denounced.

Tolerance reigned in the multicultural metropolis, with differences in race and creed mattering less than social class. However, the Christians aroused feelings of distrust and hostility in their neighbors. Their monotheism and refusal to worship the emperor caused tensions in the city. Widely despised; they were considered rabble-rousers who aimed to disrupt the Roman way of life. Historian Suetonius later described them as "an uncouth, uncomfortable set of killjoys, hating the normal pleasures of life and denying the people's gods."

Eager to exonerate himself, Nero ordered an investigation into the fire; the Christians were targeted as likely arson suspects. Dozens of witnesses came forward to report that the sect had not only declined to join the firefighting efforts, but that its members had seemed to welcome the fire. Witnesses said that some Christians, overcome by rapture, had raised their hands toward the sky and openly rejoiced. They believed that the fire heralded the end of days. Their savior, the Galilean Jesus, had prophesied a judgment day would come, during which all men would be held to account for their sins. As the fire raged, some members of the sect waited anxiously for the skies to open and Jesus to emerge and lead them to heaven.

Paul and another Christian leader named Mark had urged their followers to fight the fire and assist the injured. But another arm of the sect, led by a man called Hillel, stubbornly refused to help in any way. During the trial, Hillel said that Jesus had caused the fire and that the end of Rome was near. He cursed the city and its people—heathens whom he said deserved to die. His words caused an uproar. Found guilty of arson and declared enemies of Rome, the Christians were promptly sentenced to death.

## SAVAGE MISCALCULATION

Rome loved spectacles, and so it was decided that the executions would be made public in the most spectacular way. The emperor consulted with local artists and theater directors on how best to dispose of the condemned. A mass execution, assured Nero's advisors, would surely raise the spirits of the Roman people.

Held in the Vatican Gardens, the festivities reflected a mythological theme. The emperor, dressed as Apollo, rode on a chariot through the streets. A macabre parade of Christian prisoners, some bound and gagged, others sewn inside animal skins, followed in his wake. Lashed to the horns of a bull, one woman was dragged to death like the mythological Dirce. Nero's guards tied the remaining prisoners to stakes, doused them in oil, and "planted" them throughout the gardens. When night fell, they were set on fire, serving as grotesque human torches. Their burning bodies lit up the dark sky and provided illumination for the festivities. Their screams of agony echoed through the night.

Nearly 1,000 Christians were executed, their deaths made into entertainment. It had been an unprecedented gala event, but the emperor had misjudged his people. Many were appalled at his savagery and cruelty. His efforts to ingratiate himself with his public backfired. Nero, however, was too busy to notice. He was preoccupied with building his new palace, a colossal 300-room estate he dubbed the Golden House. He spent extravagant sums of money, depleting the treasury and nearly bankrupting the city.

## THE FALL OF THE EMPEROR

Nero was never able to regain the public's affection. In 67 A.D., Rome was on the verge of famine, largely as a result of the emperor's vast spending. Dissent brewed in the streets as well as the senate. Significant uprisings against the emperor were breaking out in the provinces. Despite these pressing matters, Nero chose to embark on a yearlong tour of Greece, leaving the care of the Roman Empire in the hands of the freedman Helius.

Nero made his way through Greece, performing for the crowds in the country's famed amphitheaters and competing in singing competitions and chariot races. The Greeks were flattered by Nero's imperial tour. In competition after competition, the Roman emperor emerged victorious. His achievements owed less to his innate talents and more to his elevated social status. No one dared upstage or best the emperor.

NEARLY 1,000 CHRISTIANS WERE TRIED AND FOUND GUILTY OF STARTING THE GREAT FIRE OF ROME. SENTENCED TO DEATH, THEIR EXECUTIONS WERE A GROTESQUE PUBLIC SPECTACLE; SOME WERE SET AFIRE, OTHERS FED TO WILD DOGS.

The Christians Thrown to the Beasts by the Romans, Leullier, Louis Felix (1811-82)

To Nero, performing had become everything; governing the empire was not a priority. The Roman populace felt betrayed and abandoned by their emperor. What's more, the collective sentiment was that he made a mockery of himself and Rome by competing for worthless trinkets in another land.

Faced with a food shortage and an absentee ruler, the public grew bitter and angry. Spain, Gaul, and Africa now refused to recognize Nero's authority. Worse still, there were rumors that General Galba, a man who Nero had sentenced to death, was planning a coup against him. Helius implored the emperor to return home, and in 68 A.D. he finally acquiesced.

Nero had neglected his office and his people for too long, and as a result, he had few remaining allies. His reputation was irreparably damaged. The senate and the Roman Praetorian Guard turned against him, supporting Galba's claim to the throne. Nero was deposed and declared a public enemy; he was the first and last Caesar to receive that ignominious designation. Shunned and humiliated, he committed suicide. Assisted by his secretary, Epaphroditus, he stabbed himself in the throat with a dagger. Nero's last words were, "What an artist dies in me!"

## LOST LEGACIES

Although Nero did not fiddle while Rome burned, it would be an understatement to say that he was derelict in his duties as an emperor after the Great Fire of 64 A.D. The last in the Julio-Claudian dynasty, Nero is remembered more for his crimes and shortcomings than his accomplishments. Historians generally consider Nero to be the worst emperor in Roman history.

Yet, Nero did accomplish many things during his reign. One of the first urban renewalists, he transformed Rome into a magnificent city. Nero's Rome was sleeker, cleaner, and more functional than it had been before the Great Fire. His extravagant Golden House stands as a grand feat of architecture. Nero designed with an eye for form and function, and under his guidance, Rome blossomed. Nero's legacy lives on in the streets and architecture of modern Rome.

SECTION II

# LIES FROM THE ANCIENTS

BUILDER, WARRIOR, KING, AND
RELIGIOUS ICON, RAMESSES II HAS
COME TO BE KNOWN AS MUCH FOR
HIS MASSIVE EGO AS THE TEMPLES
AND CITIES HE BUILT FOR HIMSELF.
HE SYSTEMICALLY ERASED THE
NAMES OF OTHER PHARAOHS FROM
PUBLIC BUILDINGS, REPLACING
THEM WITH HIS NAME.

Temple of Ramesses II (1279-13 BC) Abu
Simbel, Egypt, plate 4 from 'Le Costume
Ancien et Moderne' by Jules Ferrario,
published c.1820s-30s (colour litho),
Bramati, G. (19th century)

# CHAPTER 2

# RAMESSES II: AN ORIGINAL MASTER OF SPIN

## (1279–1213 B.C.)

I T'S MUCH EASIER TO GET AWAY WITH LYING WHEN YOU ARE a god, and as far as his people were concerned, Pharaoh Ramesses II was just that, a living incarnation of the Egyptian deity Horus.

His remarkable 67-year reign was the longest of any pharaoh, yet it could have been over before it had hardly begun. In the fifth year of his reign he marched into battle against the Hittites, intending to regain Egyptian domin-ion over the Syrian city of Kadesh, which had been won and then lost during his father's reign. After being deceived and subsequently ambushed by the enemy and abandoned by many of his men, Ramesses II took on the Hittites and man-aged to beat them back almost single-handedly.

It was a glorious victory and for the rest of his reign, Ramesses II considered it the pinnacle of his military career. He ordered his magnificent victory inscribed in hieroglyphs and images onto the walls of temples all over his empire—at Luxor, Abydos, Abu Simbel, Karnak, and the Rammeseum at Pi-Ramesses.

Three versions on papyrus fragments and thirteen versions written in three different styles (bulletin, poem, and representational) have survived. Given the intervening years, the totalitarianism of ancient Egypt, Ramesses' control over literary production, and his habit of repurposing the temples of his forebears to pay homage to himself, it's highly likely there were many more versions of this heroic event.

If only it were true. Unusually for the period, a document remains that tells the Hittite side of the story. One of the tablets excavated from the former

A TEMPLE RELIEF DEPICTS A MAGNIFIED AND FEARSOME RAMESSES II AT WAR. HE PULLS AT THE HAIR OF HIS COMBINED ENEMIES, WHO AVERT THEIR EYES FROM HIS PROUD AND POWERFUL GAZE WHILE THEIR HANDS ARE RAISED IN FEEBLE DEFENSE AGAINST THE THREAT OF HIS MIGHTY AXE.

Relief depicting Ramesses II (1279-1213 BC) smiting his enemies (painted limestone), Egyptian 19th Dynasty (c.1297-1185 BC)

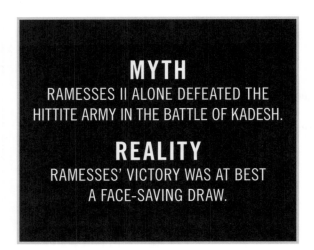

## MYTH
RAMESSES II ALONE DEFEATED THE HITTITE ARMY IN THE BATTLE OF KADESH.

## REALITY
RAMESSES' VICTORY WAS AT BEST A FACE-SAVING DRAW.

Hittite capital of Hattusas (now Boghazköy in Turkey) bears a closer resemblance to the known history than Ramesses' outlandish claims for his martial prowess. The truth is that Ramesses' glorious victory was at best a face-saving draw. He didn't recapture Kadesh, and he was in fact lucky to escape with his life. After the battle, Ramesses' army retreated back through Syria to Egypt. But by the time he got home he was a hero. What else could he be? He was a pharaoh, and pharaohs were gods.

## THE SOLDIER PHARAOHS

Ramesses II was the third of the nineteenth dynasty of pharaohs. The last of the eighteenth dynasty pharaohs, Horemheb, had no natural heirs and appointed his military commander and vizier, Ramesses I, as his successor. The eighteenth dynasty had been marked by a number of succession problems and Egypt had lost much of its power in the Ancient Near East as a result.

A major reason for Horemheb's decision was that Ramesses I had a son, Seti, who was capable of taking over from his father. Horemheb's move showed considerable foresight because Ramesses I only lived two years into his reign. Like his father, Seti had served in the army prior to his elevation to royalty. He had a particular interest in foreign policy, and once he became pharaoh, he set about restoring Egypt's former glory. To a large extent he was successful.

In the first year of Seti's reign, he led his army from Egypt into Palestine, entered Gaza, and stopped at the southern end of the Phoenician coast. The following year, Seti travelled farther up the Phoenician coast and briefly gained control of Amurru, a vassal state of the Hittites located in Northern Palestine, and also the Syrian city of Kadesh, around 500 miles from Egypt, which at the time was under the dominion of the Amorites.

Seti's northward trajectory inevitably brought him into conflict with the Hittites, who were based in central Turkey but whose empire reached into the Levant, an area bordered to the west by the Mediterranean and occupied today by Syria, Lebanon, Israel, Palestine, and Jordan. After a return to Egypt to deal with some troublesome Libyans, Seti returned to Syria where he fought the Hittites for control of Amurru. Although the battle was inconclusive, Amurru and Kadesh were ceded back to the Hittites. Nonetheless, the Hittite king, Muwatalli, offered to recognize Egypt's claim over the Phoenician states as a gesture of his goodwill.

After suppressing a revolt by the Nubians in the south of Egypt, the remainder of Seti's fourteen-year reign was largely devoted to tomb and temple building, as was the wont of Egyptian pharaohs. When Seti died in 1304 B.C., he left his son, Ramesses II, a stable domestic situation and a growing empire.

Ramesses II had taken part in his father's military campaigns. According to the hieroglyphic record, and this shows how prone to boasting the hieroglyphs were, Ramesses II had been a commander in the Egyptian army since the age of ten. By the time he was fourteen, he was co-regent, and when he became pharaoh he was still in his early twenties.

As pharaoh, he made his military mark fairly quickly. He defeated the Sherden pirates who had terrorized Egypt's Mediterranean trade and incorporated them into his army, then set up a series of forts on the border with Libya to prevent incursions. The Egyptian pharaohs, however, had great pride, and Ramesses II was itching for another chance to take on the Hittites and prove himself as pharaoh by exceeding the achievements of his father.

## SPIES, CHARIOTS, AND CHAOS

In the fifth year of his reign, Ramesses II set out with an army of 20,000 men to recapture the territory his father had effectively ceded to the Hittites. When the Ammonite king threw in his allegiance to the Hittites in preference for one with Ramesses, war between the two powers became inevitable. With more than 5,000 chariots and 50,000 men between the two armies, it would prove to be quite a battle.

Leaving an elite unit to travel up the coast of Canaan and approach Kadesh from the north, Ramesses set out with his men divided into four divisions named after Egyptian Gods: Amun, Re, Ptah, and Seth.

The more prosaic bulletin account left to posterity in Ramesses II's many temples picks up the story with Ramesses in good health in his tent south of Kadesh after enjoying a military victory at Djahi. South of the town of Shabtuna, he meets two Bedouins who tell him they were emissaries who had abandoned their loyalty to the king of the Hittites in favor of the Egyptians.

The Bedouins told Ramesses that Muwatalli was waiting together with his many allies, their armies and chariots at Khaleb, because he was too frightened of the pharaoh's might to come south and meet him. Emboldened by this news, and convinced he had obtained an advantage, Ramesses set off at the head of his Amun division toward Kadesh, leaving the three other divisions of his army to catch up.

Unfortunately for Ramesses II, the two Bedouins had not been telling him the truth. He only discovered this when his Amun division marched past Kadesh and set up camp on a mound northwest of the city. As he settled down to enjoy his rest, his scouts captured two Hittite soldiers, whom they brought to Ramesses for interrogation.

Although the details of their interrogation are not provided, it is highly likely they were tortured. This time at least, the Egyptians' informants spoke the truth. To his chagrin, Ramesses discovered that he had been deceived. Muwatalli had sent the Bedouins to spread misinformation concerning his whereabouts. In reality, he and his allies were waiting behind Kadesh to ambush the Egyptians.

The pharaoh being infallible, Ramesses' commanders confessed that they should have known that the Hittite army, numbering around 37,000 soldiers (almost twice the size of the Egyptians) was hiding behind Kadesh, ready to launch an attack. To be fair, they lacked the advantage of modern technologies such as radar and aerial reconnaissance. It would be nearly another 3,000 years before the telescope was even invented.

A RELIEF FROM THE TEMPLE RAMESSES II CARVED INTO THE MOUNTAINSIDE AT ABU SIMBEL ON THE BANKS OF THE NILE. IT SHOWS HIM MOUNTED ON HIS CHARIOT, BOW AT THE READY, AS HE CHARGES INTO BATTLE AGAINST MUWATALLI, KING OF THE HITTITES, AT KADESH.

Ramesses II (1279-13 BC) at the Battle of Kadesh, facing the army of Muwatalli, King of the Hittites, wall painting from the Temple of Ramesses II, Abu Simbel (colour litho), Bigant and Allais (19th century)

In response to this new information, Ramesses ushered the noncombatant component of his expedition (including a number of his wives) to safety, and urgently sent his vizier back to tell the rest of his army to hurry up.

The Hittites attacked.

As the Re division approached the royal camp, 2,500 of the famously formidable Hittite chariots descended and smashed through their defenses. The Hittite chariots stirred up the red Syrian dirt up with their wheels, and panic went through an Egyptian army that was probably focused on the end of a long hot day's marching and its dinner. While the Egyptian chariots were designed to defend the infantry, the Hittite chariots, which carried three warriors instead of two, were the vanguard of the assault. The thud of 10,000 hooves getting closer and closer and the clouds of dust that surrounded the chariots were enough to strike fear into the hearts of even the bravest enemy. One man controlled the horse while the other two stood ready with spears. The chariots powered through the Re division, which was stretched out over a mile on the plain.

## WHILE THE EGYPTIAN CHARIOTS WERE DESIGNED TO DEFEND THE INFANTRY, THE HITTITE CHARIOTS, WHICH CARRIED THREE WARRIORS INSTEAD OF TWO, WERE THE VANGUARD OF THE ASSAULT. ONE MAN CONTROLLED THE HORSE WHILE THE OTHER TWO STOOD READY WITH SPEARS.

With the Re division reduced to a rabble, the chariots wheeled around and headed for the pharaoh's camp. Ramesses' Amun division took the brunt of the attack as the remnants of the Re division fled back toward the camp, causing chaos in the ranks. Arrows flew everywhere. The retreating Egyptians confused the camp defenses, and many who had escaped the first charge of the chariots were slaughtered by friendly fire as the Hittite chariots set themselves to charge again.

As the dust cloud of the Hittite chariots grew nearer and the rain of arrows thicker and thicker, things were looking bleak for the Egyptians. Morale plummeted, and many soldiers simply abandoned the battle and ran for their lives. The odds were that Ramesses was about to become the first Egyptian pharaoh to be captured in battle. A total disgrace. It would cause major political instability in Egypt.

## THE SPIN BEGINS

At this point, the official history recorded in the temples becomes extremely questionable. According to Miriam Lichtheim's much lauded translation of the bulletin:

> …the forces of the Foe from Khatti [the Hittites] surrounded the followers of his majesty [Ramses II] who were by his side. When his majesty caught sight of them he rose quickly, enraged at them like his father Mont [an Egyptian God of War who Ramses often invoked by claiming a paternal link]. Taking up weapons and donning his armor he was like Seth [the red-

AN ACCOUNT OF THE BATTLE OF KADESH, GIVEN BY RAMESSES II TO SYRIA. TO SAVE FACE AFTER LOSING THE BATTLE, RAMESSES REWROTE HISTORY—INCLUDING THE OUTCOME OF THE BATTLE. HIS CAMPAIGN OF SPIN WAS A HUGE SUCCESS.

Account of the Battle of Qadesh, given to Syria by Ramesses II, New Kingdom, c.1285 BC (papyrus), Egyptian 19th Dynasty (c.1297-1185 BC)

haired Egyptian God of chaos] in the moment of his power. He mounted "Victory-in-Thebes," his great horse, and started out quickly alone by himself. His majesty was mighty, his heart Stout, one could not stand before him.

All his ground was ablaze with fire; he burned all the countries with his blast. His eyes were savage as he beheld them; his power flared like fire against them. He heeded not the foreign multitude; he regarded them as chaff. His majesty charged into the force of the Foe from Khatti and the many countries with him. His majesty was like Seth, great-of-strength, like Sakhmet [a fierce lion-headed Goddess who usually accompanied the Ancient Egyptians into war] in the moment of her rage. His majesty slew the entire force of the Foe from Khatti, together with his great chiefs and all his brothers, as well as all the chiefs of all the countries that had come with him, their infantry and their chariotry falling on their faces one upon the other. His majesty slaughtered them in their places; they sprawled before his horses; and his majesty was alone, none other with him.

My majesty caused the forces of the foes from Khatti to fall on their faces, one upon the other, as crocodiles fall, into the water of the Orontes.

The truth of the matter was somewhat different. Ramesses, rather than face the ignominy of capture, mounted his chariot and led his household troops in a series of counter-charges. He fought fiercely, inspiring his troops to take on the Hittites. However, he was helped by a number of factors.

To begin with, he was not alone as he claimed. Although his Amun division had been thrown into disarray by the Hittite attack, his personal guard, the cream of Egypt's military elite, fought with him as he mounted his rear-guard action. They were also helped by the arrival from the Canaan coast of the Ne'arin, the body of elite soldiers Ramesses had left in Amurru. With support arriving from several directions, the power of Hittite chariots, whose size made them less maneuverable than the Egyptian chariots, were forced to fight on several fronts, which mitigated the brutal power of their charges.

Perhaps more than anything else, Ramesses was also helped by the fact that many of the Hittites believed they had already won the battle and had fallen out of formation to loot the Egyptian camp. When the Egyptians and their lighter chariots wheeled and counter-attacked, the treasure-hunting Hittites were relatively easy to pick off. A number of important Hittites, including two of Muwatalli's brothers, were killed. Rather than face a resurgent Ramesses, whose Seth and Ptah divisions had yet to reach the battleground, Muwatalli made the prudent decision to retreat to Kadesh.

The following day, the two foes met again, and the battle was inconclusive. Both armies suffered heavy casualties. While Ramesses had rescued himself from the strategical naivety that almost cost him his life, the battle was far from what could be described as a victory. Despite his best efforts, he was unable to break the Hittite defenses.

In Ramesses' version of the story, he claimed that Muwatalli came to him on his knees begging for mercy. Yet the Hittites remained in possession of Kadesh while Ramesses retreated south to Damascus, then Egypt. If the Hittite side of the story is to be believed, and it makes sense because Ramesses returned several years later to try and take Kadesh again, the Egyptians were pursued by Muwatalli's army, which succeeded in taking control over Ramesses' domains as far south as the area around Damascus, which was known as Upi at the time.

## THE LEGACY OF A LIE

Ramesses had failed in his mission to capture Kadesh, had lost territories under his control, and had suffered significant casualties to his army. Yet when he got back to Egypt, he began a campaign of inscribing his "glorious victory" on the wall of temples all over the land. It was not so much a question of whether he could get away with it; Egyptian pharaohs were not at risk of being impeached by anyone. It was more a question of why.

One of the reasons is that Ramesses needed to establish his authority in the wake of his father. To come home with his tail between his legs would have undermined the legitimacy of his succession. Egypt was beginning to recover from the loss of authority experienced under the collapse of the eighteenth dynasty and while Seti had made some progress, the Hittites were strong.

By claiming victory, Ramesses helped establish the confidence of the Egyptian people in his reign. Hearing the story of his fury in battle, unwilling subjects on the fringes of Egypt, such as the Nubians, lost some of their will for rebellion while constant enemies, such as the Libyans, became less likely to attack.

Although Ramesses made a crucial strategic error in the lead-up to Kadesh, he had nonetheless managed to fight his way out of it. His willingness to believe the Bedouins and the subsequent haste that saw him separated from the main body of his army were indicative of a rash young commander still in his twenties. To his credit, he didn't make the same mistake again. In subsequent years, he went to war against the Hittites on more than one occasion. In his third campaign, he recaptured much of the terrain he lost in the second, including Upi.

In the eighth and ninth years of his reign, he extended Egyptian dominion in northern Amurru, farther north in fact than Kadesh. No Egyptian pharaoh had taken an army that far north since Thutomose III more than 100 years before. The myth of his martial prowess at Kadesh was used to strike fear into the hearts of his enemies, except for the Hittites, whom he never successfully vanquished.

## RAMESSES HAD FAILED IN HIS MISSION TO CAPTURE KADESH, HAD LOST TERRITORIES UNDER HIS CONTROL, AND HAD SUFFERED SIGNIFICANT CASUALTIES TO HIS ARMY. YET WHEN HE GOT BACK TO EGYPT, HE BEGAN A CAMPAIGN OF INSCRIBING HIS "GLORIOUS VICTORY" ON THE WALLS OF TEMPLES ALL OVER THE LAND.

The territorial gains Ramesses made in Syria and the Levant remained precarious, and city-states changed hands between the Egyptians and the Hittites on a regular basis. Ramesses's arch-enemy Muwatalli died, and the Hittites had their own succession problems. By this time, Ramesses had most likely decided that the cost of further northern incursions into contested territory simply wasn't worth the effort. At the time he had problems with Libya to the west.

Hatusillus III, the new Hittite king, had his own problems with the re-emergence of Assyrian might in Mesopotamia, threatening the eastern fringes of his empire. Although Egypt and the Hittites were worthy enemies, there were more important battles to fight.

As a result, after two years of negotiation, in 1280 B.C., in the twenty-first year of Ramesses' reign, the world's first known state-to-state peace treaty was signed between the two powers, with each side promising not to attack one another as well as provide mutual assistance in the case of attack by a third party or internal insurrection. Although the Egyptians relinquished their claims to Kadesh and Amurru, they received free access as far north as the port city of Ugarit (near Latakia in Syria) for purposes of trade, while the Hittites were allowed to use Egypt's Phoenician ports.

## HUBRIS IN HISTORY

Ramesses' lie about the Battle of Kadesh could be the first recorded attempt at snatching victory from the jaws of defeat. Arguments as to the impact of this lie have to be tempered by the fact that by the fifth century A.D., there were no people able to read hieroglyphs. Furthermore, many of Ramesses' monuments, including his entire capital Pi-Ramesses, which was doomed by the changing course of the Nile, spent centuries buried under tons of Egyptian sand. As such, his actions at Kadesh and the propagation of the lie on a massive scale were lost as a lesson to aspiring leaders for more than a millennium.

However, in the 1800s, the world of the Ancient Egyptians became an object of fascination as archaeologists and the hieroglyphs were gradually decoded. The massive statue of Ramesses II at Luxor, which was accompanied by scenes from the Battle of Kadesh, was the inspiration for Percy Bysshe Shelley's famous poem "Ozymandias," which observed the folly of human hubris. Pride was definitely a factor in Ramesses' assertion of victory at Kadesh. He was a young man, convinced of his destiny, who survived his great mistake to enjoy a long reign of self-congratulation.

An interesting parallel between Ramesses and more contemporary history can perhaps be found in the cult of the leader experienced in many totalitarian regimes. To a certain extent this began with Napoleon Bonaparte. Like the Ramessian pharaohs, he was a man of professional military talent who sought to compensate for his lack of royal birth by military victories and self-monumentalization. In his memoirs, Napoleon stated that he invaded Egypt for one purpose: glory. Thousands of years before, the pharaohs, Ramesses II in particular, had marshaled their armies for the same reason.

Napoleon, however, was more the restless conqueror-type than Ramesses. While Ramesses was happy to dishonestly immortalize his role in a great battle over the sixty-two years subsequent to Kadesh, Napoleon like his hero, Alexander the Great, was an incessant soldier.

The true political descendants of Ramesses II were the totalitarian regimes of the twentieth century. Eastern bloc dictators such as Stalin and Ceaucescu, with their fondness for commissioning statues of themselves, drew strongly from the tradition initiated by Ramesses, not least with their total disregard for the truth. Perhaps they had learned from Ramesses that if the state controlled all access to information, then the truth could be whatever they wanted it to be.

Parallels with Ramesses' Battle of Kadesh can be found in Mao's Long March and the myths of North Korea's Kim Il-Sung and Kim Jong Il. The difference is that Ramesses used military propaganda to construct political and economical stability and to increase the prosperity of his subjects, something the modern dictator has rarely succeeded in doing.

AT THE ENTRANCE TO THE TEMPLE OF LUXOR, SHOWN HERE, THE PYLONS ARE 24 METERS (79 FEET) HIGH AND CHRONICLE THE MILITARY VICTORIES OF RAMESSES II WITH SPECIAL EMPHASIS ON HIS FICTIONAL GLORY AT THE BATTLE OF KADESH. PAST THE PYLON, THERE WERE ORIGINALLY SIX MASSIVE STATUES OF RAMESSES II, FOUR STANDING AND TWO SEATED. ONLY THE SEATED ONES REMAIN, APPROPRIATE PERHAPS FOR A MAN WHOSE GREATEST VICTORY WAS A CONSEQUENCE OF CAREFUL CONCOCTION RATHER THAN BATTLEFIELD PROWESS.

Entrance to Luxor Temple, from 'Voyage dans la Basse et dans la Haute-Egypte' by Dominique Vivant Denon (1747-1825) 1802 (engraving) (b/w photo), French School, (19th century)

# CHAPTER 3

# THE GOTHS: BARBARIANS IN NAME ONLY?

## (300–700 A.D.)

T HE BARBARIANS WERE LITERALLY AT THE GATE. IT WAS 408 A.D., and the Gothic king Alaric had led his army from the eastern Roman Empire to journey westward through Greece, across the Alps, and into the heart of Italy. They now surrounded the world's capital city, controlling all means of transport in and out.

The citizens of Rome could do nothing except bide their time inside the city walls until the detested barbarians decided what to do next. They had no means of communication with the outside world and, worse, had begun to run out of food. Dead bodies started piling up throughout the city, swelling and rotting in the August sun. Then, stories of cannibalism began to spread. People were killing their own friends, it was reported, and eating them on the spot. And some people even heard tales of mothers eating their babies.

Another story making the rounds was that Serena—niece of the late emperor Theodosius, widow of the Roman general Stilichio, and surrogate mother to the present child-emperor, Honorius—had secretly conspired with Alaric to let the Goths into the city to kill everyone. The claim was based on one truth—her husband's father was a barbarian, in this case, a Vandal—and numerous leaps of logic that racists are able to make in such situations. Once a barbarian-lover always a barbarian-lover, the thinking went. The senate hastily voted to have Serena put to death; she was strangled immediately.

Two Roman delegates bravely ventured out from the city and met with Alaric to negotiate his peaceful departure. Alaric's demands included gold, silver,

ALARIC, LEADER OF THE GOTHS, PROVES HIMSELF IN BATTLE. UNLIKE THOSE IN MANY OTHER CULTURES, INCLUDING THEIR ROMAN RIVALS, GOTHIC MILITARY LEADERS WERE CHOSEN BY THE PEOPLE BASED ON THEIR SKILL AND COURAGE IN BATTLE, NOT BY BIRTHRIGHT OR THE ORDER OF GOD.

New York Public Library

> **MYTH**
> THE GOTHS WERE HAIRY, GRUNTING SAVAGES WHOSE SOLE EXISTENCE REVOLVED AROUND DESTROYING WHATEVER LAY IN THEIR PATH, INCLUDING THE ROMAN EMPIRE.
>
> **REALITY**
> THE GOTHS WERE AMONG THE MOST PROGRESSIVE OF ALL GERMANIC TRIBES, HELD HIGH-RANKING POSITIONS WITHIN THE ROMAN MILITARY, AND WANTED NOTHING MORE THAN TO FORM A PEACEFUL CONFEDERATION WITHIN THE EMPIRE.

and the freedom of every barbarian slave inside Rome. "What will you leave us?" asked the delegates. "Your lives," Alaric replied. Although they were in no real position to do so, the Romans balked at the deal. So Alaric lowered his demand for riches. But he remained firm on the freedom of all barbarians in Rome.

The deal was soon settled, and Rome's gates were opened to deliver the material and human treasures. A mass of 30,000 barbarian slaves poured out of Rome, many of them for the first time in their lives. Alaric kept his word and immediately lifted the siege, allowing for the passage of goods and food to and from the port.

## STRATEGIC SAVAGERY

Alaric and his army handled their first attack on Rome with as much (and probably more) restraint and reason as any "civilized" army of the time would have used. This was not a historical aberration; like their Romans counterparts, Gothic military leaders were often willing to use their foresight, negotiate with the enemy, and lay down their swords if it would help them strategically.

Yet the Goths and their barbarian cousins have never been able to shed their historic reputation as savages. From ancient Rome to the present day, the Germanic tribes have been portrayed as half-evolved, uncivilized beasts who did little else than subsist on undercooked red meat, have wanton sex, and swing swords at passersby.

Invented by the ancient Greeks, the term "barbarian" (Gk. *barbaroi*) itself originally connoted anyone who was not Greek, did not speak Greek, did not act Greek, and did not live in Greece—mainly Persians and Egyptians.

It's impossible to know exactly how the term originated, but one of the more accepted theories is that it is onomatopoeic: "bar-bar-bar" is what foreign languages can sound like to those without discerning ears, and so perhaps non-Greek speakers began referring to the "others" onomatopoeically. When the Romans picked the term up, they applied it, like the Greeks, to their enemies—the tribes of northern Europe. Greeks and Romans were even known to use the term pejoratively at times to refer to one another.

## FROM ANCIENT ROME TO THE PRESENT DAY, GERMANIC BARBARIANS HAVE BEEN PORTRAYED AS HALF-EVOLVED, UNCIVILIZED BEASTS WHO DID LITTLE ELSE THAN SUBSIST ON UNDERCOOKED RED MEAT, HAVE WANTON SEX, AND SWING SWORDS AT PASSERSBY.

In his essay entitled *Germany and its Tribes*, Roman historian Tacitus (56–117 A.D.) provides a painstaking description of Rome's enemies to the north. A good indicator of how Romans viewed their northern neighbors, the essay portrays Germanic barbarians as a sort of noble savage—courageous in battle but totally unappreciative of the finer things in life; religious in custom but incapable of higher thinking; dirty and smelly but hospitable and honest.

A modern historian expressed the Roman view of barbarians as people who "did not have a history but were simply part of the flow of natural history." That is, unlike the "civilized" Greeks and Romans, barbarians didn't *make* history; history *happened* to them, as it does to, say, monkeys and apes. This depiction of the barbarians has remained generally intact for more than two millennia.

Today, the word "barbaric" is used exactly as the Romans used it—to describe anyone ranging from the uncouth (loud eaters, obnoxious tourists, and the like) to the savage (anyone from muggers to terrorists). The most famous barbarian in popular Western culture is Conan, created by pulp novelist Robert E. Howard. Writing in the 1930s, Howard portrayed his subject not only as a fierce and skilled warrior, but as a smart, talented leader who, given the genre, treated women with relative respect and viewed warfare as a necessary evil. Since then, however, Conan the human has given way to Conan the barbarian, who dominates film, comic books, television, and video games. He is a one-dimensional homicidal psychopath, a man of the sword, tightly wound and itching for a fight.

One American bank has aired a series of television ads depicting prospective customers' mortal enemy—banks that charge high rates—as leather-clad barbarians running amok through suburban streets and backyards.

Another mistake made about Germanic barbarians over the ages has been the tendency to group all tribes together on the assumption that barbarians were all the same. Tacitus and his contemporaries—and, by extension, we in the present era—tend to speak of barbarians as a single group, when in fact northern European tribes, although holding many similarities, maintained certain differences in terms of religious practice, social customs, burial rites, and political practices.

Just prior to and during the Migration Period (300–700 A.D.), which marks the height of the northern tribes' incursion into the Roman Empire and beyond, the divide among tribes became even sharper. Different tribes had different goals regarding the Roman Empire, but the Goths stood out from the rest in their eagerness to attain peace with the Romans and gain acceptance into the Empire.

## UNRULY IMMIGRANTS

In 375 A.D., Roman soldiers manning watchtowers on the banks of the Danube could look across the river and see thousands of Goths amassing on the opposite side. The people composing this rag-tag horde, however, were not brandishing claymores and bellowing war cries. They were living in encampments awaiting permission from the empire to cross the river, well aware that the Huns were on the move in the north and headed toward them.

The Goths believed the Hunnic race to be the product of exiled Gothic witches having had sex with evil spirits. If the Huns reached them before they reached the southern banks, there was no doubt what would happen. Even the infants would be lucky to live.

The leader of the eastern Roman Empire, Valens, had a decision to make: Let the Goths in and have to feed and house tens of thousands of refugees or watch passively as the Huns slaughtered everyone. The second option was certainly more practical, but Valens had other concerns. He had recently lost a good portion of his army fighting the Persians. Permitting a heavy influx of Goths into the empire might make for a bit of chaos, but it would provide him with numerous males he could recruit into the Roman army to refurbish the ranks. The latter clearly outweighed the former.

Valens gave the go-ahead, and the Roman army launched one of history's greatest boat-lift operations. The great barbarian invasion of the history

PREVIOUS PAGE: IN 375 A.D., THE ROMANS HELPED GOTHIC REFUGEES FLEEING THE HUNS TO CROSS THE DANUBE RIVER TO SAFETY INSIDE THE EMPIRE. IN THIS IMAGE, THE ROMAN LEADER VALENS WELCOMES THE FOREIGNERS. HIS INTENTIONS, HOWEVER, WERE BY NO MEANS ALTRUISTIC, AND SUBSEQUENT EVENTS WOULD LEAD TO A MAJOR GOTHIC REVOLT AGAINST THE ROMAN EMPIRE.

New York Public Library

books turns out to have actually been a days-long transport of hungry, frightened Gothic refugees over the Danube in rafts and hollowed-out trees that served as boats.

The Goths didn't care what Valens' motives were. Getting their families to safety was their first concern. But they would quickly learn that putting a river between themselves and the Huns didn't necessarily mean they would be safe.

Roman officials wasted no time taking advantage of the refugees. They demanded payment for food, at times accepting children (to be enslaved) from people who had nothing else of value. The shelter the Goths were furnished with in Rome was appalling. With people dying of disease and starvation, many Goths began to wonder whether they would have been better off taking their chances with the Huns.

Even Goths who were not enslaved upon arrival existed under a sort of enslavement by proxy; the Goths were completely vulnerable to the greed of soldiers and political officials, which knew no bounds. (Reportedly, the situation was so dire for the Goths that the going rate for one dog—to be used for meat— was one human slave.)

## THE SHELTER THE GOTHS WERE FURNISHED WITH IN ROME WAS APPALLING. WITH PEOPLE DYING OF DISEASE AND STARVATION, MANY GOTHS BEGAN TO WONDER WHETHER THEY WOULD HAVE BEEN BETTER OFF TAKING THEIR CHANCES WITH THE HUNS.

Three years living under Rome's systemic corruption and logistical blunders became too heavy a price. Under the leadership of the Goth Fritigern, they organized themselves into an army and revolted against the world's greatest military power. The rebellion culminated in the Battle of Adrianople in 378, during which the Goths destroyed about two-thirds of the entire Roman force, killing up to 40,000 soldiers, including Valens himself.

## THE BUSINESS OF FEUDALISM

The victory wasn't a mere stroke of luck. The Goths had by the late fourth century become savvy military tacticians and strategists, thanks in part to the Romans themselves.

For an empire that viewed the Goths as an inferior race, it had been more than happy to develop certain relations with them long before the time of Valens. The Roman military, deployed around the known world, was not made up strictly of soldiers from within the empire.

After the Roman army's annihilation by barbarians in the Teutoberg Forest (in southern Germany) in 9 A.D., it had established the Rhine and Danube rivers as the empire's permanent northern border. From then until the Danube crossing, the Romans maintained diplomatic relations with the Germanic people living across the river. In this alliance, the barbarians served as a buffer between invaders from farther north; the Romans would assist them militarily when needed. It was a suitable trade-off for both sides.

"The war against barbarians was a business like any other; all it required was proper management," wrote Alessandro Barbero in *The Day of the Barbarians.*

The successor of Valens, Theodosius, extended his predecessor's policy to include the Goths more directly in the functioning of the empire. This was at a time when the Roman Empire was at war with itself—the Christians of Constantinople versus the pagans of Rome, fighting to decide the future religion of the Roman Empire. Simply put, Theodosius wanted to expand his military, so he initiated a policy that allowed Goths to serve more generally as mercenaries and full-fledged members of the Roman military.

It is estimated that by the end of the fourth century, 10 to 15 percent of the empire's population was composed of barbarians living in *laeti* settlements—ethnically homogenous areas in which the people could create their own laws and elect their own leaders, but were considered subjects of Rome, not full-fledged citizens, and had to supply troops to fight for the interests of the empire. The barbarian military organizations were called *foederati*, which stems from the Latin word for "treaty."

This arrangement was similar to Europe's medieval feudal system: Rome would supply the Goths with food and other sources of sustenance, and in return Gothic leaders would provide soldiers when called upon. The Goths began organizing themselves into more manageable units to facilitate their end of the pact. As their armies grew and became more organized, the Romans used them more and more.

The system worked like a dream—mostly for the Romans. It curtailed barbarian raids, put otherwise wasted farmland to good use, and produced soldiers for the army. Gothic-Roman relations were going so well that in the early 380s Theodosius allowed his niece to marry the half-Vandal Stilichio.

## BEATING THE ROMANS AT THEIR OWN GAME

The problem with the Goths was the same as with any immigrant population: Eventually, they wanted a bigger piece of the pie. A Gothic leader named Alaric, born in 375, began rising through the ranks of the *foederati*. By the age of nineteen, he was a general in charge of 20,000 soldiers and fighting for Roman interests alongside other foreign armies doing the same thing: the Huns, Alans (from Iran), Iberians, and Vandals. A proud barbarian, he wanted to see his people break free of Rome's yoke and enjoy full rights within the empire.

After the Eastern empire's victory in the bloody Battle of Frigidus against the West in 394, Alaric began to harbor greater aspirations for himself and his people. His army had suffered serious casualties in battle—possibly as many as 10,000 dead—and he believed some sort of compensation was in order. Worse, he suspected that Theodosius had sent his troops into the hottest parts of the battle with the express intention of reducing their numbers. (About this, he was probably right.)

Citing his status as loyal commander whose army had steadfastly fought and sacrificed for the empire, Alaric petitioned Theodosius to give him full Roman general status. The emperor denied his request. In response, a savage might have stormed Constantinople without much thought. Alaric, however, was no savage. He bided his time. As fate would have it, Theodosius died the following year; the empire was divided between his sons—both of them young, inexperienced, and immature. Alaric was savvy enough to know that this was his time to exploit the situation.

Alaric had his people proclaim him king of the Visigoths and led them on a tear through the Eastern empire, plundering city after city and giving the Romans little choice but to accede to at least some of Alaric's demands. The emperor appointed him *magister militum* of Illyricum (present-day Balkans), a title that put him in charge of the entire Roman army in that province. Alaric used his new status and the well-proven power of his army to attain more and more *foederati* throughout the empire. The Goth had beaten the Romans at their own game.

## CHRISTIANIZED BARBARIANS

Although Alaric was not fighting out of any known passion to spread Christianity, it was fitting that he operated on behalf of the Christian Eastern Empire against the Roman pagans of the west. After all, he and the Goths were Christians.

In addition to putting Alaric at the head of the army, his new title also raised him to one of the highest levels in the church. By the fourth century, many Goths had been raised as Arians, a sect of Christianity. Influenced by the empire in whose borderlands they lived, Goths had been converting to Christianity for centuries.

About early Gothic paganism not much is known, but historians and archaeologists have pieced together some key elements. Religion was communally practiced in such rituals as sacrificial meals and the carrying of wooden idols into battle; their main god seems to have manifested itself as a sword. The most interesting Gothic custom was the burial of warriors without their weapons. Virtually every other barbarian warrior was put in his grave armed for the afterlife. The Goths clearly had a radically different view of the afterlife than their neighbors, leading us to believe they might have viewed it as a place of peace where a warrior had no need for weaponry—perhaps more like the Christian view of the hereafter.

The Goths were introduced to Christianity by Roman prisoners during the border raids of the third century, and some began replacing their sword gods with Christ. But without a doubt the greatest influence on the conversion of the Goths to Christianity was a man named Ulfinas, an educated Goth living in fourth century Constantinople who spoke Greek, Latin, and Gothic. In 341, Ulfinas was consecrated bishop in Constantinople, and in 350 he translated the Bible into his native tongue, making Gothic, in the words of Herwig Wolfram, "by far the earliest Germanic language to reach the written stage."

## GOVERNMENT FOR THE PEOPLE, BY THE PEOPLE

For "noble savages," the Goths managed to organize themselves in a sophisticated manner. As they migrated south toward the Danube during the centuries before Christ, the leadership had begun to evolve from royalty-born kings to warrior kings. Rather than being born into their positions, the leaders emerged as those men who proved their valor on the battlefield and thus commanded respect.

Tacitus wrote about the barbarian power structure, pointing out the "kings have no unlimited or arbitrary power" and the military leaders "do more by example than by authority . . . they lead because they are admired."

As the kingship evolved, the populace held more and more sway in the selection of the king, and by the time of Tacitus, general elections were being held. (The Roman also noted that the barbarians treated their slaves comparatively better than his own people did and, when it came to women, the men "do not despise their councils or make light of their answers." The Goths, it seems, were among ancient Europe's first liberals.) Barbarians also had judges with whom kings would share power in times of emergency, in a primitive system of checks and balances.

## THE ROMAN HISTORIAN TACITUS NOTED THAT THE BARBARIANS TREATED THEIR SLAVES COMPARATIVELY BETTER THAN HIS OWN PEOPLE DID.

The history of Gothic internal politics was typical of all other nations through history, no different from that of Greece or Rome. Far from being simple debris in the "flow of history," the Goths adapted their ways of operating in the world around them according to history. While some nations have wielded more influence than others, no group of people, no matter how powerful or weak, militaristic or submissive, can claim to have done anything more than that. From the Egyptian pharaohs to the American presidency, political systems have undergone a never-ending ebb and flow of determining who should hold power, how it should be used, and what role the populace should play in this necessarily dynamic exchange.

When the gate of Rome was opened to the Goths in 410, the entirety of Europe was opened to the Germanic hordes. The Goths were followed by the Franks, and Roman Britain was later conquered by the Angles and Saxons. Later, the Slavs moved in. These great movements of people are referred to as the Barbarian Invasions or Völkerwanderung (migration).

Whatever one's view of the Goths' entry into the Roman Empire—invasion or migration—there is no doubt that Europe would look very different today had

it not been for them and succeeding barbarian tribes: Modern Western politics is a direct descendant of the Gothic power structure and political system. The Germanic tribes viewed justice as a fixed, eternal construct; the Romans linked the concept more directly with their leaders and, thus, justice was in the hand of the person who wielded the power to mete it out.

In *The Mind of the Middle Ages*, Frederick Artz writes that "when situations arose that seemed not to be covered by the old law, the Germanic idea was that more investigation was needed to find out what the old law really meant. And so law is found rather than made, and the ruler or some authority sets forth the discovery in a statute or assize."

## WHEN THE GATE OF ROME WAS OPENED TO THE GOTHS IN 410, THE ENTIRETY OF EUROPE WAS OPENED TO THE GERMANIC HORDES.

This idea extends across the ocean to the United States. Thomas Jefferson considered the founders of America as descendants of the Germanic tribes (specifically the Saxons) and the government he was helping form as rooted in the Germanic tradition. His suggestion for the new nation's seal read: "The children of Israel in the wilderness, led by a cloud by day and a pillar of fire by night, and on the other side Hengist and Horsa, the Saxon chiefs, from whom we claim the honor of being descended, and whose political principles and forms of government we have assumed."

Jefferson wanted Hengist and Horsa, Saxon chiefs who fought the Romans in Britain, depicted on the seal. He didn't get his wish, of course, but the barbarian footprint can be clearly seen in America's legal system, which invites debate, discourages absolutism, and facilitates change.

## THE "CIVILIZED" SACK OF ROME

Within two years of liberating Rome's barbarian slaves, the Goths and Romans were at it again. On the night of August 24, 410, Rome's gates were opened (possibly by a rankled slave), and the Goths poured into the city unopposed. They torched buildings near the gate to create a beacon and went to town.

The Goths lived up to their reputation as rapists and pillagers; "[t]he private revenge of [thirty] thousand slaves was exercised without pity or remorse; and

THIS EIGHTEENTH CENTURY FRENCH DRAWING WITH THE NONE-TOO-SUBTLE TITLE "BARBARIANS DEFEATED BY A BOOK" IS TYPICAL OF THE WESTERN CONCEPTION OF BARBARIANS AS ILLITERATES. REALITY: THE GOTHS NOT ONLY READ BOOKS, BUT WROTE THEM, TOO. BY THE END OF THE FOURTH CENTURY, THE GOTHS HAD THEIR OWN WRITTEN ALPHABET AND A VERSION OF THE CHRISTIAN BIBLE IN THEIR OWN LANGUAGE.

Corps de Garde (Barbarians Defeated by a Book) (red chalk over graphite on laid paper), Loutherbourg, Philip James (Jacques) de (1740-1812)

the ignominious lashes which they had formerly received were washed away in the blood of the guilty and obnoxious families," wrote Edward Gibbon in *The Decline and Fall of the Roman Empire: Volume II.*

And yet, as invasions of ancient world capitals went, Alaric's was relatively tame. While he allowed his troops free reign of the city, he placed limitations on their looting and killing. He demanded that citizens who took refuge in any place of Christian worship were to remain untouched, and that all churches and religious objects were to be left intact. By most accounts, Alaric's command was actually followed. Some Roman citizens even reported being escorted to a church by Goths themselves.

In ancient warfare, this type of behavior was rare indeed. One of the most influential Roman Catholic theologians, St. Augustine, was a contemporary of Alaric. His masterwork of theology, *City of God*, which he began writing in 413, was inspired by the sack of Rome, and Alaric's behavior plays a major part in it. Augustine argues that the barbarian conqueror's benign approach (by ancient standards) was a direct result of Christ's power and the influence of Christianity on the barbarians. Some historians and writers view Augustine's take on the subject as silly and pompous, and Augustine himself as just another arrogant Roman refusing to see the Goths as human beings with minds of their own. But perhaps they miss the point.

Augustine, after all, would likely attribute *anyone's* sense of morality and decency to the grace of Jesus, including (and especially) his own. From a historical perspective, it doesn't much matter whether Gothic mercy during the sack of Rome was compelled by the power of Christ or the result of Goths naturally being somewhat civilized. (Augustine would see no difference between the two.)

Since the beginning of Western thought, which itself is heavily influenced by Christianity, merciful behavior has been equated with civilized behavior; only savages commit the barbaric act of mass murder. In one of history's most famous events, the Goths proved that they were barbarians in name only.

# LIES FROM THE RENAISSANCE

THOUSANDS STRONG, ENGLISH
TROOPS UNDER EDWARD II AND
SCOTS UNDER ROBERT THE BRUCE
CLASHED AT BANNOCKBURN
IN THE DECISIVE BATTLE OF
THE SCOTTISH WAR FOR
INDEPENDENCE.

# CHAPTER 4

# ROBERT THE BRUCE: THE ARACHNID AND THE MONARCH

## (1314)

R IDING INTO BATTLE THAT JUNE DAY IN 1314, ROBERT THE Bruce's gilded and jeweled crown gleamed brightly in the Scottish mid-summer sunlight. The burly monarch reached up, adjusted the crown, and thrust it more firmly down over his leathern helmet. Kings did not normally wear their crowns into battle, but the Scottish king was making a statement.

Not one to choose a sturdy warhorse, the king sat astride a diminutive palfrey, a pony-sized steed favored by royalty and high-ranking nobles for its smooth and easy gait. He guided the frisky animal back and forth before the assembled Scottish spearmen, archers, and men-at-arms, exhorting them to battle. He knew his force would be badly outnumbered, but he appealed to their patriotism and bravery.

A fourteenth-century mounted king might ordinarily remain in the rear, guiding the movement of troops. Robert rode ahead of the formation, clearly exposed, as an example. He carried neither sword nor spear, only a battleaxe.

To the English force massing opposite him, across the sun-hardened marshland of Bannockburn, he was sending a message, too. Friend and foe alike were being notified that after a series of English invasions of the high-land nation, and some ignominious defeats, the thirty-nine-year-old Scottish monarch was defiantly drawing a line in the sand. Here the War for Scottish Independence would be fought, and the outcome would rest in his hands. The message was clear: Robert the Bruce was back, both as an inspiration and a target.

OPENING THE DECISIVE BATTLE OF BANNOCKBURN IN 1314, SCOTTISH KING ROBERT THE BRUCE, RIGHT, WIELDS HIS BATTLEAXE AGAINST THE CHARGING ENGLISH KNIGHT, SIR HENRY DE BOHUN, AND STRIKES HIM DOWN WITH ONE BLOW.

Encounter between Robert Bruce (1274-1329) and Sir Henry de Bohun (1276-1322) illustration from 'British Battles on Land and Sea' edited by Sir Evelyn Wood (1838-1919) first published 1915 (colour litho), Walton, Ambrose de (fl. 1900-15) (after)

On the English side, gazing across the scrubby gorse, a cocky, ambitious, young knight saw an opportunity. Sir Henry de Bohun, twenty-three, was the son of a high-ranking English noble family. Long overshadowed by his older brother Humphrey, he was eager to rise in the ranks of England's army and gain respect from his peers, who brushed him off as simply a bumptious youth.

The glittering crown of the Scottish king had caught his eye. The king was out in the open, unguarded by aides or retinue, an easy, inviting target. What a chance! De Bohun could strike a blow for the English cause while simultaneously covering himself with the glory he had long sought. Without a word or indeed a further thought, de Bohun leveled his lance, spurred his horse, and rode full tilt directly at the Scottish king.

The suddenness of this move by a lone horseman caught both sides by surprise. Scottish spearmen and English archers alike stood transfixed as the solitary figure slashed through the gorse toward his target. The "target" was transfixed, too, but by no means immobile. While the palfrey twitched nervously, Robert the Bruce gripped the reins and watched the young man's advance. Then, as de Bohun approached so closely that Robert could smell the horse and hear his snorting, the monarch suddenly swung his steed to the left, presenting the rider the full flank of the little horse. The startled de Bohun swerved, and his lance thrust harmlessly by. As the two almost touched, Robert stood up in the saddle, raised his battleaxe and brought it down sharply on the young man's crown. With a single blow, he split both helmet and skull.

As de Bohun fell to the ground and the now-riderless horse floundered away, a cheer went up from the Scottish ranks. Men thronged around their heroic leader, congratulating him, praising the deed and his bravery but at the same time chiding him for his headstrong and reckless behavior. Robert brushed them away and ignored their compliments. He shook his head and glanced downward.

"I broke my axe," he muttered mournfully. "It was my best axe." He tossed away the shattered haft, wheeled his horse, and prepared for battle.

## THE SPIDER AND THE WARRIOR KING

King Robert was the son of two formidable Scottish nobles and had claimed the throne seven years earlier, in 1307, after a series of protracted disputes and struggles. His father was Robert de Brus, Sixth Lord of Annadale, and his mother the equally formidable Marjorie, Countess of Carrick, who is said to have imprisoned her intended husband and kept him under lock and key until he agreed to marry her. Through both parents the younger Robert traced his ancestry back five generations to the Scottish king David, giving him a disputed claim to the Scottish throne.

As leader of the Bruce clan, he immediately faced conflicts with other Scottish nobles and then had to deal with an English cross-border invasion into Scottish territory. In attempting to throw back the invaders, he was badly humiliated by a surprise attack and forced to flee the country in 1307. He reached tiny Rathlin Island off the northern coast of Ireland and holed up, alone, in a muddy hillside cave.

Many legends have grown up around that period of exile. According to the version taught to generations of Scottish schoolchildren, Robert lived a solitary existence, without human companionship or even animals for friends.

Then one day he spotted another living creature sharing the cave. A tiny spider was valiantly trying to spin a web across the cave mouth. Starting from one wall of the entrance, the spider attempted to hurl a strand across to the opposite wall. Each time the strand fell short. Robert watched fascinated as the spider patiently tried and tried and tried again. Seven times, Robert counted, the strand dropped before reaching its target. It was the same number of times he had been set back in his campaign against the English.

"If the spider fails again, I shall take it as an omen that I should give up the struggles," Robert allegedly said to himself. "If the spider succeeds, I shall leave this cave and take up my responsibilities again." On the eighth try, the gossamer strand reached the far wall, and the spider industriously began spinning a full web. Inspired by the creature's persistence, Robert immediately left the cave, returned to the wars, and triumphed over the English.

Moralistic Scotland loved the story, because of the lesson for children of "try, try again," somewhat like American acceptance of Parson Weems' fable about George Washington refusing to fib about the fallen cherry tree.

But skeptics have long since picked holes in the enchanting and uplifting tale. For one thing, Robert himself never told the story, nor did any contemporary writer. It surfaced for the first time 500 years later in the writings of Sir Walter Scott, to be repeated in the poems of Robert Burns. (Indeed true skeptics, digging further, have found an almost identical legend in other cultures, including that of the ancient Greeks.)

No one has ever identified the cave itself—there is no such hillside cave on Rathlin Island, it was found—nor pinpointed the time Robert is said to have lived there. And finally, true naysayers note that to exit the cave Robert would have had to break through the industrious little creature's handiwork. That would make him the ultimate ingrate, hardly an example for schoolchildren.

## THE HAMMER OF SCOTLAND

What probably brought Robert out of hiding was the report that King Edward of England had died in July 1307 while on his way to yet another campaign against Scotland. Edward had been succeeded by his feckless young son, to be known as Edward II, as king and therefore leader of the king's armies. Even Edward II's generals didn't trust the young man in the heat of battle.

Edward I, on the other hand, was known—and dreaded—north of the border as "the Hammer of Scotland." Called Edward Longshanks because he was more than six feet tall, the warlike Edward harbored a ruthless and relentless determination to unify all of Britain—England, Scotland, Wales, plus surrounding islands—under one crown. *His* crown. For thirty years, he waged war against the Scots with the aim of bringing them under his thumb.

First, though, he had concentrated on Wales, the rocky, craggy protuberance on England's west flank. Hemmed in and protected by the rugged terrain, the proud Welsh people had developed their own culture and nurtured their own language unrelated to English, a lilting, rhythmic tongue lending itself to music and poetry.

THE RUTHLESS AND DETERMINED KING EDWARD I OF ENGLAND, KNOWN AS "THE HAMMER OF SCOTLAND," WAGED WAR AGAINST THE SCOTS FOR THIRTY YEARS WITH THE AIM OF BRINGING THEM UNDER HIS THUMB.

Edward I (1239-1307) King of England (engraving), English School, (19th century)

Edward opposed such unbridled independence, seeing it as a threat to his one-kingdom dreams; besides the Welsh frequently raided across the border, stealing sheep and making themselves a nuisance and then retreating into their forbidding hills and crags. They needed to be punished for these transgressions. Edward sent in his armies, and within a few months in 1301 the Welsh had surrendered and given up their sovereignty.

According to legend, Edward won them over with a classic, devious ruse. He promised the independent Welsh their own ruler, someone who had been born in Wales and didn't speak a word of English. And Edward made good on the promise, in his way. His newborn son who eventually became Edward II was anointed from birth as Prince of Wales, a title that still survives for the oldest son of a ruling British monarch. The infant's mother had indeed given birth to him in Wales' Caernavon Castle. And of course, only days old, he didn't speak a word of English. Or a word of anything else.

## OF KINGS AND COUNTRIES

With Wales behind him, Edward could now turn his full attention north to Scotland, with the aim of assimilating the fiercely independent and ethnically distinctive Scots. The country was riven by rivalries and factions among the nobles, immortalized by Shakespeare in his classic tragedy *Macbeth*.

King Alexander III was elderly and ill, and his only legitimate heir, Prince Alexander, was also ill, with no male offspring. Historically, at the death of a king or to establish a royal right of succession the Scottish thanes—nobles—had met to choose a new monarch, usually from within their ranks.

This practice stopped when Alexander III's House of Canmore opted for primogeniture, giving the throne to the dying monarch's firstborn son. Falling back on tradition, Alexander III had convened earls, counts, bishops, and large landowners to discuss how the new monarch would be chosen. Before they reached a decision, in 1283 the young prince died. And his father followed him in 1286. That left only one person in the direct, if tenuous, line of succession. Margaret, "the Maid of Norway," was Alexander's granddaughter, product of an arranged political marriage to Eirik II of Norway. She was three years old.

Who should rule? One faction insisted the little girl should be named queen, regardless of her age. Lineage was important. The old king had foreseen this possibility and appointed three "guardians" to rule in her name until she was older, or until some other heir was named.

Others came forward to press their claims. The two leading claimants were John de Balliol, from a large land-owning family, who traced his ancestry back four generations as the great-great-great grandson of King David II, and Robert de Brus, now the Earl of Carrick. The earl, who similarly had four generations of royal descent, was the father of Robert the Bruce. And no compromise among the three factions seemed possible.

## EDWARD TAKES UP THE "GREAT CAUSE"

Edward, the English king, then inserted himself and magnanimously offered to referee the dispute, which became known as the "Great Cause" and dragged on for years. But meanwhile, Edward insisted that all factions, the guardians and other nobles, accept his decision and also recognize the English king as their "overlord," making them part of the English domain.

It would be a temporary arrangement, just for a little while until the line of succession was straightened out, Edward assured them. This arrangement would stabilize the country. A bit exhausted, all contestants astonishingly agreed. But then Margaret—she was then nearly seven—died when the ship taking her to Norway to visit her grandmother went down in a storm. That left the Balliol and Bruce factions the last men standing. All claimants sent delegates to Edward to plead their case. After a prolonged interval, Edward endorsed John de Balliol as King John, the new monarch. The Bruces accepted the decision grudgingly.

Balliol—now King John I—soon learned that when Edward said "overlord," he meant just that. *He* was now Scotland's boss. The country henceforth would be ruled from London. Scotland would be part of Edward's kingdom, just as he had wanted. The new Scottish "king" found his directives repeatedly overruled by London and was several times called on the English carpet to explain himself forthwith.

Finally, in 1296, when Edward ordered John to furnish Scotch troops for a war against Scotland's longtime ally France, John, backed by some other Scots but not the Bruces, decided enough was enough and refused to obey. Edward accused him of treason and clapped him in the Tower of London, where he

ON TRIAL FOR HIS LIFE:
AFTER LEADING A SUCCESSFUL
UPRISING AGAINST THE ENGLISH,
SIR WILLIAM WALLACE—
"BRAVEHEART"—WAS CAPTURED,
TRIED IN AN ENGLISH COURT, AND
SENTENCED TO A GRISLY DEATH.

The Trial of Sir William Wallace
at Westminster, Scott, William Bell
(1811-90) (attr. to)

remained for three years. Then Edward compelled him to abdicate and declared the throne vacant. Scotland rebelled. Edward sacked the Scottish stronghold city of Berwick, killing men, women, and children and destroying the town. A new panel of guardians took over and defied the English monarch, whereupon Edward sent his massive army across the border.

Mel Gibson has memorialized the struggle that followed in the film *Braveheart*. After the abdication of King John, the English "kidnapping" of the Stone of Destiny, on which Scottish kings were crowned, and its removal to Westminster Abbey, and subsequent Scottish defeats, English forces seemed to have the country subdued. They even convened a rump Scottish parliament under Edward's banner.

But then the noble William Wallace, a.k.a. Braveheart, rallied the Scottish forces and revolted against Edward, forcing him to send in yet more troops and inflaming the populace. Wallace soundly defeated the English at the battle of Stirling Bridge. Wallace was appointed guardian and led several triumphant raids into English territory. But Edward's reinforcements overwhelmed the Scots at the Battle of Falkirk, and Wallace fled to France.

The Bruces, father and son, had sworn fealty to Edward as part of the "Great Cause." After all, they owned property on both sides of the border and felt loyalty to England as well as Scotland. Now they renounced that oath and, with others, sent troops into the field to resist the English advance. They were badly outnumbered and no match for Edward's armies. The young Bruce, now in his thirties, was repeatedly defeated in small engagements near the border. The losses drove him into exile on Rathlin Island.

## A DIFFERENT KIND OF WAR

When Robert returned to the Scottish mainland after the death of King Edward in 1307, he fought a different kind of war. Gone were the set-piece battles of masses of armored knights struggling in an open field. Instead he turned to guerrilla tactics, ambushing and surprising the English invaders and picking off their forts and strongpoints one by one. Castle after castle, whether held by the English or merely thought to be sympathetic to the invaders, fell to him or surrendered to the inevitable when his force abruptly appeared at their gates.

Soon much of southwestern Scotland was out of English hands and became Robert's domain. For seven years, he kept the English off balance, and they were unable to consolidate their rule. He became such a master of guerrilla fighting that he has developed an international reputation, up there with Mao and Ho Chi Minh.

The Bruces had always considered the crowning of John Balliol as King John I of Scotland to be rank injustice. In 1307 with John off the throne and exiled in France, and Edward out of the picture, Robert concluded that the throne was vacant and the time had come to press for a Bruce right to the crown. The Bruce clan, after all, represented the closest surviving relatives of the deceased Alexander III.

## ROBERT THE BRUCE BECAME SUCH A MASTER OF GUERRILLA FIGHTING THAT HE HAS DEVELOPED AN INTERNATIONAL REPUTATION, UP THERE WITH MAO AND HO CHI MINH.

Technically he and John Comyn, a wealthy land baron and a nephew of Balliol, had been named co-guardians in 1306, succeeding William Wallace after his capture and grisly execution in 1305 in which Wallace had been hanged, then quartered and his body parts distributed for public display in Scotland, Wales, and other parts of the island to warn other would-be rebels against foolish thoughts of insurgency.

However, things had become so tense between the Comyns and Bruces that a third guardian, Bishop William Lamberton, had been appointed to keep them apart. He was, to the say the least, unsuccessful. An angry Robert one day accused Comyn of betraying him to the English king in the hope of receiving Bruce lands as a reward. The confrontation took place before the high altar of the Grayfriars monastery in Edinburgh.

Robert then accused Comyn of treachery. Voices rose higher and higher until an enraged Robert unsheathed his broadsword and brought it down on Comyn's skull. Robert escaped, but later heard that Comyn had survived. Two Bruce henchmen then went out and finished the job. With the path to the throne now seemingly clear, Robert persuaded the Scottish nobles and bishops in 1307 to anoint him king. He became Robert I.

## A NEW AND BELLIGERENT KING

Edward II, England's greenhorn king, had his own notions about who should rule Scotland and how to go about it. It was foolish, he decided, to fight for castles or fortifications or cities. His job was to seek out the Scottish army and destroy it once and for all. With his burgeoning strength and reputation, Robert I was in the way. He would have to be exterminated. The only questions were when and how.

When the young king's father had invaded Scotland, he had penetrated more than ninety miles inland, making a headquarters in Edinburgh, the largest city and ostensible capital. Everything south of that line the English Plantagenets considered their turf. Accordingly they had built a fortified Stirling Castle thirty miles west of Edinburgh on the River Forth.

**ROBERT'S FIRST ESTIMATE WAS THAT HIS FORCE WOULD BE OUTNUMBERED TEN TO ONE. EVEN WHEN HE REVISED THE NUMBERS DOWNWARD, HE STILL COUNTED AT LEAST THREE ENGLISHMEN FOR EVERY SCOT.**

After years of fighting their way through English-held territory, in 1313 the Scots under Robert the Bruce's brother Edward surrounded the castle and besieged it. Rather than resort to a protracted siege and subsequent loss of life, Edward had struck a deal with the English commander. He would lift the siege temporarily. If the castle was not relieved and the siege lifted by reinforcing English troops by midsummer the following year, 1314, the English would yield and leave the fort, unarmed, but also unharmed by the besieging Scots. It was a tactic that had worked before, and brother Edward considered it a smart ploy. Older brother Robert was angered but by the deadline had come to see the deal as a godsend.

King Edward II liked it, too. He saw it as a win-win situation for himself. If relief arrived in time, the castle would remain in English hands, a black eye for Robert and the Scots. If Robert decided on combat and open warfare, he would come up against Edward's overwhelming forces. The English would surely crush him and bring Scotland to heel.

Robert, however, had been looking for a place to fight the English on his own terms and in a location of his own choosing. On the approach to the castle lay a patch of level ground known as Bannock Burn. A small stream, or "burn" in Gaelic, ran through it; in the rainy winter the stream and a lacework of tributaries flooded the little plain, but as the rains stopped it dried out and was planted with wheat, oats, and barley. A narrow, curving road bisected its fields.

Robert saw it as an ideal battleground. Using a technique he had perfected in his guerrilla campaigns (and that the Vietnamese were to use equally successfully centuries later), he had his men dig holes three feet deep, fill them with branches or twigs, and then cover them again with sod. Although the ground appeared solid from a distance, it was actually riddled with disguised pits—the origin of the term "pitfall"—to snag unwary soldiers and prove particularly hazardous to cavalry. For good measure, Robert had his men plant steel spikes in the pits. The dusty road would furnish the only sure footing for horses or men.

After de Bohun's disastrous exhibition of daring, Robert retreated behind his lines to study Edward's massing army. What he saw was not encouraging— the battle would be extremely challenging. His first estimate was that his force would be outnumbered ten to one. Even when he revised the numbers downward, he still counted at least three Englishmen for every Scot.

Indeed the odds were even greater than that. The English infantry, armed with long spears, numbered 16,000; they were backed up by more than 2,000 cavalry, plus longbowmen. Robert faced them with about 7,000 infantry plus a cavalry force of 500 and small formations of archers and men-at-arms. Each infantryman carried a seven-foot, steel-tipped spear and wore a helmet, a thick, knee-length padded jacket, and armored gloves. The foot soldiers were augmented by archers and heavily-armed men-at-arms, nobles usually mounted but fighting on foot that day.

Robert had divided his army into three commands. His trusted lieutenants Thomas Randolph, the Earl of Moray, and Sir James Douglas commanded the left and right wings, and brother Edward commanded the center. Robert himself led the rear guard and directed the battle from the center.

## THE ROLLING HEDGEHOG

The English advantage in numbers ironically proved their undoing. As the English drove toward the Stirling Castle bastion, King Robert's tactic of sowing the little plain with "pepper pits" forced the advancing troops to mass toward the center of the field and clog the road. That route was already being used by cavalry and congested with horses and men.

As the English cavalry pressed forward, Robert's deputy Randolph met them with an innovative formation called a "schiltron." Highly-disciplined spearmen, moving in unison, planted themselves in the path of the advancing English and stood their ground. The steel tips of their spears protruded menacingly from the mass at different heights and angles. The formation was appropriately nicknamed the "hedgehog" because it resembled a huge porcupine with quills extended.

As the cavalry thrust forward, pushed against the unforgiving wall of sharp blades by comrades behind, screaming horses and men alike were impaled on the forest of spears. And while they were thus stymied, they were easy prey for archers. The English turned and ran.

A recurrent theme in motivational lectures describes an inept leader as one who keeps repeating an unsuccessful action again and again and still expects different results. King Edward II was a brave man but a slow learner. Next day he was at it again. But this time he avoided the road and sent his men directly across the Bannock Burn. He was astonished to see a large Scottish force emerge from a woodland bordering the battlefield and advance on his front. The Scots suddenly dropped on their knees and prayed.

"Look! They pray for mercy!" Edward cried. "For mercy, yes," said an aide. "But from God, not from you. These men will conquer or die."

Enraged, Edward ordered his men to attack. It was the same story. Attempting to avoid the pitfalls and the forbidding terrain, the men crowded together. As a forest of advancing spears came toward them, their sheer numbers prevented them from moving or getting into position. Scottish archers now sent volleys of arrows into the disorganized horde. Trying to avoid the arrows, they became so closely packed that if a man fell wounded, or simply lost his footing, he was likely to be trampled or suffocated.

"Lay on! Lay on! Lay on! They fail!" the cry went up from the Scottish ranks. Now the excited Scottish rear guard and camp followers snatched up weapons and came charging into the floundering mass. Thinking they were being attacked by the Scottish reserve, the English turned tail and fled. Some tried to swim the River Forth and drowned. Others tried to cross the Bannock Burn but tumbled down the steep, slippery banks until the stream was filled with fallen men. Many who escaped the battlefield tried to head home to

England, ninety miles away, and were cut down and killed en route. According to some estimates, fewer than half of Edward's 16,000 foot soldiers made it back across the border.

The luckless Edward, bellicose to the end, tried loudly and frantically to rally his dissolving army, but to no avail. His personal bodyguards finally surrounded him, snatched him, and forcibly carted him away from the battle, still shouting.

His reputation in tatters, Edward survived and retained his throne until 1327, when he was murdered. The battle cemented Robert's position as king of Scotland and established him as one of the country's greatest heroes, immortalized now in a mammoth statue near the Bannock Burn battlefield.

It took ten years, however, for the English Parliament to grudgingly accept Scottish sovereignty. In 1603 the two kingdoms were united as one with the coronation of James VI of Scotland as James I of England. Scotland, however, retained its feisty independent streak; the Church of Scotland and the Bank of Scotland are just two examples. Many of the United Kingdom's political leaders have been Scottish, including the 2008 prime minister, Gordon Brown.

As for the little spider that supposedly inspired it all, the industrious eight-legged worker, like the others from the Wars of Independence, has scuttled into history.

# CHAPTER 5

# THE BLOODY RECORD OF HERNÁN CORTÉS

## (1500s)

THEIR HORSES' HOOVES MUFFLED, THE SPANISH TROOPS AND their Indian allies filed silently through the darkened streets of Tenochtitlán, the fabled city of the Aztec empire. It was raining lightly, and just past midnight on July 1, 1520. Hostility was on every side, but they were not alarmed. "The Aztecs do not fight at night," they had been assured by their commander, the conquistador Hernán Cortés.

Then a lantern suddenly shone brightly in the darkness, and a woman's voice shattered the stillness. Out for water, she heard the hoof beats of the enemy's horses and spotted the shadowy ranks. "Come quickly! Come quickly!" she shouted. "Our enemies are leaving! They are running away!" From a temple top, a priest called out: "Mexican chiefs, your enemies are leaving! Run for your canoes of war!"

The huge war drum atop the city's giant pyramid sounded, its notes echoing through the city and arousing the populace. Within minutes, volleys of stones, sticks, timbers, anything that could be dropped or thrown, cascaded from the rooftops, knocking marchers to ground. A torrent of arrows pelted them. Men and women brandishing clubs, stones, and makeshift weapons attacked the fallen, many of whom were weighted down with gold and other loot and could scarcely struggle to their feet. Others rushed to set up the much rehearsed defense of the island city.

In 1520, Tenochtitlán had a population estimated at 200,000. It had been constructed on a blob of land in a volcanic lake in the Valley of Mexico, where the great metropolis of Mexico City stands now. The arriving Spanish marveled at the

Cemalacatitlā.

Quezallan.

Xaltelolco.

Quetzaltenāco.

RUTA que siguio HERNÁN CORTÉS en la Conquista de MÉXICO.

# MYTH
HERNÁN CORTÉS WAS
A MONSTER RESPONSIBLE FOR
THE MASSACRE THAT FOLLOWED
THE FALL OF TENOCHTITLÁN,
THE AZTEC CAPITAL.

# REALITY
CORTÉS'S INDIAN ALLIES WERE
RESPONSIBLE FOR THE MASSACRE,
WHICH CORTÉS TRIED TO STOP.
A SEVERE OUTBREAK OF
SMALLPOX WAS A MAJOR
CONTRIBUTOR TO THE FALL
OF TENOCHTITLÁN.

city, which rivaled in its urbanity the great cities of Europe. Tenochtitlán was linked to the shore by bridges and causeways, set up to allow sections to be dismantled quickly to forestall any attack. Thus Cortés' men had brought with them a makeshift span to cross any gap in a bridge or causeway.

Led by Cortés himself, the Spanish soldiers, plus a few hundred Indian allies, now headed for the critical causeway, which would lead them to friendly territory. At its far end, a road would carry them to the land of the Tlaxcalans, many of whom were fighting alongside them. The Tlaxcalans and Aztecs had long been enemies, and the Tlaxcalans were thirsting for a fight.

## TO CAPTURE, NOT TO KILL

But when Cortés' force reached the causeway, they found their way blocked by a massive mobilization of Aztecs, a phalanx of trained defenders. The elite Aztec warriors fought with swords fashioned from obsidian, a black volcanic rock that could be honed to an exquisitely sharp thinness and is even today used in fine surgical scalpels. They did not ordinarily aim to kill opponents, but to wound and capture them, often to sell as slaves or use for sacrifice. A stunning blow to the back of the head was their favorite method of dispatching a foe.

The Spanish had brought brass cannon, the primitive, muzzle-loading arquebus, and men on horseback, none of which the Aztecs had ever encountered and that terrified them at first: the cannon as much by its deafening roar as the casualties inflicted; the mounted warriors because they seemed like some sort of mysterious primitive beast, half man and half four-footed animal, like the centaurs of mythology.

In the hand-to-hand "Battle of the Bridges," both proved more hindrance than help. The cannon could not be fired at short range, and the artillerymen, swarmed over by sword-wielding Aztecs, could not fire them. The cavalry could not maneuver in the close quarters. Horses and men plunged off the causeway into the water below. Cortés himself was knocked from his horse. The horse's legs were broken, and Cortés was saved by one of his lieutenants.

## THE NIGHT OF SADNESS

Somehow the vanguard of the retreating column managed to reach the far shore. Many of them plunged into the water and tried to swim the last yards across the final channel, where they were set upon by angry Aztecs in their war canoes. Others simply floundered until their armor and pocketed loot dragged them beneath the surface. The cannon were completely lost. A mare laden with gold bullion and treasures utterly disappeared; it had been a trove destined for the Holy Roman Emperor Charles V, who was king of Castile and Aragon, which Ferdinand and Isabella had combined into modern Spain, and of Burgundy in France, the Hapsburg lands of Austria, and seventeen Hapsburg provinces in the Netherlands. In one stretch where the causeway flanked a canal, the waterway became so clogged with Spanish bodies that others used them for footing in their eagerness to flee.

Spanish chroniclers afterward called the bloody debacle "La Noche Triste"—the "Night of Sadness." The Spanish death toll was conservatively estimated at 450—some estimates ranged as high as 1,700—along with virtually all their Tlaxcalan allies, perhaps several thousand of them.

The rout was in sharp contrast to the scene short weeks before, when Cortés stood atop the city's great pyramid beside the abashed Aztec Emperor Montezuma and proclaimed a "New Spain" pledged to King Charles V and the Cross of Christianity. It seemed the end of the vainglorious conquistador's career. But within another year, in 1521, Cortés was back atop the pyramid in triumph. This time his victory had been assured by a silent, unrecognized ally that launched Spain as a dominant power in the Western Hemisphere and the world for several centuries to come.

## YOUNG MAN IN A HURRY

Hernán Cortés grew up in a small town in western Spain's semi-arid Extremadura region. His was a distinguished but somewhat impoverished family. Born in 1484 or 1485—historians disagree—he had to be wet-nursed in infancy. The sickly boy was sent off at age fourteen to the University of Salamanca, Spain's most prestigious center of learning. His family hoped for a legal career, but after two years of studying law and Latin, the adventurous youth returned home.

Spain in 1501 bubbled with tales of Columbus' voyages to the "New World" and the riches to be found there. The restless sixteen-year-old was eager to see for himself, and his disappointed parents agreed. Either the military or the Indies, they said. A distant relative, Nicolas de Ovando de Caceres, had just been appointed governor of the Spanish Caribbean–island colony of Hispaniola (now Haiti and the Dominican Republic) and arranged for the youth to accompany him. But just as the ship was about to embark, his passage was canceled because he was injured. Supposedly he fell out a window escaping from a married woman's bedroom.

The young man reached Hispaniola not long afterward. By 1504, he had established himself in the capital, Santo Domingo, as a citizen with a small plot of land. Along with the land he was given a *repartimiento* of Indian slaves to work the fields and a few small mines. He took part as a soldier in the further conquest of Hispaniola and Cuba. With his minimal university training in law, bolstered by a few months in a notary's office in Seville, he was named notary for the town of Azusa. Although diligent about watching his slaves work, the young man mostly spent his hours drinking, gambling, and pursuing Indian women.

In 1510 Cortés accompanied a gold-prospecting expedition to Cuba, assigned as the expedition's treasurer responsible for seeing that the "quinto," or one-fifth of the proceeds, was earmarked for the emperor. His coolness in command and leadership abilities so impressed the new governor, Diego Velázquez, that he chose Cortés, fluent and apparently learned, as his secretary. He also installed the young man as *alcalde*, or mayor, of Cuba's capital city, Santiago.

Velazquez had an itch to expand his—and the Spanish empire's—domain beyond the known islands identified by Columbus. He dispatched his nephew, Juan de Grijalva, to sail westward in search of other lands that might be claimed by Spain. There was also the persistent rumor of a city of gold out there, beyond the horizon, not to mention peoples who should be shown the glories of Christianity. When Grijalva did not immediately return and no word was heard of him, his alternately worried and avaricious uncle in 1519 decided to mount a new expedition to search for him. It was also to carry the Cross and investigate the rumors of a gold bonanza. He chose thirty-four-year-old Cortés as its leader.

## DISAGREEING WITH THE BOSS

Cortés, however, had a somewhat rocky relationship with Velázquez, who twice had him jailed. Although Cortés had fathered a child by an Indian slave woman, he had never married until he began courting the governor's sister-in-law Catalina Juárez. After a while, Velázquez decided Cortés was simply toying with Catalina's affections, and had no intentions of marriage. At his urging, she sued Cortés for breach of promise. Velázquez jailed Cortés until he yielded and became Catalina's husband.

Another falling out disrupted the proposed Mexico expedition. Velázquez had issued Cortés a document outlining his duties and responsibilities and authorizing him to commission vessels and crews, enlist soldiers, and acquire supplies. He was to file a plan for the voyage and its mission, with particular emphasis on Grijalva's rescue. All claimed property would belong to the emperor, Charles V, along with one-fifth of the profits. The government and Cortés, now owner of sugar cane, sugar mills, and gold mines, were to share the costs and split the remaining proceeds.

Velázquez strongly suspected that Grijalva might have indeed located the fabled city of gold and claimed it for his own. He might right now be living there in tropical splendor, cutting out the governor back in Hispaniola and His Majesty in Spain. There was the secondary fear that Grijalva and his crew might have been seized by savages and enslaved or killed.

Cortés was busily chartering vessels and outfitting them when one of Grijalva's little ships reappeared. The captain brought what seemed good news of a successful voyage. Grijalva, as directed, had charted the coastline of the "island" of Yucatán (actually a peninsula, as Cortés was to demonstrate). He had been welcomed by the Mayan natives who had cooperated fully, showered him with gold offerings, fed him fine foods, and demonstrated the fertility of the soil.

They had also located two Spaniards who had been cast ashore earlier and knew the territory, the people, and the language. These two had remained behind for a Spanish foothold in the territory. They had confirmed the tales of a rich city in the interior (which they had not seen), a city of gold whose inhabitants were the Mayans' bitter enemies. The Mayans would certainly greet the Spanish warmly and join any effort to find and conquer the inhabitants of the city of gold.

## "IS THIS ANY WAY TO SAY GOODBYE?"

Hearing all this, and also concerned about the money Cortés was spending, Velázquez reneged on his contract with Cortés. If the area was so tempting and easily captured, and with so much being invested, he wanted control for himself, not by any possible freebooter. He sent Cortés a message countermanding his earlier commission. Cortés was forbidden to leave port. Cortés by now had rounded up 600 men bent on adventure and possible wealth and chartered six ships. He was not about to be relieved of command. He pretended not to have received the order.

Turning his back on his possessions and his wife in Santiago, on November 18, 1518, he prepared to set sail. At daybreak Governor Velázquez came to the quay and confronted him. Cortés met him in a small boat, flanked by armed guards.

"How is this, my friend?" the governor called out. "Is this any way to say goodbye to me?"

"Forgive me, but these things have all been thought out before they were ordered," Cortés called back. "What are now your orders?" When Velázquez didn't answer immediately, Cortés directed his captains to cast off.

Velázquez had him pursued as he left port and docked at other Spanish settlements, but the voluble Cortés was not to be swayed. At each call, Cortés boasted of the riches he expected to find just beyond the horizon. He was a convincing talker. By the time he pushed off from the last port, San Cristobal de la Habana, his fleet had grown to eleven ships, with an estimated fifty or more sailors. He also had sixteen horses, which would prove valuable in days to come. He had enlisted a total of nearly 700 men. Half the Spanish males in Cuba had signed on with him.

## ANYONE HERE SPEAK SPANISH?

On February 18, 1519, Cortés waved farewell to Cuba, rounding its westernmost point, Cape San Antonio, for the short hop to the "island" of Yucatán. Although a brief crossing, it was not an easy one. A heavy storm scattered the little fleet, and at least one vessel was lost and several damaged before they limped into the harbor of Santa Cruz, on the small island of Cozumel (now a popular beach resort). They were to remain there nearly a month, making repairs, taking on

# BEGINNING "THE AGE OF EXPLORATION"

When Christopher Columbus "discovered" the "New World" in 1492 and returned boasting of hidden riches beyond Europe's wildest dreams, the news galvanized the acquisitive instincts of France, Portugal, England, and especially the Spanish court of Ferdinand and Isabella, Columbus' original backers. All were excited by the lure of gold, silver, and precious metals, plus fertile and resource-rich lands inhabited only by easily-quelled savages.

Columbus himself made four exploratory voyages to the Caribbean, planting the flag of Spain and the cross of Christianity wherever he went. Spain then founded a thriving colony on Hispaniola, the island now shared by Haiti and the Dominican Republic. Portuguese sea captain Ferdinand Magellan, flying the flag of Spain, set off on what became an epic round-the-world trip that extended European reach into the far Pacific. In his wake, Spain colonized and Christianized a group of 7,000 islands that were named the Philippines. Another Spanish adventurer, Francisco Pizarro, invaded the Inca Empire in South America with a mere handful of men. That foray begat the colony of Peru. King Henry VII of England tapped Italian John Cabot to seek a western passage to the Indies; Cabot reached what is now Newfoundland, and his voyage eventually led to English colonies in North America.

This exploratory flurry drew on the legacy of a Portuguese prince, Henry, who became known as Prince Henry the Navigator. A soft-spoken, generous, quiet man, from early youth Henry was obsessed by a dream of enriching his tiny Iberian country.

He first focused on Africa, the giant continent that lay just across the Straits of Gibraltar from Iberia. In 1415, aged twenty-one, he convinced his father, King John I, to seize control of Ceuta, a Moorish port opposite Portugal on the North African coast. Ceuta was used by the Barbary pirates as a base from which they raided Portuguese towns, capturing residents and selling them in the African slave markets.

Ceuta was also near the terminus of the trans-Saharan caravans that brought coveted spices, silks, and other Oriental products to the West. Henry saw the profitable trade possibilities for his country, but he hoped for a more reliable delivery method, via a sea route to the so-called "Spice Islands" (now Indonesia).

But the ships that plied the Mediterranean were too slow and heavy for such trips. So Henry commissioned the design of a lighter, faster ship with triangular Arab sails instead of the European square rigging, giving them more maneuverability and allowing them to sail into the wind. The new, two-masted vessel, usually running a length of twenty to thirty meters, was called the caravel. In the latter half of the fifteenth century, encouraged by Henry until his death in 1460, Portuguese caravels sailed around and mapped the African continent, including its stormy southernmost point, which was named the Cape of Good Hope. In 1498, well after Henry's death, Portuguese commodore Vasco da Gama fulfilled Henry's dream, leapfrogging in a caravel across the Indian Ocean from East Africa directly to India.

The caravel greatly accelerated the subsequent Age of Exploration. Most of the explorers who capitalized on Henry's pioneering sailed in caravels. The list included Columbus. The *Nina* and the *Pinta* were both small caravels, about twenty meters long with a beam of seven meters, and Columbus praised the *Pinta* as his favorite vessel for its speed and agility. The vessel that completed Magellan's circumnavigation was a caravel. Six of Cortés's fleet were caravels. They were ideal for his purposes because their shallow draft and maneuverability enabled them to move speedily over shallows and explore small creeks and inlets as places for landing.

water and food, erecting a cross, and parleying, and sometimes skirmishing, with the Mayans.

On arrival, the conquistadors were greeted by two naked men approaching in a dugout canoe and carrying bows and arrows. The two made signs that seemed friendly, and one called out in Spanish, "Gentlemen, are you Christians? Whose subjects are you?" When told they were vassals of the king of Castile, the two men fell to their knees and thanked God for deliverance.

They had been part of a group of twenty who set out in an open boat from the Spanish settlement of Darien, in Panama. They had been bound for Santo Domingo when the boat ran aground and was broken up in the shoals. Half the twenty died; the others were captured, and the two who survived watched horrified as their mates were sacrificed and eaten.

Imprisoned in cages, they managed to break out and were sheltered but held as slaves by rival Mayan chieftains. That had been eight years before. One of them, Geronimo de Aguilar, a thirty-year-old priest, had taught himself several Mayan dialects while in captivity. Cortés had been frustrated in communicating with the Mayans and needed an interpreter. Aguilar was just what he had been looking for. He signed on and remained with the conquistador throughout the expedition.

Once they left Yucatán and Mayan territory, Aguilar would be of less help. But he would prove his usefulness as Cortés hopscotched along the coast before choosing Vera Cruz for an anchorage. This would be the jumping-off place for the push inland toward the rumored city of gold, and on Palm Sunday, 1519, a local chieftain presented him with ten Indian female slaves. One of them was a comely young woman who spoke both Chontal Maya and Nahuatl, the languages of the local region and that of the Aztec empire. That meant she could talk to Aztecs in Nahuatl and then with Aguilar in Maya, who could then translate what he heard into Spanish, a cumbersome but effective process. After a Palm Sunday mass and the traditional procession with tree branches substituting for palms, the young woman was baptized and confessed to the Christian faith. She soon picked up rudimentary Spanish, too, and was to play a key role in events of the next few years.

Known in the local dialect as Malinali, she was given the baptismal name Marina and soon became known as "La Malinche." She was said to be in her early twenties and "beautiful as a goddess," although pictures at the time hardly confirm it. Many conflicting stories have developed around the La Malinche legend, inspiring films, novels, and plays, often with a feminist twist. She is portrayed as the educated daughter of an important chieftain who was killed in battle, after which she was sold into slavery, and then given to Cortés. She remained at Cortés' side throughout the Mexican campaign, serving as an interpreter and also a liaison with local groups, and she was said to be his most influential adviser. She also became his mistress and bore him a son. And she played key roles as Cortés advanced toward Tenochtitlán and the heart of the Aztec empire.

## TOWARD THE CITY OF GOLD

Cortés and his "holy company" set out from Vera Cruz in early August 1519. He had with him 350 men under arms, 20 crossbowmen, and 20 arquebusiers. He also brought nearly 100 Cuban Indian slaves.

Vera Cruz and Mexico City—Tenochtitlán—are separated by some 250 miles of forbidding terrain, including mountains as high as 10,000 feet, coastal swamp, jungle, thick forests, and a scorching dry salt lake. In the 1500s it was also populated by distinctly unwelcoming tribes, either allied with or intimidated by the Aztecs. The Spanish fought several small skirmishes, but their main weapon was fear. At the first sign of resistance, the artillery would fire a few rounds, and the roar and smoke caused the opposition to melt away.

Two important cities lay in Cortés' path. Both, about sixty miles south of Tenochtitlán, had strained relations with the Aztecs. The warlike populace of Tlaxcala, a city of some 100,000, had thwarted several Aztec attacks, and although the Aztec emperor Montezuma said he had the city "in a cage" and could walk in whenever he chose, the Tlaxcalans openly jeered with the kind of "bring 'em on" bravado that would be heard five centuries later. Cholula was a sophisticated city of religious shrines, fine art works, and tapestries. Well defended, the Cholulans were technically allies of the Aztecs but maintained an arm's length relationship, focused more on diplomacy than fighting.

Cortés' curving route took him to Tlaxcala first. He explained to the Tlaxcalans that his mission was friendly, that he hoped they would furnish food and water for his hungry, thirsty troops, and that he was a representative of a great far-off king. His motives were religious, too: He was bringing the message of the one true God. The Tlaxcalans challenged him, and Cortés attacked. A vicious three-day battle ended with Tlaxcalan surrender and an offer to join the Spanish in battle against the hated Aztecs.

Cholula was taken with little fighting; the Cholulans decided that the Spanish would be temporary guests. Cortés made it clear he was more than a guest. He knocked down and destroyed idols in the city's temples and summoned the city's chieftains to discuss terms of surrender.

## CORTÉS THE BUTCHER

What happened next, still controversial 500 years later, was to fuel Cortés' reputation as an unprovoked and bloody butcher. As with Tlaxcala, he demanded—"requested" in some histories—that the city provide the troops with food and water.

It was August after all, hot and humid even at the 7,000-foot altitude, and his men were famished and thirsty. The Cholulans said they were sorry, but they hadn't the resources. Cortés' little army had added more than a thousand Tlaxcalans; that was too many mouths to feed. If the Tlaxcalans were hungry, they could go home.

Cortés tried another tack. He assembled the city's chieftains, a kind of grand council, in the courtyard of the main temple. He delivered a florid sermon condemning human sacrifice, explaining that in the eyes of the one true god all men were brothers and should not be killed in the name of religion. The Cholulans listened politely. They could furnish limited food, they said, adding that they couldn't let fellow human beings starve, because that would violate traditional Cholulan hospitality, but it would take time to organize the food and prepare it for their guests. They were obviously stalling and were possibly in league with the Aztecs. Cortés ordered the gates locked. Spaniards and Tlaxcalans fell on the men, the cream of Cholulan society, and massacred them all. The best guess was 3,000 dead.

Cortés afterward blamed his new allies, the Tlaxcalans, for the bloodshed. Some of his associates said the onslaught was simply a military necessity. If they were to take Tenochtitlán, they couldn't leave such formidable potential enemies in their wake.

A TRIUMPHANT CORTÉS IN ARMOR AND A DEFERENTIAL MONTEZUMA IN GAUDY PLUMES GREETED EACH OTHER IN THIS IMAGINATIVE PAINTING FROM THE SIXTEENTH CENTURY. TERRIFIED, MONTEZUMA INITIALLY REFUSED TO MEET THE SPANISH EXPLORER, WHOM HE THOUGHT MIGHT BE THE DEITY QUETZELCOATL.

The Encounter between Hernan Cortes (1485-1547) and Montezuma II (1466-1520) from 'Le Costume Ancien ou Moderne' by Jules Ferrario, Milano, c.1820 (colour litho), Gallina, Gallo (1796-1874)

CONQVISTA DE M

POR CORTES. N. 7.

Vltimo conbate de mexi
por tierra y las fuerzas por las tres
que van aneota, y por la laguna
ponteras quindan un crudo corria
tu Gua: Pedro de alvarado el de c
chiblas y por los huertas a la T.
fernan Cortes ————
Calçada de S. Juan ————
Christoual de Oli ————
Pedro de Aluarade ————
Calçada de tacuba ———— 3
Gonsalo de sandoual ———— 4
Calçada de Guadalupe ————
Sacerd. de Idolo ———— 6
G. Filiber o va Padilla ————

News of the slaughter sent tremors down Montezuma's spine. The Aztec religion was filled with superstition and legend. And legend said that the year of I-Reed on the Aztec 14-month calendar was bad for kings. The white deity Quetzelcoatl would appear and ascend the Aztec throne. Disaster would overtake Tenochtitlan. I-Reed was the current year, Montezuma realized. And those invaders with the white faces might have been sent by Quetzelcoatl. Their pale complexioned leader might be the great god incarnate. What would be the fate of the Aztec empire then? Of Montezuma himself? "What can we do? We are finished," he cried to his court.

The emperor summoned two trusted aides and dispatched them as emissaries to Cortés. They were laden with gifts of gold and silver, fine cloth, and beautiful feathers, and were told to promise young maidens and offer payment of regular tribute if the invaders would just go away. Cortés assured the emissaries that his intentions were peaceful. But he must meet with Montezuma face to face. That would not be possible, he was told. Montezuma was ill. The road ahead was impassable. Provisions to feed the army could not be found en route. The city zoo was filled with wild animals, alligators and lions, which would devour the Spanish if let loose. No summit conference. It could not be done. Sorry.

The emissaries remained with Cortés as he moved forward, imploring, offering. At one point a man dressed as Montezuma appeared. Cortés greeted him, but then some Tlaxcalans appeared and began to laugh. The man was an impostor; a Montezuma relative dressed in the emperor's royal robes. Montezuma himself apparently arranged the deception, hoping it would satisfy Cortés and that he would go away.

## A MAGNIFICENT ENTRANCE

Finally, on November 8, 1519, nearly a year after Cortés departed Hispaniola, he and his company arrived at Tenochtitlán. Crossing the grand causeway leading to the main gate, they entered in a grand procession that awed the Aztec onlookers. First came four armored men on horseback—Cortés' most trusted lieutenants. Then a flagbearer carrying the royal banner of Castile. Then a troop of infantry with drawn swords, followed by crossbowmen in plumed helmets, more horsemen, and finally Cortés himself on horseback. More than 1,000 Indian allies followed.

Montezuma had decided by now that royal protocol required an Aztec prince to greet a royal visitor personally. He met Cortés carried on a litter under a resplendent canopy of green feathers decorated in gold, silver, and jade, adorned with flowers and garlands. Cortés dismounted, and Montezuma stepped down from the litter. The two clasped hands, then delivered flowery speeches translated by Marina and Aguilar. Cortés interpreted Montezuma's polite and seemingly abject words of welcome such as "I bow down to you" to mean that the emperor was submitting himself to the representative of the Spanish king. To Cortés' mind, Montezuma was pledging to become a vassal of Charles V. Mission accomplished.

Six days later, Cortés made the new relationship plain. An Aztec-allied tribe had attacked a Spanish outpost near Vera Cruz. Ostensibly to learn who had ordered the attack, Cortés entered the royal palace with fifty armed guards, marched into the throne room, and effectively imprisoned Montezuma. He announced that the emperor was being held hostage until he knew the truth about the attack. Thereafter guards surrounded Montezuma day and night. He remained emperor in name, but Cortés called the shots. As for the attack on the outpost, Montezuma insisted he had nothing to do with it; the perpetrators were a renegade group of Aztec allies.

Tenochtitlán's population was sullen but endured the arrangement with only minor resistance until April 1520. The two men held friendly (translated) conversations and discussed policy together. Cortés mollified Montezuma with a promise he would return to Spain; he began ship construction.

Then Cortés learned that Spanish vessels had arrived in Vera Cruz with 600 armed men, supposedly assigned to capture Cortés and replace him as captain-general. Cortés mustered half his men and headed for Vera Cruz. He surprised their commander, Pánfilo de Narváez, routed him out of bed, jailed him, squelched minor resistance, and recruited the defeated Narvaez troop remainders into his own army. He turned back toward Tenochtitlán, which, unknown to him, had fallen into chaos.

## THE SLAUGHTER OF TOXCATL

When Cortés departed for Vera Cruz, he left a few more than 100 men and designated his most valued associate, Pedro de Alvarado, as the Spanish

commander and de facto governor. Before leaving, at Montezuma's request, Cortés had authorized a giant celebration on May 16 of the feast of Toxcatl, one of the most important Aztec festivals. He emphasized that there must be no human sacrifice, nor idol worship. Several days before the festival was to begin, Montezuma asked Alvarado to repeat the permission. Alvarado did, again repeating the ban on sacrifice.

As preparations continued, Alvarado became increasingly nervous. Visiting the main square where the festivities were to take place, he saw stakes being driven into the ground and was told surreptitiously by Tlaxcalans that these were meant to bind sacrifices, who would be Spanish. The largest stake would be for Alvarado himself. Then the Mexicans stopped providing food, and the natives who worked for the Spanish disappeared. Figures of the Virgin Mary installed by Cortés in the main temple were replaced by figures of Aztec idols. Alvarado became convinced that an uprising was in the making, timed to the fiesta. He allowed Toxcatl to go forward until all Tenochtitlán's nobles were amassed in the main square and the fiesta reached its climax in a frenzied dance by all the nobility.

Then Alvarado had the exits blocked. He assigned sixty men to guard Montezuma and kill those around him. The other sixty were to enter the temple and attack the nobles at the height of the dance. When the gates were secure, Alvarado gave the order "*Mueran!*"—"Let them die." His men methodically chased down and killed all the nobles, then turned to the unarmed spectators, and killed them, too. The number of dead was said to be at least 3,000; other estimates ran as high as 10,000.

The city erupted. Rioting began, with people clamoring to enter the temple. A general alarm was sounded from the great war drum, and men flocked to the armories to receive weapons. The Spaniards retreated to their quarters and were besieged there. A frightened and desperate Alvarado took Montezuma to the top of the pyramid at knife point and told him to quiet the crowd, to no avail. The emperor had lost his god-like image. Stones were thrown; "What saieth Montezuma, O fool?" an outraged spectator cried. "Am I not one of his warriors?"

The news of the bloody turmoil reached Cortés in Vera Cruz two weeks later, in early June. It was brought by four weeping messengers sent by Montezuma, then reinforced by a Spanish officer. "Your captain whom you left in the city of Tenochtitlán is in grave danger," the officer reported. "They have made war against and killed many. It would be good if you went back quickly."

Cortés immediately reassembled his force, strengthened by some 400 troops of Narvaez's men who had joined him, and headed north. He arrived late on June 24 to find the embattled garrison near starvation, its food supply almost totally cut off. Alvarado's men were rebelling, short of gunpowder and subsisting on fetid drinking water from a well that they dug in the courtyard. Cortés had hoped to take over the country without fighting; now he found that dream destroyed.

In an attempt to salvage it, he went to Montezuma and told him to halt the disorder. The emperor protested tearfully that he was powerless. The

Spanish had robbed him of everything—his dignity, his authority, his sway over his people, his sacred status. The people were beyond his control. Cortés nonetheless marched him to the top of the pyramid on June 27 to address the crowd. A hail of stones, spears, bricks, and wood slabs greeted the once revered figure. Montezuma was struck three times by sharp stones in the chest and abdomen. Aides carried him down the pyramid, mortally wounded. He died three days later, on June 30. It was said he was baptized a Christian on his deathbed, with Cortés at his side, but this was never proven.

That same night, Cortés decided to abruptly evacuate his depleted and weakened force, and by 1 AM the next morning, in a steady drizzle, he ordered an ignominious retreat from the "city of gold" he had coveted and so majestically entered a short time before. La Noche Triste was a sorrowful night indeed.

## THE COMEBACK KID

But by no means was it to be a full withdrawal. Choosing a different but more difficult route out of Tenochtitlán, Cortés managed to elude pursuit. After an epic painful trek, in which the starving troops were forced to eat grass, he reached Tlaxcala, home of his staunchest allies. There he dug in, rearmed, reinforced, and made plans for his return.

First, Cortés set out to win over to his cause all the surrounding tribes. Those who he could not convince by words, he chose to subdue by force. In an exceedingly brutal and bloody campaign, he allowed his allies freedom to sacrifice and cannibalize as they wished. By late 1520 much of central Mexico was under his control, willingly or not. Then he ordered the construction of a fleet of nineteen forty-foot brigantines on one of the satellite lakes around Tenochtitlán. He was determined to cancel the power of the swarming warrior-laden canoes that had created havoc on La Noche Triste.

But his domination of the country was aided by an unexpected ally. Smallpox, rampant in Europe, had inadvertently been imported to Hispaniola and Cuba by voyagers and colonizers. The deadly disease ran wild through the native population. The Spanish themselves were scarcely affected because most of them, like Cortés himself, had been exposed in childhood and were thus immunized. The disease was then carried to Mexico and Tenochtitlán from Hispaniola by an African slave bearer who had accompanied Narvaez and joined Cortés on his return to the city. Shortly after La Noche Triste, the disease erupted and swept through the local population, striking down much of the priesthood and the military leadership and eventually killing Montezuma's successor as emperor, his brother Cuitlahuac. At least one-quarter of the Aztec population of 200,000 died of the disease, and twice that number were seriously sickened.

The combination of disfiguring "pox," high fever, and agonizing death that devastated natives while sparing whites claimed many warriors and their leaders, and it also robbed others of the will to fight, convinced the disease was the wrath of the white man's god or a form of witchcraft.

Massing his allies, Cortés on June 23, 1521, set out to retake the great city. He launched his brigantines, gained superiority on the lake, surrounded the city, and then slowly squeezed. Repeated bloody battles broke out on the bridges and causeways. On August 13, the conquistador himself intercepted the latest emperor, Montezuma's cousin Cuauhtemuc, and took him prisoner. Cuauhtemuc begged Cortés to kill him, because surrender would mean he had failed his people and his gods, but Cortés persuaded the unhappy man to remain. He now proclaimed "New Spain" as part of the Spanish domain, with himself as the king's representative. The sickly child of Extremedura had come far from his humble beginnings and left a bloody trail behind him, along with a stained and disgraced reputation.

# CHAPTER 6

# THE GALILEO AFFAIR: A HISTORIC COLLISION OF SCIENCE, RELIGION, AND EGO

## (1633)

T HE WAITING WAS EXCRUCIATING. HIS MIND RACED, YET Galileo Galilei remained very still, sitting quietly in a wooden chair, his hands folded in his lap. Confined to a small but comfortable suite inside the Holy Office, he awaited the verdict that would decide his fate. Summoned by the Commissary General, Galileo came to Rome to answer charges of heresy regarding his book *Dialogue on the Two Great World Systems (Dialogo sopra i due Massimi Sistemi del Mondo)*. The sixty-six-year old physicist was exhausted. The imprisonment and the accusations against him had taken a toll on his health.

Released in February 1632, *Dialogue* was stirring up controversy in intellectual and nonsecular circles across Italy. The work, which Galileo considered one of his great achievements, discussed the merits and deficiencies of two conflicting theories on the order of the universe, the Earth-centered Ptolemaic theory, and the sun-centered Copernican theory.

Since the fifteenth century, the Roman Catholic Church and most of Europe embraced geocentrism, which held that a motionless Earth was the center of the universe. Introduced by Aristotle and expounded on by Claudius Ptolemy, geocentrism formed the basis of European thought on astronomy. It also confirmed what was observed by man's senses.

More important, the Ptolemaic system confirmed what was written in the Holy Scriptures. According to numerous passages in the Bible, the Earth stood still. *Psalms 93:1* and *96:10* state, "Yea, the world is established; it shall never be moved." And *Psalm 92:1* declares that God "fixed the Earth upon its

## MYTH

THE PHYSICIST GALILEO WAS CONDEMNED AND IMPRISONED BY THE ROMAN CATHOLIC CHURCH BECAUSE HIS WORK CONFLICTED WITH THE TEACHINGS OF THE BIBLE.

## REALITY

HIS TRIAL FOR HERESY WAS THE CULMINATION OF A CAMPAIGN TO DISCREDIT HIM THAT WAS SPEARHEADED BY HIS ENEMIES AND RIVALS—AND INFLAMED BY GALILEO'S OWN HUBRIS.

foundations, not to be moved forever." Further, Saint Thomas Aquinas, one of the Church's most beloved and respected theologians, embraced the Ptolemaic system.

The Copernican theory, on the other hand, contradicted the Holy Scriptures. Astronomer and Catholic cleric Nicholas Copernicus introduced heliocentrism as an alternative to the Ptolemaic system in his seminal work *On the Revolutions of the Heavenly Sphere (De revolutionibus orbium coelestium)*. According to the heliocentric, or Copernican theory, the sun was the center of the universe, and the Earth revolved around it. Copernicus, who dedicated the book to Pope Paul III, died on the day *Revolutions* was published, unaware that a preface had been added that undermined his revolutionary theory. Unsigned, the preface states that the theory is meant as a mathematical tool for calculating the movements of the planets, and it appears to be written by the author. In fact, it was the work of Andreas Osiander, a Lutheran philosopher who oversaw the book's publication. Although the Roman Catholic Church allowed *Revolutions* to be published, it had insisted the book carry a disqualifier, explaining that the alternate system was to be considered purely "hypothetical." To secure permission for publication, Osiander added the preface.

First published in Germany in 1543, *Revolutions* took Copernicus years to complete and broke new ground. However, upon its release, the work was met with much derision and was largely dismissed by scientists and theologians. Church reformer Martin Luther condemned it. Less than a century later, Copernicanism would ignite the intellectual passions of the brilliant physicist Galileo Galilei. The theory formed the basis of his *Dialogue on the Two Great World Systems*.

Presented in the form of a Socratic-type debate between three characters, the *Dialogue* offered arguments for and against the Ptolemaic and Copernican theories. An enlightened man of science, the character Salviati makes a compelling case in support of the Copernican theory. The neutral Sagredo is a wealthy, knowledge-seeking aristocrat. Simplicio, the third character, is an Aristotelian philosopher, who argues rather ineffectually for the Ptolemaic model of the solar system. Salviati, who represents Galileo's views, emerges the clear winner of the debate.

Charged with heresy, Galileo could easily have fled Italy and escaped the authority of the Inquisition. Yet, he chose to stand trial and defend himself. The scientist considered himself a good Catholic and felt that heresy was "more abhorrent than death." After traveling for twenty-three days, Galileo arrived in Rome on February 13, 1633. Ill and depressed, he spent the next two months with friends, recuperating at Villa Medici. In April, he surrendered to the Inquisition. No common prisoner, Galileo was housed in a three-room suite in the Holy Office, and a servant was at his disposal. The physicist was allowed visitors, but he could not leave the premises.

## GALILEO'S FALL FROM GRACE

It was a far cry from the triumphant tour of Rome that Galileo made in 1624. His old friend Cardinal Barberini had just been appointed Pope Urban VIII. The new pontiff feted Galileo and encouraged his "favorite son" to continue his work exploring the heavens. The pope fancied himself an intellectual; the idea of sponsoring major scientific discoveries greatly appealed to his vanity.

During a succession of private meetings, Galileo tried unsuccessfully to convince the pontiff to reverse a Church edict against promoting and teaching the Copernican theory. The pope admitted that he did not approve of the edict but felt that because the Copernican theory could not be proven, it *must* be treated as a mathematical device, not as a factual discovery. He gave Galileo permission to write about Copernicanism but only in hypothetical terms. Pope Urban asked that his own view—that nature, as created by God, is far too complex to be understood by man—be included. He believed Galileo would bring him fame. The pope was right, but it would not be the fame he hoped for.

Galileo spent the next five years working on the *Dialogue on the Two Great World Systems*. He submitted the book to the Church and received

official approval. Published in 1632, the *Dialogue* was an enthusiastic, unapologetic endorsement of heliocentrism. Although Galileo's allies were thrilled with the book, they were also wary. In Galileo's eagerness to overturn the prevailing geocentric system, he had thrown caution to the wind. Despite his promise to Pope Urban to remain neutral, Galileo zealously defended Copernicanism in the book—albeit through the character Salviati. Described as "the laughingstock of this philosophical comedy" Simplicio is the character Galileo chose to express the pope's views about the universe—a colossal misstep.

## SINCE THE FIFTEENTH CENTURY, THE ROMAN CATHOLIC CHURCH AND MOST OF EUROPE EMBRACED GEOCENTRISM, WHICH HELD THAT A MOTIONLESS EARTH WAS THE CENTER OF THE UNIVERSE.

The *Dialogue* caused a scandal. Critics claimed it brazenly defied a Church edict forbidding the promotion of Copernicanism. Galileo's enemies—and there were many—told the pope that he had been ordered by Chief Church Theologian Cardinal Robert Bellarmine not to defend the Copernican theory back in 1616. Galileo had failed to mention the warning during his meetings with the pontiff. His enemies also convinced the pope that the physicist had modeled Simplicio after him. Blinded by his own ambition, Galileo had inadvertently insulted one of his dearest friends. Pope Urban felt humiliated and betrayed. Galileo promptly lost his most important and powerful ally.

## THE TRIAL OF GALILEO IN 1633

Galileo was officially charged with defying the Church's edict forbidding the defense of the heliocentric theory and for publicly "holding as true the false doctrine taught by some that the sun is the center of the world." The tribunal claimed that he had been personally warned not to teach or promote the theory in 1616—a charge that is not altogether accurate. According to the written indictment, the Church theologians decreed the following:

1. The proposition that the sun is in the center of the world and immovable from its place is absurd, philosophically false, and formally heretical; because it is expressly contrary to Holy Scriptures.

2. The proposition that the Earth is not the center of the world, nor immovable, but that it moves, and also with a diurnal action, is also absurd, philosophically false, and, theologically considered, at least erroneous in faith.

Ten cardinals heard Galileo's case. Over a two-month period, officers of the Inquisition interrogated Galileo eighteen times. The prosecution's case was bolstered by a suspect injunction against Galileo dated March 3, 1616. The injunction, which may have been planted in Galileo's file by an enemy, states, incorrectly, that Cardinal Bellarmine "had admonished [Galileo] to abandon his opinion which he has held up to that time, that the sun is the center of the spheres and immobile and that the Earth moves, and had acquiesced therein."

Galileo was understandably flummoxed. He insisted he never saw the letter, nor had he been served with any injunction. In his defense, he said that he had never been forced to abjure his position on heliocentrism, as the tribunal was now claiming. As proof, he offered up a letter from Bellarmine stating that "Galileo has not abjured, either in our hands or in the hands of any other person here in Rome, or anywhere else as far as we know, any opinion or doctrine which he has held; nor has any salutary or any other kind of penance been given to him."

Galileo also pointed out that Church authorities, including the Supreme Inquisitor, had signed off on the *Dialogue*. The book was not written in his voice, in the first person, but rather as a dialogue between three men. He did not understand why the book was now being prohibited when it had already received official approval.

Two cardinals, sympathetic to Galileo, worked to spare him and proposed a lenient sentence. Commissary General Father Vincenzo Maculano received permission to approach Galileo extra-judicially with a deal, the seventeenth century equivalent of a plea bargain. For an admission of guilt—an honest acknowledgement that he had erred in defending and advocating heliocentrism in the *Dialogue*—Galileo would be sentenced to private penance and temporary house arrest. Realizing the odds were against him, he agreed to the deal.

Pope Urban, who was still smarting from his perceived betrayal by his old friend, overruled the sentence and decreed that the *Dialogue* was to be forbidden

and Galileo was to be forced to formally abjure, by threat of torture. Because of his age and ill health, there was little chance that Galileo would be subjected to torture. Galileo was well aware that the threat was an empty one. Still, the sentence, meted out by his old friend, hurt him deeply.

## MISTRUTHS, MYTHS, AND MISCONCEPTIONS

The trial and conviction of Galileo Galilei is considered one of the greatest scandals in the history of Christianity. For centuries, Galileo's name has been used as a battle cry against the perceived tyranny of the Roman Catholic Church. The physicist is consistently portrayed as the voice of science and reason, as an educated man battling an unyielding, unenlightened Church.

Two ironies are at work here. The first is that the Church was responsible for much of the early progress in astronomy; many of the leading astronomers in the seventeenth century were also members of the clergy. The second is that despite his conviction for heresy, Galileo considered himself a good Catholic who strove to square his responsibilities as a scientist with his faith. He would most likely be dismayed to learn that his name was being used to besmirch the Church.

## THE MYTH OF GALILEO BEING CONFINED TO A DANK JAIL CELL AND TORTURED IS JUST THAT, A MYTH.

The myth holds that Galileo, the scientist, tried to enlighten the close-minded Church, arguing that reason and science should be given precedent over faith. In reality, both Galileo and his judges believed that science and the Bible must be reconciled, and that they could not stand in contradiction. The Galileo Affair, as it has come to be known, was not a battle of reason versus religion, but of good science versus bad science. We know today that the earth orbits the sun, but Galileo lacked the scientific instruments necessary to prove this fact. It would take another hundred years for such instruments to be developed.

The charges brought against Galileo were motivated by personal vendettas. With his acerbic wit, sarcasm, and refusal to compromise, Galileo had made many enemies, including Pope Urban VIII. He routinely attacked rival theories and the men who proposed them. He mocked his opponents mercilessly

KNOWN AS THE "HAMMER OF THE HERETICS," CHIEF CHURCH THEOLOGIAN CARDINAL ROBERT BELLARMINE WAS A DEDICATED SCHOLAR AND A KEY FIGURE IN THE COUNTER-REFORMATION. HE WAS CANONIZED IN 1930 BY POPE PIUS XI.

New York Public Library

and insulted their intelligence. Such bully tactics did not sit well with his victims, many of whom had been former allies. Years after the trial, a Jesuit astronomer remarked that if Galileo had not offended the order, "he would not have fallen into trouble, he would be able to write on any subject he wished, even the rotation of the Earth." Several cardinals assigned to Galileo's case believed that the trial was intended not to protect doctrinal purity but to punish Galileo. History bears this out.

## GALILEO QUARRELED OFTEN WITH HIS COLLEAGUES, CRITICIZING THEIR THEORIES, DISMISSING THEIR IDEAS, AND REFUSING TO CONCEDE ANY OF THEIR POINTS. HE REFERRED TO THOSE WHO DISAGREED WITH HIM AS "INTELLECTUAL PYGMIES."

The myth of Galileo being confined to a dank jail cell and tortured is just that, a myth. Galileo was forced to formally abjure, and the *Dialogue* was banned. While the sentence issued by Urban was unduly harsh, it was never enforced. Galileo's daughter, a Carmelite nun, was permitted to say his penance for him, and the physicist was allowed to live out his days at home, under a loosely-enforced house arrest. He spent the remainder of his life working on the *Discourses on Two New Sciences*. Presented as another discussion between the fictional characters Salviati, Sagredo, and Simplicio, the book offered Galileo's views on kinematics (the study of the motion of objects).

## THE MAKINGS OF A BRILLIANT PHYSICIST

Born in Pisa in 1564, Galileo Galilei was the eldest child of Vincenzo Galilei and Giulia Ammannati. Vincenzo was a talented but poor musician who struggled to support his wife and six children. He encouraged Galileo to become a doctor. Galileo enrolled in medical school but dropped out after two years, deciding to study mathematics instead of medicine.

In 1589, Galileo was appointed to the chair of mathematics at the University of Pisa. He was an independent spirit, an iconoclast who eschewed blind philosophical faith. He was drawn instead to reasoned argument. Stubborn and opinionated, Galileo quarreled often with his colleagues, criticizing their theories, dismissing their ideas, and refusing to concede

any of their points. He referred to those who disagreed with him as "intellectual pygmies." Galileo routinely disparaged Aristotle, whose work was widely revered in academia.

"Few there are who seek to discover whether what Aristotle says is true," he confided to a friend. "It is enough for them that the more texts of Aristotle they have to quote, the more learned they will be."

The gifted young man quickly alienated himself from the other educators at the University. He also incurred the wrath of Giovanni de Medici, son of the Grand Duke of Tuscany's son, when he lambasted a machine de Medici invented to dredge the harbor of Leghorn. It seems that Galileo's capacity for scientific discoveries was rivaled only by his knack for making enemies.

Galileo took a mistress, a local woman named Marina Gamba, with whom he fathered three children out of wedlock. Oddly, the devoutly Catholic Galileo declined to marry his lover and legitimize his offspring. He dispatched of his

GALILEO'S LONG-TIME FRIEND MAFFEO BARBERINI (SEEN HERE IN PORTRAIT) WAS ELECTED TO THE PAPACY IN 1623. BARBERINI CHOSE THE TITLE POPE URBAN VIII.

Architectural scheme with a portrait of Pope Urban VIII (1568-1644) in a cartouche probably 17th century (w/c), Italian School

daughters Virginia and Livia, sending them to live at the convent of San Matteo. Both girls became nuns and lived in abject poverty. Their mother later married an older man who adopted Galileo's son, Vincenzo. Although a devoted academic and scientist, Galileo was an ineffectual father.

In 1592, he left Pisa for a more prestigious, and lucrative, position at the University at Padua. There, Galileo developed interests in a range of topics including kinematics of motion, optics, astronomy, tidal theory, and instrumentation. He made numerous discoveries in both pure and applied science.

## THE DISPUTE OVER THE COSMOS

Galileo had long been interested in Copernican theory. In May 1609 he learned that a Dutchman had invented a new magnifying device to view the heavens. The physicist immediately drew up plans for a device of his own. Galileo's telescope permitted him to observe the night sky as never before. His celestial discoveries confirmed for him that Copernicus had been right: The universe was a sun-centered system, and the planets, including Earth, orbited the sun. Jupiter's moons and the phases of Venus showed that the planets—at least not all of them—did not orbit the Earth. This fact disproved the Aristotelian-Ptolemaic system. Galileo assumed the Church would now adopt the Copernican theory. Then again, he still had the Tychonic system to contend with (see "Unraveling the Mysteries of the Heavens" on page 113).

Galileo made his first public endorsement of Copernicanism in 1613 with *Letters on the Sunspots*. He continued to vigorously defend the theory in subsequent letters and debates. Not content to treat Copernicanism as a hypothesis only, Galileo continually trespassed on theological ground—a scandalous thing for a layman to do. He insisted the scriptures be reassessed to incorporate his new discoveries. Galileo argued that the Bible was designed to teach mankind about religion, not the natural world. He cited works from St. Augustine and St. Thomas Aquinas that bolstered his position.

In Galileo's 1615 *Letter to the Grand Duchess*, he wrote, "As to rendering the Bible false, that is not and never will be the intention of Catholic astronomers such as I am; rather, our opinion is that the Scriptures accord perfectly with demonstrated physical truths. But let those theologians who are not astronomers guard against rendering the Scriptures false by trying to interpret it against propositions which may be true and might be proved so." Many theologians were outraged.

In 1615, Carmelite friar and respected theologian Paolo Antonio Foscarini published a book that attempted to reconcile the Copernican theory with Holy Scripture. News of the work gave Galileo hope that the subject was ripe for reexamination by the Church. He believed that Foscarini's support was just what he needed. He was wrong. There were now two men openly advocating for Copernicanism. This antagonized the more conservative members of the clergy. A contentious debate over the private interpretation of the Holy Scripture had been one of the reasons behind Martin Luther's split with the Church in 1517. Now, the Church feared Foscarini and Galileo might stir up a new theological revolution.

Galileo's rivals claimed, incorrectly, that there were a growing number of "Galileans" promoting Copernicanism on the physicist's behalf. Still smarting from the Protestant Reformation, the Church moved to assert its authority. Copernicus's *Revolutions* was banned until it could be "corrected," and Cardinal Robert Bellarmine reminded Foscarini and Galileo that the Council of Trent "prohibits expounding the Scriptures contrary to the common agreement of the holy Fathers."

Bellarmine, an educated, calm, and fair man, met privately with Galileo and counseled him to treat the theory as a mathematical device, a hypothesis only. The Church was not banning the theory, he explained, but would only accept it as fact if it could be proven conclusively. In that event, the Church would need to reexamine its interpretation of the Holy Scripture, Bellarmine allowed. Galileo was not officially enjoined from discussing Copernicanism. He was, however, in a difficult position. Convinced the theory was correct, Galileo could not possibly prove it to be so. To the naked eye, the stars appeared to remain still. This reinforced contemporary consensus that the Earth was immobile. Galileo's telescope was too weak to observe the star's parallax shifts as the Earth orbited around the sun.

## POISON PEN LETTERS AND THE LEAGUE OF PIGEONS

Galileo's unorthodox views, predilection toward sarcasm, and increasing preoccupation with heliocentrism made him a controversial celebrity. He continued to make enemies and became embroiled in a series of bitter disputes with members of the scientific community. His archrival Lodovico delle

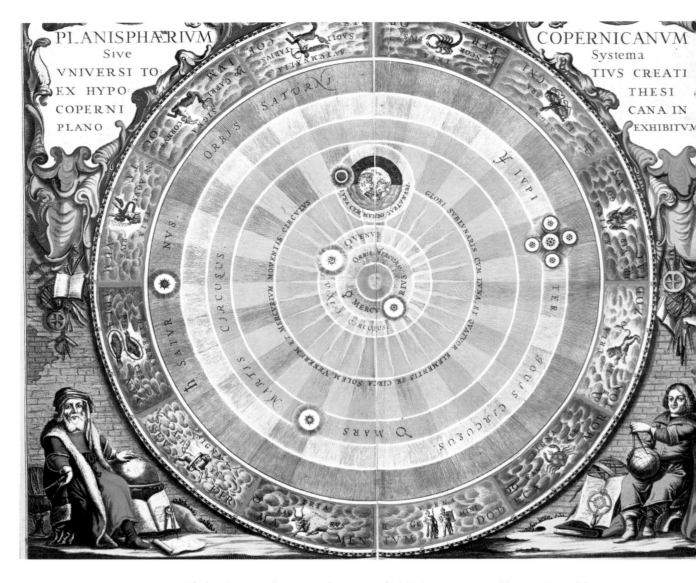

Colombe was determined to ruin Galileo's reputation. He was joined by a group of theologians Galileo dubbed the "Pigeon League" (Colombe means "dove" in Italian). In terms of achievement and intellectual brilliance, the group was no match for Galileo. The group could not best the physicist intellectually; it decided to bait him with a scriptural argument. The ploy worked. Galileo was too stubborn and too vain to remain silent on the issue.

Galileo counted the Jesuits among his allies, but his hubris and sarcasm soon alienated the order. Galileo claimed credit for the discovery of sunspots, despite the fact that the Jesuit astronomer Christopher Scheiner had written about them two years earlier. Scheiner proposed that sunspots were really small stars orbiting and eclipsing the solar body. Galileo not only disagreed with him, but viciously attacked the Jesuit in print, writing the following in his first book, *The Assayer:*

"Others, not wanting to agree with my ideas, advance ridiculous and impossible opinions against me; and some, overwhelmed and convinced by

PICTURED IS THE COPERNICAN HELIOCENTRIC SYSTEM AS ENVISIONED BY THE GERMAN ARTIST ANDREAS CELLARIUS IN HIS CELEBRATED SEVENTEENTH CENTURY WORK *ATLAS COELESTIS SEU HARMONIA MACROCOSMICA.*

The Copernican System,'Planisphaerium Copernicanum', c.1543, devised by Nicolaus Copernicus (1473-1543) from 'The Celestial Atlas, or the Harmony of the Universe' (Atlas coelestis seu harmonia macrocosmica) Amsterdam, c.1660, Cellarius, Andreas (17th century)

## UNRAVELING THE MYSTERIES OF THE HEAVENS

In 1608, Dutch lens crafter Hans Lippershey invented the first practical telescope. Dubbed the "Dutch perspective glass," Lippershey's telescope could only magnify objects thrice. The lens crafter's designs were disseminated around Europe. Galileo received news of the telescope in Padua and immediately set out to build one of his own. The telescope he created was much more powerful than Lippershey's and, according to Galileo, magnified objects "nearly one thousand times larger and thirty times closer than when seen with the naked eye."

Galileo used his new instrument to study the heavens. What he saw astounded him. The moon was not smooth, nor perfectly round as was believed; it had valleys and crevices and its surface resembled the Earth. Jupiter had a quartet of satellites circling it! He observed Venus and discovered that the planet was revolving around the sun, not the Earth. This led Galileo to believe that the Earth was neither motionless, nor the

central focus of the solar system. These discoveries turned the Ptolemaic theory of the cosmos on its head.

The up-and-coming astronomer described his exciting discoveries in *Starry Messenger (Sidereus Nuncius),* a pamphlet he dedicated to Cosimo II de Medici, the Grand Duke of Tuscany. He named Jupiter's moons the "Medicean Stars" in the Duke's honor. The Duke was flattered and appointed him mathematician and philosopher of his court. Galileo would continue his celestial observation under the patronage of the Duke.

*Starry Messenger* was widely circulated in Italy. The text contradicted the accepted geocentric view of the cosmos, and it naturally caused a sensation. Galileo's discoveries, like Copernicus' before him, were met with skepticism. However, once the leading Jesuit astronomers obtained a telescope, they confirmed Galileo's claims. The Jesuits gave him their support. Still, they were not willing to abandon geocentrism. Instead, they compromised,

adopting the system proposed by Tycho Brahe.

Danish astronomer Brahe had rejected the Aristotelian-Ptolemaic system as well as the Copernican theory. According to Brahe, all the planets orbit the sun, while the sun and the moon revolved around a motionless Earth. Unfortunately for Galileo, his celestial discoveries fit just as well in the Tychonic system as they did in the Copernican one. What's more, the Tychonic system did not contradict the Holy Scripture, making it especially appealing to the Church. Galileo was clearly frustrated. He was also a man on a mission. Although he could not prove the Copernican theory, he was determined to convince the world of its accuracy.

In 1611 Galileo traveled to Rome to discuss his celestial discoveries with the leading scientists and theologians. He received a warm welcome, and he was even granted a private audience with Pope Paul V.

my arguments, attempted to rob me of that glory which was mine, pretending not to have seen my writings and trying to represent themselves as the original discoverers of these impressive marvels."

In reality, neither man discovered sunspots. That honor belonged to Johann Fabricius, a German whose pamphlet on the subject was published months before Scheiner's.

Galileo's stunning rebuke of Scheiner deeply offended Jesuits. The belligerent physicist also engaged in a heated debate over comets with Jesuit mathematician and astronomer Horatio Grassi. Once again, Galileo used his pen as a sword, writing in *The Assayer*, "Let Sarsi [Galileo's pseudonym for Grassi] see from this how superficial his philosophizing is except in appearance. But let him not think he can reply with additional limitations, distinctions, logical technicalities, philosophical jargon, and other idle words, for

## THE CHURCH APOLOGIZES

In 1822, the Catholic Church lifted the ban against Copernicus's *On the Revolutions of the Heavenly Sphere* and allowed heliocentrism to be defended as fact. In 1979, Pope John Paul II reopened the Galileo case. In 1992, the Church investigation concluded that:

"Certain theologians, Galileo's contemporaries, being heirs of a unitary concept of the world universally accepted until the dawn of the seventeenth century, failed to grasp the profound, nonliteral meaning of the Scriptures when they described the physical structure of the created universe. This led them unduly to transpose a question of factual observation into the realm of faith.

"It is in that historical and cultural framework, far removed from our own times, that Galileo's judges, unable to dissociate faith from an age-old cosmology, believed quite wrongly that the adoption of the Copernican revolution, in fact not yet definitively proven, was such as to undermine Catholic tradition, and that it was their duty to forbid its being taught. This subjective error of judgment, so clear to us today, led them to a disciplinary measure from which Galileo had much to suffer. These mistakes must be frankly recognized, as you, Holy Father, have requested."

Pope John Paul II officially acknowledged that the Earth moved and issued a formal apology for the prosecution of Galileo.

Today, Galileo Galilei is considered to be the father of modern science. His work and his intellect have inspired countless scientists, artists, intellectuals, and even musicians. A spacecraft, the four large moons of Jupiter, a pop song, and a play by esteemed dramatist Bertolt Brecht have been named in his honor. Galileo's final work was "so great a contribution to physics," maintains the award-winning physicist Stephen Hawking, "that scholars have long maintained that the book anticipated Isaac Newton's laws of motion."

I assure him that in sustaining one error, he will commit a hundred others that are more serious, and produce always greater follies in his camp."

Up until this point, the Jesuits had been Galileo's biggest supporters. His vicious attacks on members of their order would cost him dearly. The Jesuits remained silent when Galileo's enemies, led by the League of Pigeons, repeatedly urged Church authorities to bring charges against him for heresy. Their determined campaign eventually led to Galileo's trial in 1633.

## GALILEO'S ENDURING LEGACY

On April 30, 1633, Galileo recanted his belief in heliocentric system before the Inquisition. He said:

> I have been judged vehemently suspected of heresy, that is of having held and believed that the Sun is at the center of the Universe and immovable, and that the Earth is not at the center and that it moves. Therefore, wishing to remove from the minds of your Eminences and all faithful Christians this vehement suspicion reasonably conceived against me, I abjure with a sincere heart and unfeigned faith these errors and heresies, and I curse and detest them as well as any other error, heresy or sect contrary to the Holy Catholic Church.

> And I swear that for the future I shall neither say nor assert orally or in writing such things as may bring upon me similar suspicions; and if I know any heretic, or one suspected of heresy, I will denounce him to this Holy Office, or to the Inquisitor or Ordinary of the place in which I may be.

Contrary to popular belief, Galileo did not mutter defiantly, "And yet it does move!" (Eppur si muore!") After abjuring, he was sentenced to house arrest for the remainder of his life and ordered to recite daily penance. Galileo spent his remaining years working on his final book, *Discourses on Two New Sciences,* which recounted many of his scientific discoveries. While writing the book, the physicist lost his sight. He died in 1642 in Florence.

# LIES FROM THE TIME OF THE REVOLUTIONS

Hand-colored woodcut of a 19th century illustration
by Darley / North Wind Picture Arcives / Alamy

MILITIA FIRE AT BRITISH SOLDIERS
DURING THE BATTLE OF LEXINGTON
IN 1775. THE PICTURE REFLECTS
MORE OF THE MYTH THAN THE
REALITY. ACTUALLY, THE MILITIA
WERE DRAWN UP IN THE OPEN ON
LEXINGTON COMMON AND WERE
HIT BY A BRITISH VOLLEY AS THEY
DISPERSED. FIRING FROM BEHIND
STONE WALLS WAS EMPLOYED
DURING THE BRITISH RETREAT
FROM CONCORD.

# CHAPTER 7

# PAUL REVERE: THE NOT-SO-LONE HORSEMAN

## (1775)

*"Listen my children, and you shall hear,
Of the midnight ride of Paul Revere,
On the eighteenth of April, in Seventy-five;
Hardly a man is now alive
Who remembers that famous day and year."*

PAUL REVERE CALLS THE LEXINGTON MINUTEMEN TO ARMS. ACTUALLY MILITIA OFFICERS, ALERTED BY REVERE, WILLIAM DAWES, AND OTHERS, CALLED UP THE TROOPS. THE OFFICERS OF THE HIGHLY ORGANIZED COLONIAL MILITIA SUMMONED MEMBERS WITH DRUMS, BEACON FIRES, SIGNAL GUNS, CHURCH BELLS, AND, IN ONE CASE, A TRUMPET.

Hand-colored woodcut of a 19th century illustration by Darley / North Wind Picture Archives / Alamy

HENRY WADSWORTH LONGFELLOW WROTE HIS FAMOUS POEM back in 1860. Now everybody remembers the Boston silversmith's famous ride to warn the local militia of the arrival of the British Redcoats. What we remember, though, is not quite the way it was.

We remember the lone rider spreading the alarm "to every Middlesex village and farm," right up to "the bridge at Concord town." We know that the result of his ride was the first armed conflict in what became the American Revolutionary War, but we can't explain how a mortal man and a mortal horse were able to reach everybody in a county and bring out hundreds of armed men. Some of us know that there were one or two more riders that historic night, but few remember that there were dozens more.

Most important, we don't remember that Paul Revere himself was part of a vast organization, part of which he had built himself and most of which had been developing for more than a century.

## THE RISE OF THE SONS OF LIBERTY

Paul Revere was one of the patriot leaders in Boston. We should note that "patriot" was not a compliment in the late eighteenth century—at least, not in England.

When Dr. Samuel Johnson said, "Patriotism is the last refuge of scoundrels," he wasn't just mincing words. A patriot was someone who believed his first loyalty was to his homeland, not his monarch. Anyone who believed that was, to an eighteenth-century English gentleman, a scoundrel. As it happened, there were a lot of "scoundrels" in the American colonies, especially those in New England.

During the last war with France, which ended in 1763, England had built up an enormous (for the eighteenth century) military establishment. The British government felt that it was only right and proper that the American colonies contribute to the maintenance of this establishment, which had been created for their protection. The colonists didn't.

They were already paying taxes that had been those authorized by their colonial assemblies, assemblies composed of people they had elected. The colonists could not vote for members of the British Parliament, which had authorized the new taxes. Besides, if the military existed to protect the American colonies, the colonists could ask, "Protect us from what?" Since the colonies were founded, the major threat had been France. France, defeated in the last war, was no longer a threat.

The British government passed a number of tax measures, which brought increasing resistance from the colonists, some of it violent. Resistance groups, generally called the Sons of Liberty, began to organize. In Boston, there were seven independent groups. Many of them shared membership. Paul Revere belonged to five of them, more than any other man but Dr. Joseph Warren, who became president of the Provincial Congress.

Committees of Correspondence were formed to keep like-minded people in all the colonies informed of developments. The committees had couriers, called "expresses," to carry messages to other committees. Paul Revere was an express. He made many rides from Boston to Philadelphia, New York, Portsmouth, New Hampshire, and Exeter, New Hampshire, as well as to other towns in Massachusetts.

Revere was about the only high-ranking Son of Liberty who was a "mechanic," someone who worked with his hands—in his case, silversmithing. He organized other "mechanics" into a spy ring to keep track of British troop movements.

## MOUNTING TENSIONS

Revere's spy ring learned that the British were sending two regiments to Fort William and Mary in Portsmouth, New Hampshire, to secure the gunpowder and cannons kept there. At the time, the fort was garrisoned by only six invalid British soldiers. Revere rode to Portsmouth, about sixty miles away, and told the Patriots (who also called themselves Whigs, the name of the English party opposed to the incumbent Tory party) about the plan. About 400 New Hampshire militiamen forced the British commander at the fort to surrender and moved all the military supplies out of the fort before the British troops arrived.

General Thomas Gage, commander of all British troops in North America, had his own spy ring, which included Dr. Benjamin Church, who ranked just below Dr. Warren in Patriot circles. Church's real role was never known until long after the Revolution. General Gage knew that the Sons of Liberty were caching gunpowder, bullets, muskets, and cannons in several places in Massachusetts. He learned that at Salem, a number of ships' guns were being converted to field pieces and that the Patriots had eight recently imported field guns there as well. He sent 240 men of the 64th Foot (infantry) under Lieutenant Colonel Alexander Leslie to collect them.

Revere's "mechanic" spies watched them depart, but British soldiers detained them so they couldn't report what they had seen. However, the marching "lobster-backs," as the Redcoats were known, were seen by many men in nearby Marblehead who gave the alarm in Salem. The Colonial militia raised a drawbridge and confronted Leslie's troops while other townsmen hid the guns. More and more armed colonists began arriving.

Leslie agreed to a compromise proposed by a local minister: The militia would lower the bridge if the British would march no farther than the forge, around 100 yards away. If they found no cannons, they would turn around and go back to their base.

In both of these incidents, a key element was an institution that was, at this time, probably unique to British North America—the militia (see "The Militia" below).

## THE LEGEND OF THE THREE-WAY SPLIT

There is a widely published opinion that in 1775, about a third of the colonists wanted independence from Britain, a third were loyal to the Crown, and a third were neutral. The proposition sounds like something dreamed up by British historians.

Actually, only a small minority in early 1775 wanted independence. But a huge, overwhelming majority in New England said they were struggling for their "rights as Englishmen," especially no taxation without representation and the right to a trial by a jury of one's peers. (Some new English laws specified a trial for certain offenses in England, but they were never enforced.) These people had complete control of the militia, something no minority could achieve.

At this time the passion for liberty was perhaps less fervent in the Middle Colonies, such as New York and Pennsylvania, but the Tory minority there was

GENERAL THOMAS GAGE, COMMANDER OF BRITISH FORCES IN NORTH AMERICA, SENT TROOPS TO CONCORD TO CONFISCATE MILITARY SUPPLIES THERE. THE TROOPS ROUTED A SMALL PARTY OF MILITIA IN LEXINGTON, BUT WERE DRIVEN OUT OF CONCORD AND HARASSED ALL THE WAY BACK TO BOSTON. GAGE'S AMERICAN WIFE IS BELIEVED TO HAVE TIPPED OFF THE PATRIOTS.

Portrait of General Thomas Gage, c.1768 (oil on canvas mounted on masonite), Copley, John Singleton (1738-1815)

## THE MILITIA: AMERICA'S PECULIAR INSTITUTION

Militias, armed citizens organized to fight, had existed in Europe since the Dark Ages, but in the era of strong, centralized monarchies, most of them absolute, the militias had faded away.

In France and many Continental powers, owning weapons in the eighteenth century was a criminal offense. In Britain, such ownership was greatly restricted, and there was no provision for calling up an organized militia. In the American colonies, however, militias were a necessity. Raids by Native Americans were an ever-present possibility, and until the last war, so were attacks by European, especially French, troops as a result of wars begun in Europe.

All colonies had laws requiring every free man except ministers to possess a musket or rifle, ammunition and a bayonet, sword, or hatchet. Every town had a militia and held "muster days" for drilling the troops. After the final French defeat, the militia laws were laxly enforced, but tensions with the "mother country" had renewed interest in the militia, especially in New England.

still small and had no representation in the militia. In the South, especially in the Carolinas, there were more Tories, but they had little affection for the British Crown.

In the Carolinas, the hardscrabble farmers in the uplands tended to be Tories because the rich merchants on the coasts were Whigs. The lowlanders had been oppressing the uplanders. The two had fought a war, the War of Regulation, shortly before the Revolutionary War began.

When Paul Revere set out on his historic ride, he didn't have to rouse every villager and farmer. He contacted the leaders of the militia, and they in turn, sent out other messengers. They also lit bonfires, fired signal guns, beat drums, and rang church bells. Revere also called on Congregational ministers, who had their own network. And, of course, he called on his old friends, the leaders of the Sons of Liberty.

## GAGE'S UNDERCOVER MEN

General Gage learned that the Whigs were also hiding military stores in

Worcester and Concord. Worcester, Massachusetts, was a hotbed of Patriotism; colonists there were openly threatening violent resistance to any British expedition. Besides, it was forty miles from Boston. The general had to know any particularly dangerous spots, places where dissident Whigs could stage ambushes. So he had two bored young officers, Captain John Brown and Ensign Henry De Bernier, walk to Worcester and check out the route. They were to dress in plain country clothes and pretend to be surveyors.

The spying did not get off to an auspicious start. The officers brought along a batman (a military servant), "our man John," and when they stopped at a tavern, banished him to a separate table. A black waitress took their order, and one of the officers tried to make small talk.

"This is a fine country," he said, forgetting that he was supposed to be a native of the country.

"So it is," said the waitress. "And we have got brave fellows to defend it, and if you go up higher you will find it so."

The next time the officers stopped, they promoted their servant to an honorary officer and let him sit at their table. They slept at a tavern owned by a known Tory, who warned them not to go farther, but they continued on to Worcester. Everywhere they went they attracted attention and saw groups of country people staring at them. They began to fear for their lives. Then it started to snow. Brown and De Bernier blessed the weather, because it kept the local people inside. The snow did not facilitate traveling, though. On the last leg of their trip, they walked thirty-two miles through ankle-deep snow.

Gage decided to go to Concord instead of Worcester.

## "ONE IF BY LAND, TWO IF BY SEA"

The failure of the British expeditions to Portsmouth and Salem and even the unwanted attention his two spies attracted convinced Gage of the need for the utmost secrecy. Before the Concord expedition began, a screen of mounted British officers armed with pistols and swords would intercept any Patriot expresses. The troops would march after almost everyone was in his bed.

> PAUL REVERE ARRANGED WITH A COUPLE OF SONS OF LIBERTY TO HANG ONE LANTERN ON THE STEEPLE OF THE OLD NORTH CHURCH IF THE REGULARS TOOK THE LAND ROUTE AND TWO IF THEY LEFT BY BOAT.

At this time, Boston's Back Bay really was a bay, not a tract of filled land. From the air, Boston would have looked like a huge pollywog projecting into the harbor. The town of Charlestown, across the water, had the same shape. There were two ways the troops could exit Boston: over the narrow neck of land, heavily guarded by British troops, or across the water to Charlestown. There were no troops in Charlestown, so there might not be Whig spies watching them, Gage thought. He was inclined to start with boats.

Paul Revere knew the British were about to move, but he didn't know how they'd leave Boston. That information was important. He arranged with a couple of Sons of Liberty to hang one lantern on the steeple of the Old North Church if the regulars took the land route and two if they left by boat. Ironically, the rector of the Old North Church was one of the few Loyalists in Boston. Two lanterns appeared, and Revere, waiting in Charlestown, began his ride.

## A SOMEWHAT OPEN SECRET

The British troops were not told where they would be marching; none but those on Gage's innermost circle were told. Right after he learned of the expedition, Lord Percy, Gage's second-in-command, saw a group of citizens talking on Boston Common. He asked one of them what they were so earnestly discussing.

"The British troops have marched, but they will miss their aim," the man said.

"What aim?

"Why, the cannon at Concord."

Percy was shocked.

There was a strong suspicion then and now that the Sons of Liberty were getting their information from General Gage's American wife. As a high-ranking, confidential source, she trumped even Dr. Church.

But the British troops themselves were responsible for other leaks. A farmer named Josiah Nelson heard some of the mounted officers Gage had sent out to intercept any Whig expresses. It was dark, and Nelson mistook one of the riders for an American farmer.

"Have you heard anything about when the Regulars are coming out?" he asked.

The officer then displayed a startling amount of overreaction. He drew his sword and struck Nelson on the scalp, cutting him severely. He told the farmer that if he spoke to anyone about the incident, they'd come back and burn down his house. Nelson went home and let his wife dress his scalp. Then he picked up his weapons, mounted his horse, and left to alert his neighbors. The word was out even before the two official expresses, Paul Revere and William Dawes, began to ride. Actually, there was a third official express, but his name is lost to us.

## REVERE CAPTURED

The Committee of Safety (the Patriot group organized to defend against British raids) told Revere and Dawes that even more important than warning the people of Concord to hide their weapons and ammunition was warning Sam Adams and John Hancock, who were in Lexington. One of the missions of the British expedition was to arrest those two Patriot leaders.

Dawes, a tanner whose business required him to frequently leave Boston, took the land route. He was known to the guards and was able to talk his way past them. Revere left from Charlestown and joined Dawes much later. On the way to Lexington, each courier stopped to warn the militia commanders, ministers, and Patriot leaders. These officials sent out their own couriers and activated a variety of prearranged signals to call up the militia.

Revere got to Lexington and the two Patriot leaders first, but was soon joined by Dawes. Unfortunately, Hancock didn't want to leave. Revere and Dawes set out for Concord. On the way, they met young Dr. Samuel Prescott, heading home after a long night of courting his fiancée. Prescott was an ardent Son of Liberty and offered to help them spread the news. Because the British screeners seemed to be everywhere, Revere told his companions there was a good chance they might be captured. Therefore, they should split up and try to alarm every farmhouse in the area. Suddenly, a crowd of British officers surrounded them. The Americans spurred their horses, and both Prescott and Dawes got away, although Dawes' horse threw him and ran away. Revere was captured.

## PAUL REVERE NEVER GOT THE CHANCE TO WARN EVERY INDIVIDUAL FARMER, BUT BY CONTACTING COMMUNITY LEADERS, HE WAS ABLE TO SPREAD THE WORD NEAR AND FAR.

The British gloated that they now held "the noted Paul Revere." Revere didn't deny that he was an express. But he warned them that the country was rising, and if they continued on, they would be dead men. As they rode on, the officers heard the rattle of drums, the clanging of church bells, the booms of signal guns, and saw the glow of beacon fires. These alarming noises and sights came from their front and their rear. More guns, more bells, and more drums. The British grew nervous.

Finally, they released Revere and rode back toward Lexington and the main body. Revere, unhorsed and hampered by high, heavy boots and spurs, trudged back to Lexington, determined to get Hancock and Adams to move. He knew that Prescott, a good rider mounted on a splendid—and fresh—horse had gotten to Concord. So Paul Revere never got the chance to warn every individual farmer, but by contacting community leaders, he was able to spread the word near and far.

Finally, bowing to the combined arguments of Revere, Adams, and his fiancée, Dorothy Quincy, Hancock agreed to leave. Revere then helped Hancock's secretary, John Lowell, hide a large trunk full of incriminating papers. As the two men were moving the trunk out of a tavern, the vanguard of the British column, accompanied by the officers who had captured Revere, appeared. They ignored the two men lugging the trunk. Their eyes were focused on a small body of militia on Lexington Common.

## THE REDCOATS ARRIVE

All the time Paul Revere had been riding, the British column had been marching toward Lexington. Early on April 19, 1775, they arrived in Lexington. The column was composed of the flank companies of each regiment in the Boston garrison.

Each regiment had two flank companies, one of light infantry and one of grenadiers. Grenadiers were big, strong men, originally trained to throw hand grenades. Early grenades proved to be too dangerous to their users, and became obsolete, but armies kept the big men as shock troops. Light infantry were quite different from grenadiers. They were wiry, quick moving men, trained to think for themselves instead of always waiting for orders. Their tactics were adaptations of the tactics of American Indians and American rangers. Men in both types of flank companies were considered the elite of the army.

The light infantry, commanded by a marine officer, Major John Pitcairn, were the vanguard. Behind them were the big grenadiers with the commander of the entire column, Colonel Francis Smith. The troops were not happy. Their boats had put them ashore at the wrong place, and they had to wade through freezing water that ranged from thigh-high to waist-deep.

When the light infantry got to Lexington, they found a group of about sixty militiamen waiting for them on the town common.

"Disperse, ye damned rebels, and lay down your arms!" Pitcairn yelled.

Militia Captain John Parker looked at the British column of 280 light infantry and decided there were too many. "Let the troops pass by. Do not molest them, without they being first," he told his troops.

As the Regulars came closer, Parker told his men to disperse, but keep their muskets. Somebody fired a shot. The light infantry charged huzzaing and firing. Seven militiamen were killed and nine wounded. One British soldier was lightly wounded.

After that incident, the British troops learned for the first time that Concord was their destination. Some of the officers were appalled at the idea of marching farther into hostile territory, but the men fired a victory salute and gave three cheers. Their discomfort forgotten and confident that the "rebels" could offer only feeble resistance, the Redcoats marched out of Lexington. But as they were leaving Lexington, more militia were entering. Parker soon had twice as many men as he had during the fight. Soon, they, too, would be leaving for Concord.

## THE MILITIA MAKES ITS STAND

When the British troops arrived in Concord, there were few military stores in town. On April 7, when they learned that Gage had determined to seize the supplies in Concord, the Committee of Safety had sent Paul Revere to the militia commander in Concord to warn him. The commander, Colonel James Barrett, who led a five-company regiment of Middlesex militia, had many of the stores in his house. Prescott's arrival had spurred the citizens to move the rest of the supplies out.

The British found only some wooden gun carriages, 500 pounds of lead bullets in sacks, and some barrels of flour. They burned the wooden gun carriages and threw the flour and bullets into a pond. Water, of course, had no effect on the lead bullets, and because the troops didn't bother to break open the watertight barrels, it had no effect on the flour, either. They also dug up three buried cannons, but they couldn't move them without the gun carriages they had burned.

PREVIOUS PAGE: THE BATTLE OF LEXINGTON AS IMAGINED BY WILLIAM BARNES WOLLEN, A TWENTIETH CENTURY PAINTER. AS THE PICTURE SUGGESTS, THE PATRIOT FORCES WERE GREATLY OUTNUMBERED BY THE BRITISH.

The Battle of Lexington, 19th April 1775, 1910 (oil on canvas), Wollen, William Barnes (1857-1936)

They found no men of military age in the town. Then they heard fife and drum music. Two regiments of the Middlesex militia—500 men—were marching on the other side of the North Bridge. They were marching to *The White Cockade*, a song of the Jacobite rebels of 1745, that used the tune of *Highland Laddie*, a traditional Scottish air (which British bagpipers played in 1942 as their army moved up to attack the Germans at El Alamein). To the British, who had derided the colonial militia as an ineffectual rabble, the sight was something of a shock.

More shock was to come. Captain Walter Laurie took three companies of light infantry to guard the North Bridge. He ordered them to prepare for street firing. They formed a long column, four abreast. In eighteenth-century street fighting, the first rank would fire and immediately run to the rear while the second rank fired and followed them. As the first rank was reloading, the third and fourth ranks would be firing. This made it possible for soldiers with muzzle-loading muskets to keep up a continuous fire, sweeping a narrow, built-up street. The trouble with this tactic was that Concord had scattered houses, not narrow, built-up streets.

Somehow, even in spite of Lexington, the militia had the idea that the British would fire only blanks to scare them. They marched to the bridge, keeping time with the fife and drum. The nervous light infantry fired without orders. American Captain Timothy Brown heard a bullet whiz by.

"God damn it, they're firing ball," he yelled.

"Fire, fellow soldiers!" another militia officer shouted.

The militia were marching two abreast on an angle to the bridge. That meant their firing line was about 200 men. The light infantry firing line was four abreast.

A long, ripping volley, producing a cloud of white smoke, burst out of the militia line. Twelve Redcoats went down. Eight got up again and ran to the rear, followed by all the others. The militia volley was actually pretty poor shooting; the colonists were firing on the king's soldiers, and they were very, very nervous.

The light infantry ran back to headquarters with tales of thousands and thousands of rebels moving into Concord. Colonel Smith decided that his troops had carried out their assignment and there was no reason to stay in Concord. He sent a rider to Boston to ask for reinforcements and marched his troops back the way they had come.

## THE MILITIA VOLLEY WAS ACTUALLY PRETTY POOR SHOOTING; THE COLONISTS WERE FIRING ON THE KING'S SOLDIERS, AND THEY WERE VERY, VERY NERVOUS.

The march back was a nightmare. Militia contested every step. Sometimes they stood in line and traded volleys in the standard European fashion. More often, they used light infantry (or Native American) tactics, firing from behind stone walls or from concealed positions. Militia General William Heath took command of the rebel forces and got them to completely encircle the British column, moving ahead of the Redcoat advance guard and closely following the rear guard.

Gage sent Lord Percy off with reinforcements. His Lordship was in such a hurry that he neglected to take along extra ammunition wagons. He rescued Smith's troops, but his own soon began to run out of ammunition. Gage sent up six wagon loads of ammunition driven by grenadiers. They ran into a militia "alarm company." Members of alarm companies were troops considered too old for most fighting. They were called up only when there was a genuine alarm— just before the women and children were thrown into the fray.

This company was commanded by David Lamson, a free black man. He ordered the wagons to stop. The big grenadiers laughed at the old coots and whipped their horses. The old coots shot one horse in every wagon, stopping the wagons, killing two sergeants, and wounding the officer in charge. The rest of the grenadiers leaped off their wagons and ran for their lives. They surrendered to the first civilian they saw, an old woman working in her garden. She took them to the local militia captain and told them, "If you ever live to get back, tell King George that an old woman took six of his grenadiers prisoner."

PREVIOUS PAGE: BRITISH GRENADIERS RETREAT UNDER FIRE FROM CONCORD IN 1775. THE BRITISH LOST HEAVILY TO COLONIAL MILITIA FIRING THEIR MUSKETS FROM BEHIND TREES AND STONE WALLS. CONTRARY TO THE LEGEND, THIS WAS ONE OF THE FEW MAJOR ENGAGEMENTS IN THE REVOLUTIONARY WAR DURING WHICH THE AMERICANS ACTUALLY USED THESE NATIVE AMERICAN TACTICS.

Hand-colored woodcut of a 19th century illustration by Howard Pyle / North Wind Picture Archives / Alamy

Percy sent a courier back to beg for more ammunition, and the British eventually reached Charlestown. Of the 1,750 British involved, 73 were killed and 174 wounded. Patriot losses were trifling.

The militia didn't go home. More poured in from all over New England—tough frontiersmen from what was to become the independent republic of Vermont, mountaineers from New Hampshire, and uniformed elite units such as the Governor's Foot Guard from New Haven, Connecticut, led by a firebrand named Benedict Arnold.

The American Revolutionary War had begun.

CHAPTER 8

# THE BASTILLE: REPRESSIVE PRISON OR LUXURY HOTEL?

## (1789)

IF THE LEGEND OF THE FRENCH REVOLUTION IS TO BE BELIEVED, on July 14, 1789, a crowd of 1,000 angry, liberty-loving citizens descended on the Bastille, the famous Parisian prison, with the intention of releasing those prisoners held in atrocious conditions at the pleasure of His Majesty, Louis XVI.

They surrounded the great building and demanded that Governor Bernard-Rene de Launay hand over control of the institution. As de Launay vacillated, the crowd grew and became more forthright in its demands. Eventually it forced open one of the drawbridges protecting the imposing citadel. The soldiers guarding the Bastille fired on the angry mob trying to extricate the poor souls suffering inside.

When the revolutionaries wheeled in cannon with the intention of blasting their way through to the inner sanctum, de Launay, after chickening out of a threat to blow the building and everyone in it to kingdom come, surrendered and one of the great emblems of the tyranny of France's Ancien Regime had fallen to the people. The prisoners were liberated and a great blow for the revolution had been struck. The Ancien Regime, with its tri-partite political system in which authority was vested in the monarchy, aristocracy, and clergy, was on shaky ground.

The fall of the Bastille was a major symbolic event that was an important aid to the initial success of the French Revolution. Yet between the legend and the actual history there is considerable disparity. Rather than the act of one great

A CONTEMPORARY PAINTING SHOWS THE STORMING OF THE BASTILLE ON JULY 14, 1789, AN EVENT MANY CONSIDER TO BE THE PREEMINENT SYMBOL OF THE FRENCH REVOLUTION. YET EVEN THIS PAINTING DRAMATICALLY OVERESTIMATES THE DEGREE OF VIOLENCE INVOLVED ON THE GREAT DAY.

The Taking of the Bastille, 14th July 1789, late 18th century (coloured engraving), French School, (18th century)

**MYTH**

THE BASTILLE WAS A BASTION OF TORTURE, EVIL, AND POLITICAL OPPRESSION, WHERE INNOCENT CITIZENS WERE HELD BY THE TYRANT LOUIS XVI.

**REALITY**

ONLY SEVEN PRISONERS WERE HELD IN THE BASTILLE, WHERE THEY LIVED IN RELATIVE COMFORT AND EASE.

liar, it is a tissue of lies, boasts, rumors, misperceptions, omissions, and mysteries that coalesced into a myth, concocted, used, and believed by many, but never actually controlled by anyone.

The idea of the Bastille as a bastion for torture, evil, and oppression developed over centuries, yet for most of its career as a prison it was a relatively pleasant place to be incarcerated, so much so that some prisoners even protested against their release. Far from being a centerpiece of Louis XVI's tyrannical rule over his people, at the time of its storming the Bastille only had seven prisoners: four common criminals, a young noble deposited there at the request of his family, and two madmen who, after being released, were subsequently incarcerated at Charenton, a lunatic asylum.

Louis XVI's advisers had little notion of the Bastille as an important symbol of the regime. In fact at the time it was stormed, there were plans to demolish the Bastille because it cost too much money to run. The main reasons for the hold the Bastille continued to have on the public as a kind of bogeyman building were literary and historical. Little was actually known of what went on inside the building, and numerous former prisoners, including the leading enlightenment thinker Voltaire, capitalized on this by penning popular accounts of the Bastille that emphasized its evilness, in contrast to the relatively comfortable conditions inside.

Part of the lie of the Bastille is that its reputation for tyranny far exceeded the actual circumstances of incarceration. Of course, it must be remembered that the Bastille was still a prison where people could be incarcerated at the whim of the king. However, the release of these unfortunates was not the primary concern of the mob that descended on the prison on July 14. After having liberated 30,000 muskets from the Hotel des Invalides in the morning, the mob stormed the Bastille with the primary goal of obtaining barrels of gunpowder that had been taken there for safekeeping.

The inaccuracy of the reputation of the Bastille before its storming fed into its metamorphosis into the dominant symbol of the French Revolution thereafter. The truth therefore is somewhat irrelevant. It is a classic case of history belonging to the victors. As an act of liberation, storming the Bastille was chaotic and unconvincing. Yet as a symbol of liberty, it continues to have tremendous resonance.

## BASTILLE BEGINNINGS

The Bastille began its life not as a prison but as a fortress, which is the word's meaning in French. Charles V of France ordered it built between 1370 and 1383 to defend Paris from the English during the Hundred Years War in which the English Plantagenets fought the French House of Valois for the throne of France.

The Bastille was located on the eastern side of the city, near Fauborg Street in the Marais quarter, a poor area built over a former swamp. Four-and-a-half-stories tall, it was designed to protect the Porte de St. Antoine and was surrounded by its own moat, fed by the waters of the Seine. The Bastille had eight closely-spaced towers, roughly 77 feet. (23.5 meters) high, which were linked by walls, creating a rectangular edifice that contained two courtyards and an armory.

Following the Hundred Years War, the French continued to use the Bastille primarily as a military citadel. Important personages visiting Paris as guests of the king stayed there; as such, it was a hotel for VIPs well before it became a prison.

The use of the Bastille as a prison was pioneered by Cardinal Richelieu (1585–1642), the enormously influential chief minister of Louis XIII, who has also been credited with the foundation of the modern secret service and the modern nation state. Richelieu designated the prison as a state prison, a place where people could be imprisoned at the king's pleasure without any trial. The means used to carry out these arrests were known as "lettres de cachet", a letter from the king informing a person of his imprisonment. A lettre de cachet didn't say why the person had been arrested. Nor did it tell him how long he was going to be imprisoned.

In Richelieu's time, up to fifty-five people were incarcerated in the Bastille on this basis. Their ranks included people Richelieu suspected of plotting against

him, monks and priests who were either heretics or deranged, noblemen accused of various crimes, foreign spies and prisoners of war, and French officers jailed for military offences.

The talent pool of the Bastille was extended under the reign of the Sun King Louis XIV to include journalists and other writers who fell afoul of important personages. Rarely, however, were writers imprisoned because of their philosophies. Instead, it was usually for the writing of scurrilous, satirical, or libellous verse.

From 1685, when the staunchly Catholic Louis XIV revoked the Edict of Nantes, which had legislated religious tolerance in France, the writers were also accompanied by Protestant and Jansenist activists. The population of the Bastille

was further fleshed out with duelists caught in the act as well as the perpetrators of sensational crimes such as poisoning, witchcraft, and forgery.

Richelieu instituted the practice that the identity (and social rank) of the Bastille prisoners should be kept secret. The natural consequence of this is that people began to fill in the gaps for themselves, and the Bastille began to develop its mystique as a place of diabolical punishment. Its prisoners came to include many of France's best (and worst) writers and journalists, so it should be no surprise that small facts grew into large, terrible, and often untrue stories. Although the mystique of the Bastille was useful perhaps as a deterrent, it could also be used symbolically by people who wished to incite public sentiment against the Bourbon Monarchy.

# L'HOMME AU

*l'Homme au Masque de Fer, ou plutôt son histoire, qui a si long-tems fixé les recherches d'une infinité d'Auteurs*
*l'avoient plongée jusqu'à présent. Des papiers trouvés à la Bastille nous apprennent que cette dénomination n'à jamais a*

MASQUE DE FER.

*...rtir enfin du ténébreux Cahos où la discrétion barbare d'intermédiaires Ministériels
...à Louis de Bourbon, Comte de Vermandois, Fils naturel de Louis XIV né le 2. 8.bre*

AN IMAGE DEPICTS THE MYTHICAL
MAN IN THE IRON MASK, PERHAPS
THE BASTILLE'S MOST FAMOUS
PRISONER. IN REALITY, THE MASK
WORN BY THIS MYSTERIOUS
PRISONER WAS MADE OF
VELVET. HIS IDENTITY REMAINS
CONTESTED TO THIS DAY.
THIS IMAGE IDENTIFIES HIM
AS LOUIS DE BOURBON, AN
ILLEGITIMATE SON OF LOUIS XIV.
IT IS HIGHLY UNLIKELY THAT THIS
WAS THE CASE.

The Man in the Iron Mask (d.1703)
imprisoned in the Bastille, print of
1789-90 which identifies him as
Louis de Bourbon, Comte de Vermandois,
son of Louis XIV (1638-1715) and
Louise de la Valliere (1644-1710)
(colour engraving), French School,
(18th century)

## THE MAN IN THE IRON MASK

This dual effect can be seen in the most famous tale of the Bastille, the big fib otherwise known as the Legend of the Man in the Iron Mask, which nonetheless became one of the main reasons for the public's identification of the Bastille as a venue for unspeakable acts.

The diary of Lieutenant Etienne du Junca, an official at the Bastille from 1690 until his death in 1706, records on Thursday, September 18, 1698, the 3 PM arrival of a new governor of the Bastille, Bénigne d'Auvergne de Saint-Mars. With him, du Junca wrote, was a "longtime prisoner, whom he had in custody in Pignerol, and whom he kept always masked, and whose name has not been given to me, nor recorded."

The prisoner was placed in a room on the third floor of the Bertauderie Tower with two other prisoners, one imprisoned as a "retailer of ill speech against the state," and the other accused of sorcery and debauching young girls.

Saint-Mars had been governor of the citadel of Pignerol from 1665 to 1681, so by 1698, the mystery prisoner had been in captivity for at least 17 years. Du Junca's later remarks point to the fact that the prisoner was well treated, acted like a gentleman, and had no complaints. He was allowed to attend Mass on Sundays and holidays, but he had to keep his face covered by a "black velvet mask." Du Junca's report is the only mention of a mask, and note that it is black velvet, not iron. Five years later, on November 19, 1703, du Junca recorded the death and burial of the "unknown prisoner, who has worn a black velvet mask since his arrival here in 1698."

The man in the iron mask, immortalized by Alexander Dumas in his 1848 novel *The Vicomte of Bragelonne: Ten Years Later,* the final in the d'Artagnan Romances trilogy whose most famous volume is *The Three Musketeers,* was actually a man in a black velvet mask. Yet the mystery shrouding the Bastille and the lack of records kept on its secret prisoners allowed this legend to mutate into something entirely different.

In 1751, Voltaire, who not incidentally enjoyed two stints in the Bastille, wrote that his enigmatic predecessor wore an iron mask that was riveted around his head and had a "movable, hinged lower jaw held in place by springs that made it possible to eat while wearing it." The image caught the public's imagination and despite its falsity became a powerful tool employed by one of

# WHO WAS THE MAN IN THE BLACK VELVET MASK?

Voltaire's image of the man in the iron mask was not the only way the French author and philosopher mangled the truth of this prisoner to undermine the Ancien Regime. The reason for the man being masked, argued Voltaire, was to prevent his identification. Since at the turn of eighteenth century, celebrity culture did not exist, Voltaire supposed that the need to mask a prisoner meant he would be highly recognizable, most likely through a familial resemblance to the king, the one face in the realm that was known to everyone.

Voltaire conjectured that the man behind the mask was none other than the older half-brother of Louis XIV, who was imprisoned because he caused doubts as to the legitimacy of the king's succession. Another theory supposed it was Louis XIV's twin brother sequestered from birth for the same reason. There was no evidence at all for either theory.

With no conclusive evidence to determine who the masked man was, speculations have grown wilder over the years. Perhaps the most outlandish was that the masked man and elder brother of the king sired a child in prison to a woman who took the child to Corsica and raised him under her own name of Bonaparte, thus proving

that Napoleon was by birth a legitimate inheritor of the throne of France.

There have been theories that the man was the product of a tryst between the queen mother and a Moor, or was actually a woman. It's been suggested the man in the iron mask was the playwright Molière, whose death in 1673 was staged and who remained a prisoner of the king for another three decades. Why this might be the case has never been adequately explained. Other largely conspiratorial theories have supposed the man was English, usually either Charles II's rebellious illegitimate son, the Duke of Monmouth, or a progeny of Oliver Cromwell.

Given that the prisoner had accompanied Saint-Mars since his days in Pignerol, his probable identity is usually reduced to one of two men. The first was Antonio Ercole Matthioli, a politician from Mantua whose double dealings in sensitive diplomatic negotiations over the sale of the stronghold of Casale led the French to abduct and imprison him. On his arrest warrant was the special order of the king that "no person shall know what happened to this man." When pressed by his mistress, Madame de Pompadour, who had become

intrigued by this enigmatic figure, Louis XV told her he was the minister of an Italian Prince. Marie Antoinette received the same answer from her husband, Louis XVI.

Those in favor of this theory also point to the fact that when he died in the Bastille, the masked man was buried under the name of Marchioly, a small change from the Marthioly, which was the common Francification of the Italian's name. At the time it was also an Italian upper-class custom to wear a face mask when going out in the sun.

The other likely contender is Eustace Dauger, apparently a valet, and also a prisoner of Saint-Mars at Pignerol. At the time of his arrest, the secretary of state wrote to Saint-Mars, saying that "You must never, under any pretences, listen to what he may wish to tell you. You must threaten him with death if he speaks one word except about his actual needs. He is only a valet, and does not need much furniture."

Instructions were left for the governor to feed him personally and isolate him from the rest of the prison populace. While the timing of Dauger's arrest and imprisonment fits the known facts, no one actually knows who he was. Most likely he was imprisoned under a false name

and the reasons given for his confinement range from being the valet of a prominent French Huguenot and thus valued for the information he might have, someone hired by the state secretary as an assassin, or the black sheep of a prominent family who was engaged in schemes of debauchery, sodomy, and Satanism.

About the only certain truths in the case of the man in the iron mask is that he never wore one and that we will never know for sure who he was. Yet this legend helped establish the notoriety of the Bastille perhaps more than anything else.

the ideological progenitors of the French Revolution to undermine the legitimacy of the Ancien Regime.

## A FIVE-STAR PENITENTIARY

European prisons of the premodern era evoke images of dingy dungeons infested with rats, their inhabitants chained to walls with their arms, legs, and even necks in manacles. One thinks of a diet of vermin-infected gruel and bad water as likely to poison a person as quench the thirst. The opportunity to perform one's ablutions is limited, which the stench of the prisoner's cell attests to. Communication is forbidden, yet the honeycomb network of dungeons hums with the groans of broken men, tortured with everything from the iron maiden (a hinged casket with metal spikes inside), hot pokers, floggings, fingernail removal, and the rack.

The Bastille was nothing like this. Yet as the enlightenment took hold of France in the eighteenth century, writers and journalists increasingly found themselves incarcerated. Many took their revenge by breaking the vow of silence concerning their experiences that was a condition of release and publishing lurid memoirs of their confinement. The more lurid they were, the hungrier the public was to hear them. To some extent they were the eighteenth century equivalent of tabloid newspapers such as *News of the World* and the *New York Post*. And they were far more prone to taking liberties with the truth.

In René Auguste Constantin de Renneville's *Histoire de la Bastille*, he talks of

The castle where cruelty, misery, and persecution howl,
Which should make the bottom of hell shudder in amazement,
Which would make the devil feel dread if he lived here,
Is now subject to the wild Bernaville . . .

Mortals, be frightened by this image of hell,
A tyrant rules here, the devil is his slave,
For Satan punishes only the guilty,
But Bernaville may cut down Innocence herself.

De Renneville spent more than a decade in the Bastille between 1702 and his release at the intercession of England's Queen Anne in 1713. The Bernaville mentioned above was the governor of the Bastille during his incarceration. While a decade is a long time to spend cooped up against your will, the meals Renneville experienced suggest that the hell he was describing was at least a French hell to the extent it still maintained a certain pride in the quality of its cuisine, as is evidenced by the description of his first meal here.

"The turnkey put one of my serviettes in the table and placed my dinner on it, which consisted of pea soup garnished with lettuce, well simmered and appetizing to look at, with a quarter of fowl to follow; in one dish there was a juicy beefsteak, with plenty of gravy and a sprinkling of parsley, in another a quarter of forcemeat pie well stuffed with sweetbreads, cock's combs, asparagus, mushrooms, and truffles; and in a third, a ragout of sheep's tongue, the whole excellently cooked; for dessert a biscuit and two pippins. The turnkey insisted on pouring my wine. This was good burgundy, and the bread was excellent. I asked him to drink, but he declared it was not permitted. I asked if I should pay for my food, or whether I was indebted to the king for it. He told me that I only had to ask freely for whatever would give me pleasure, that they would try and satisfy me and His Majesty paid for it all."

## LIFE IN THE BASTILLE WAS FAIRLY RELAXED. PRISONERS WERE ABLE TO VISIT EACH OTHER IN THEIR CELLS OR PLAY BOULES IN THE COURTYARD, AND SOME ENJOYED CONJUGAL VISITS FROM THEIR WIVES.

Such gourmet rations are a consistent theme in accounts of the Bastille. If one of its inhabitants happened to be a nobleman, he was permitted to bring a servant and furnish the rooms with beds and comfortable chairs. The king supported more indigent prisoners and paid them an allowance. For much of the Bastille's history, if a prisoner didn't fully spend his allowance, he was permitted to keep the remainder. In the seventeenth century, there were cases of people pleading for their sentences to be extended so that they could save enough money to get their finances in order before returning to the harsh economic realities of the outside world.

Although the lower dungeons were still in use during the reign of Louis XIV and Louis XV, they were used only to punish transgressions of the prison rules. For the most part, life in the Bastille was fairly relaxed. Prisoners were able to visit each other in their cells or play boules in the courtyard, and some enjoyed conjugal visits from their wives. Others were even allowed to spend the day in town before returning to the jail at night.

## LOUIS XVI: BASTILLE REFORMER

It was mainly from the trumped-up memoirs of disaffected inhabitants that the Bastille earned its sinister reputation. Among these authors was lawyer Simon Nicholas Henri Linguet, whose 1783 *Memoirs sur la Bastille* affected the fervor with which the castle was stormed in 1789. Yet his account of his two-year stretch in the Bastille from 1780–82 was vastly exaggerated in its description of the horrors and entirely self-serving in its attempt to arouse the sympathy of the liberal-minded public (and the well-off intelligentsia of the salons who were fond of patronizing tragic causes) to increase his fame.

Ironically, having helped incite the storming of the Bastille, Linguet became a casualty of the Terror, when the Jacobin faction of the revolutionaries under Robespierre seized control of the government and purged around 40,000 citizens in the space of less than a year. Arrested in 1793, he lost his head to the guillotine in 1794. In addition to Linguet, one of the most famous latter-day prisoners of the Bastille was ersatz aristocrat, con man, and probable lunatic Jean Henri Latude (a.k.a. Danry), a three-time escapee of the French prison system, whose incarceration was his only real claim to fame. His original crime was to send poison to Madame de Pompadour, then a letter to warn her in the hope of a reward. Although his memoirs were published subsequent to the storming of the Bastille, he was picked up as a cause by the important salon personage Madame Negros, whose intercession secured his very public (and lucrative release) in 1784, and thus his story became widely known. Yet his conduct in the prison system was frequently violent. He deliberately sabotaged possible release dates to maximize the gain from his incarceration. Determined to become an aristocrat, even if only by self-invention, his imprisonment hardly qualifies as a grievous injustice.

The same can be said for the Marquis de Sade, who was removed from the Bastille, allegedly for shouting out his window, "they are massacring us in here!" just days before it was stormed. He had been arrested under the king's lettre de cachet for a variety of crimes, including raping, drugging, sodomizing, and torturing his servants.

ALTHOUGH OFTEN PORTRAYED AS A TERRIBLE TYRANT BY THE REVOLUTIONARIES, LOUIS XVI, SHOWN HERE, WAS ACTUALLY SOMETHING OF A REFORMER, IF A BIT TOO SLOW FOR THE TIMES. DURING HIS REIGN, HE ACTUALLY IMPROVED CONDITIONS IN THE BASTILLE AND WAS THINKING OF GETTING RID OF IT BECAUSE OF THE NEGATIVE (IF NOT ENTIRELY ACCURATE) REPUTATION IT HAD AMONG THE CITIZENS OF PARIS.

Louis XVI (1754-93) (oil on canvas), Lefevre, Robert (1755-1830)

The real history of the Bastille also gives the lie to the commonly held belief that Louis XVI was a terrible tyrant. During his reign he actually improved conditions in the Bastille and his other state prisons. Torture was banned, and in 1776 so was the use of the cold and damp dungeons. Legal reforms also meant that lettres de cachet now had to indicate the probable duration of imprisonment. Between Louis XVI's accession to the throne in 1774 and July 14, 1789, only 240 people were imprisoned in the Bastille. It was never full, meaning the best rooms were used, and in terms of food, clothes, and furnishing, the conditions were benign.

Despite this, the Bastille remained unpopular mainly through the lies of former inmates such as Linguet and Latude. Realizing this and that the expense of maintaining the prison might better be diverted to improving Paris' police force, there were plans as far back as 1784 to close the Bastille, then knock it down. In several proposals, the prison would be replaced by a public square. One planned to put a statue of Louis XVI at the center of this square, to be made from the melted down chains, bars, and locks of the prison.

## A MEAGER HAUL

On July 14, when Bernard de Launay eventually surrendered and the citizens of Paris invaded the Bastille, they were gratified to discover the gunpowder they were looking for but somewhat surprised and disappointed to discover only seven prisoners. Initially it was supposed there must be secret dungeons and tunnels where the true evil of the Bastille was concealed, but a concerted search found no evidence of any such thing.

The beneficiaries of perhaps the greatest symbolic moment in the French Revolution were four forgers, common criminals who might have been incarcerated in any old jail; a mad Irishman, prone to thinking he was Julius Caesar and God, who had originally been arrested for second-rate espionage; and another lunatic, Tavernier, who had been arrested for his part in an assassination attempt on Louis XV. After being carried through the streets of Paris in triumph by their liberators, it wasn't long before these two were admitted to the asylum at Charenton. The final prisoner was the Comte de Solages, who had been imprisoned under a lettre de cachet at the request of his family for sexual deviancy that included incest.

## SIGNIFICANCE OF THE BASTILLE

As the stormers of the Bastille went through it, finding little evidence of the evil they imagined went inside its walls, they started to make things up. A toothed wheel paraded as an instrument of torture was actually part of a printing press, while a medieval suit of armor was described as an iron corset used to render prisoners completely immobile.

Someone even managed to "discover" the nonexistent iron mask, while bones found on the cellar floor, most likely belonging to soldiers killed in the half-dozen or more attacks on the Bastille over the centuries, were produced as those of the man in the iron mask.

It's always easier to mythologize a place that has no material existence. By February 1790, the Bastille had been demolished and turned into revolutionary relics that were sold throughout France at a profit. In June 1790, the National Assembly issued a special decree: "Stirred by legitimate admiration for the heroic intrepidity of the conquerors of the Bastille . . . who have exposed and sacrificed their lives to shake off the yoke of slavery and bring freedom to their country, the Assembly agrees that each of the conquerors of the Bastille who is able to bear arms shall at public expense receive a coat and full set of weapons, according to the uniform of the nation."

Nine hundred and fifty-four people signed up. Not all of them had been there. The true facts of the Bastille proved to be helpless in the path of the tall tales that established its sinister reputation. The Bastille became an evil symbol that helped lead to the eventual downfall of the Ancien Regime. If the angry mob had failed in storming the Bastille, it's quite possible the revolution could have faltered. As such, the importance of the Bastille to the success of the French Revolution cannot be denied, and it is a crucial moment in a series of events that helped create the modern world. Even today it resonates for many as a symbol of freedom in the fight against tyranny. Yet just because the Bastille remains a powerful symbol doesn't mean that the grounds for this were true.

# LIES FROM THE AMERICAN WILD WEST

IN A PAINTING BY NEWELL CON-
VERS WYETH (1882-1945), JESSE
JAMES AND MEMBERS OF HIS
GANG, INCLUDING HIS BROTHER
FRANK, ARE SEEN HIDING OUT IN
THE WOODS IN MISSOURI. MANY
BELIEVE THE NOTORIOUS BANDIT
AND NINETEENTH CENTURY ROBIN
HOOD WAS NOTHING MORE THAN A
COLD-BLOODED KILLER.

The James Brothers in Missouri
(oil on canvas), Wyeth, Newell Convers
(1882-1945)

# CHAPTER 9

# JESSE JAMES: AMERICAN ROBIN HOOD OR SERIAL MURDERER?

## (1860s–1880s)

**B**URSTS OF STEAM SPAT FROM THE TRAIN'S VALVES AS IT pulled to a stop in Centralia, Missouri, on the morning of September 27, 1864. A small contingent of men on horseback approached the locomotive, excited but cautious.

A man in his mid-twenties wearing a cavalryman's hat atop his head of wavy, shoulder-length brown hair stood out from the rest. Clearly, he was the leader. His men deferentially pulled their horses back from the train as he approached, waiting to hear his command. The leader briefly trotted his horse up the train line, looking through the windows at the frightened faces inside as he decided what to do next. When the train arrived, he and his eighty or so followers— guerrilla soldiers fighting for the Confederate cause—had been in the midst of sacking the small town, a bastion, they believed, of Union sympathizers. Not unlike a scene from a Wild West movie, the group had descended upon Centralia out of the blue, firing their guns in the air as they raced through the town center, robbing people at gunpoint in their own houses, looting stores and homes, and horsewhipping anyone within reach. Any Centralia citizen who read the newspaper headlines would have immediately identified the carnival of violence as the work of William "Bloody Bill" Anderson and his crew.

Anderson's nickname was well earned. The previous year, he had ridden with Quantrill's Raiders, the most famous and feared of all Confederate guerilla forces in Missouri, and he had taken part in the slaughter of about 200 men and boys in Lawrence, Kansas. Anderson, by all reports, was the most gleeful killer of

JESSE JAMES, RIGHT, AND HIS BROTHER FRANK POSE FOR THE CAMERA IN 1870. TOGETHER, THEY SERVED IN THE CIVIL WAR IN THE NOTORIOUS CONFEDERATE GUERILLA FORCE OF "BLOODY BILL" ANDERSON. AFTER THE WAR, THEY BEGAN ROBBING BANKS AND TRAINS. FRANK DECIDED TO END HIS CRIMINAL CAREER AFTER A BOTCHED JOB THAT NETTED ALL OF TWENTY-THREE DOLLARS AND ENDED IN THE DEATHS OF TWO GANG MEMBERS.

Frank (1843-1915) and Jesse James (1847-82) c.1870 (b/w photo), American Photographer, (19th century)

**MYTH**
JESSE JAMES WAS AN AMERICAN VERSION OF ROBIN HOOD, STEALING FROM THE RICH AND GIVING TO THE POOR.

**REALITY**
JESSE JAMES WAS A CONFEDERATE VIGILANTE WHO KILLED AND STOLE WITHOUT MERCY, GIVING NOTHING BACK TO THE POOR.

all the raiders, and he single-handedly murdered more Lawrence residents than any of his comrades.

As Bloody Bill sized up the situation, a lanky sixteen-year-old member of his gang with sandy hair and piercing blue eyes steadied his horse, one hand on the reins. Brand-new to the war, Jesse James gripped a revolver tightly in his other hand. His brother Frank, four years his senior, was nearby. Frank, like Anderson, had been a member of Quantrill's Raiders, but he had been injured in a battle and sent home to recover. By the time Frank's wound healed, Anderson had broken from Quantrill to form his own group. By then, Jesse and Frank's mother, Zerelda, had decided Jesse was old enough for war and sent her two boys out to fight for the Confederate cause in which she strongly believed. They immediately joined up with Anderson.

When Bloody Bill found out that a large group of Union soldiers traveling home on furlough were on the train, he made his decision. He moved his men to their car and ordered the soldiers to step off the train, where he made them line up and take off their uniforms. He spent the next few minutes waxing poetic on how he expected no quarter in this war and in turn would give none, and how for "honor's" sake he would not let any captured enemy soldier live.

"Every Federal soldier I put my finger on," Anderson announced, "will die like a dog." He told his guerrillas to ready their weapons. A split-second of crackling rolling gunfire was the last sound the unarmed Union soldiers would ever hear. In a moment, each of the approximately twenty-five lay dead next to the train tracks.

Young Jesse James would earn a reputation in Anderson's band as a dedicated and disciplined fighter. Unlike many other inexperienced soldiers in the guerilla contingent, James would patiently hold his trigger until the perfect moment during an ambush and fearlessly charge straight at the enemy during a frontal assault.

Until now, though, he had probably not killed anyone in cold blood; if he had killed anyone, it was an armed soldier, and it was during a battle. What James contributed to at the Centralia train depot was mass murder. Far from being repulsed by what was patently a war crime, James was unfazed, perhaps even exhilarated. In fact, in the short time he spent with Anderson, he came to view him as a war hero and leader. When Anderson was killed soon after Centralia—hunted down and shot dead by Union Major Samuel Cox of Gallatin, Missouri—James vowed to avenge the murder of his hero.

## THE MYTH OF THE NOBLE OUTLAW

American popular culture often portrays Jesse James as the epitome of the "good" bad guy. In addition to numerous songs and Internet fan sites, the robber and murderer from Missouri has been featured in at least fifty Hollywood movies and made into an action figure for children. He has at least one annual festival named after him, complete with barbecue, fire truck rides, and chainsaw carving demonstrations. James even made an appearance on the sitcom *The Brady Bunch*, which, incredibly, offers one of the more accurate depictions of Jesse James—as a violent, homicidal fanatic who killed innocent, unarmed people without remorse.

The more popular perception of James as a Robin Hood–type figure appears in writings such as *Cowboy Songs and Other Frontier Ballads,* the 1910 book that launched author John Lomax's career, thanks largely to a foreword by Theodore Roosevelt. In it, Roosevelt alluded to one of the most famous folk songs of its time, "The Ballad of Jesse James." The song depicts the most famous bandit who ever lived as a generous, good-natured man who "stole from the rich and gave to the poor," and who was treacherously shot in the back by "a dirty little coward" who had "ate of Jesse's bread and slept in Jesse's bed." Roosevelt couldn't help but see the parallel with Robin Hood and wrote:

"There is something very curious in the reproduction here on this new continent of essentially the conditions of ballad-growth which obtained in medieval England; including, by the way, sympathy for the outlaw, Jesse James taking the place of Robin Hood."

A testament to the power of incomplete information, misunderstood facts, and historical unawareness, Roosevelt's commentary has been misinterpreted by Jesse James fans over the past century. Writers and bloggers on the subject like to say that Theodore Roosevelt "proclaimed" Jesse James the "American Robin Hood," implying that he was a fan of the legendary outlaw. It's doubtful that Roosevelt, a former police commissioner New York City, would have glorified a cold-blooded killer like Jesse James. Indeed, his statement does no such thing. Roosevelt "proclaims" nothing. He simply made an observation of fact: American ballad writers viewed Jesse as Robin Hood's counterpart.

## BUSHWHACKERS VS. JAYHAWKERS

Jesse James came into the world at the perfect time and in the ideal place to forge a career as the most famous outlaw of his time. He was born in 1847 to Robert and Zerelda James in Clay County, Missouri, which had become a slave state under the Missouri Compromise.

When Jesse was seven years old, however, the Kansas-Nebraska Act was passed, overturning the 1820 Missouri Compromise and opening up the possibility for Missouri and Kansas to outlaw slavery by popular vote. More than three-quarters of Missouri's population was pro-slavery, but the less-settled Kansas territory was up for grabs.

The territories soon descended into violent struggles between the two sides. As abolitionist settlers from the Eastern states descended upon Kansas and Missouri en masse to swing the vote their way, slavery supporters earned their nickname "bushwhackers" by raiding abolitionist settlements, with anti-slavery "jayhawkers" responding in kind. In 1855, John Brown conducted his bloody raid in Kansas, murdering five pro-slavery settlers, after which the two sides entered into a minor terror-style war, ten years before the Civil War broke out.

The James family, which owned seven slaves, lived in the middle of it all. Clay County was only one county away from the Missouri-Kansas border, with the relatively heavily populated Kansas City just to its south. Jesse's father Robert, a Baptist preacher, had left the home in 1850 to spread the Word in the gold mining camps, and he died of cholera within three months.

Their mother, Zerelda, remarried twice, was an unapologetically vocal supporter for the Confederate cause. That, combined with her oldest son's bushwhacking exploits, put the James' farm in the sights of Union intelligence gatherers during the Civil War. (The fact is, Zerelda did pass information to Confederate guerillas whenever she could.)

On more than one occasion, Union sympathizers harassed the family. Once, in the summer of 1863, a group of local Union militiamen—not Union troops, but Federalist-supporting citizens who had formed their own group, much as Quantrill and Anderson had done—arrived on the farm looking for information on the whereabouts of the Confederate raiders. Jesse and a slave were tending to the tobacco crops when the militiamen suddenly appeared. They grabbed Jesse by the scruff of the neck and dragged him across the field to the house. Zerelda characteristically approached them head-on, shouting obscenities at her hated neighbors-turned-enemies.

Ignoring Zerelda and her man-sized bravado, they focused their attention on the more timid half of the couple, Zerelda's third husband, Ruben Samuels. The militiamen had come prepared. They took out a noose, put it around Samuels' neck, and pulled it tight, threatening to hang him if he didn't provide information. Samuels pleaded ignorance to every question they shouted at him.

Their patience at an end, the militiamen threw the other end of the rope around a tree branch and pulled Samuels off the ground. They let their kicking, choking victim down before he was strangled to death, but Samuels suffered a permanent injury to this throat. Jesse could only sit and watch this brutality with horror—and hatred.

## APPLYING THE LESSONS OF BLOODY BILL

Jesse James had entered the war a committed Confederate; by 1865, he was a fanatic. His loathing for the Union had been potent during the war and was fired up afterward by the same thing that infuriated most rebels: Reconstruction, which, among other acts perceived as injustices, disenfranchised former Confederate soldiers and sympathizers from the political process.

After the war, the boy nicknamed "Dingus" (in his early teens, Jesse accidentally shot off part of his finger and exclaimed "Dingus!" to avoid swearing) quickly displayed the leadership qualities and temperament of a world-class outlaw. As a veteran of Bill Anderson's legendary marauders, he (as well as his brother) commanded immediate respect. Anderson's group was known by Confederate sympathizers as an elite group of warriors, and anyone who served with them was known as a special brand of soldier.

Still seething over their defeat in the war and their perception that the Union was treating ex-Confederates unfairly, many bushwhackers turned to crime. These

# A SOUTHERN BELLE WITH ATTITUDE

Whatever authoritative void the death of Jesse's father, Robert James, might have left in his childrens' lives, his wife, Zerelda James, more than made up for.

Nearly six-feet tall and possessing a powerful temper that could frighten even her friends, Zerelda was staunchly political and backed the pro-slavery movement with fierce intensity. No dainty Southern belle, she applauded the bushwhackers' border raids and every murder they committed, and she would give a tongue-lashing to anyone who didn't agree with her.

Anger and self-righteousness don't pay the bills, though. With no source of income after her husband's death, Zerelda was on the verge of losing the farm. She quickly married a wealthy farmer twice her age, Benjamin Simms. At the age of fifty-two, however, Simms had no interest in raising Jesse, Frank, and their younger sister, Susan. He and Zerelda separated and soon afterward, he died.

In less than two years, Zerelda was married again. The third time was a charm. Dr. Ruben Samuels was three years younger than her and

was more interested in her children than Simms had been. He took legal guardianship over the children, gave up his physician practice, and moved to Zerelda's house to become a farmer—all seemingly under the orders of Zerelda.

Near the end of the war, her collaboration with Confederate guerillas was so well known that she came to the attention of top Union brass in the area. In January 1865, Union officials issued order No. 9, which required the departure of the James clan, along with ten other local families, from Missouri within twenty days. Zerelda, Ruben, and Susan packed up and were moved to southern Nebraska.

Eventually, she would come back to Missouri. After Jesse's death, Zerelda spread a small bed of river stones on the ground beneath his tombstone. She invited sightseers to take a stone with them as a memento—for twenty-five cents apiece. When the stone supply ran thin, Zerelda would go down to the river and collect more.

men never accepted the end of the war. Missouri was perhaps the most ravaged state in the war, and the political scene was hot as ever. Unless a man could prove that he had not served in the Confederacy, he would be summarily barred from holding public office, voting, and even preaching in a church. Three-quarters of Missouri's men were removed from public life and left powerless.

As a result, the Radical Republicans took over the government and eventually gave civil rights to all former slaves. With no Union army left to fight, bushwhackers focused their fury on banks and trains—symbols of creeping industrialism and Yankee encroachment. Every dollar stolen, every train derailed was a victory. And if a former Union soldier or Republican politician were murdered in the process, so much the better. Of course, the riches gained—tens of thousands of dollars on occasion—was surely the main draw, a fact almost always ignored by writers and movie-makers enamored with antebellum-minded bandits.

Jesse and Frank James quickly established names for themselves in the burgeoning new industry of bank and train holdups. Many historians credit them with "inventing" the daylight bank robbery in Liberty, Missouri, situated in Clay County, where the James boys lived. On February 13, 1866, a group of men on horses entered town. Two of them walked into the bank, and one approached the counter to request change for a ten-dollar bill. As one of the two cashiers stepped up to the counter, the man put a revolver in his face and demanded all the cash in the bank. The cashier complied.

After being handed nearly $60,000, the robbers forced the two men into the vault and shut the door. Assuming the door would automatically lock, they ran out of the bank and mounted their horses. The employees pushed the unlocked door open and shouted into the street that the bank had just been robbed. One of the riders, panicking, turned and shot and killed a nineteen-year-old boy who happened to be standing near the bank. It was the first known bank robbery of its kind, and a reward was immediately posted for the bandits.

Many believe that Jesse and Frank were the perpetrators. The pair lived only a few miles from the bank, and other known bushwhackers were spotted near the scene firing their guns as they fled. Everyone in town seemed to know the robbers were former bushwhackers, and many knew about Jesse and Frank's past. One witness who claimed to know the James brothers provided a positive iden-

tification but retracted it when his life was threatened. Nevertheless, no hard evidence linked them to the robbery.

## MURDER AND REVENGE IN GALLATIN

The first crime unquestionably committed by Jesse James occurred on December 7, 1869, in Gallatin, Missouri. Shortly after noon, Jesse and a partner (probably Frank) entered the Daviess County Savings Association. As the perpetrator did in Liberty, Jesse asked to cash in a bank note, this time worth $100. The cashier, a local Democratic leader named John Sheets, sat down at his desk to fill out a receipt.

Jesse eyed the bankman carefully. He silently pulled out his revolver and drew a bead on him. A deafening blast resounded throughout the small building. Sheets must have felt as if he were hit by a truck. Before Sheets had time to realize he had been shot in the chest, Jesse put a bullet in his head.

The killer grabbed a folder from a desk, and the two criminals fled. As they began galloping out of town, Jesse's horse reared, and he fell from the saddle. His foot got caught in the stirrup, and he was ingloriously dragged for fifty feet before freeing himself. At this point, Gallatin's citizens had rallied and were on the heels of the two bandits. Jesse quickly mounted his partner's horse, and the two escaped from the town center. Within about a mile, the robbers were relieved to see a lone man riding his horse. Jesse James wasted no time pulling out his gun and making it clear that the horse was going with him. The rider, of course, submitted to the request.

For all that trouble, the haul amounted to little or nothing in cash. But stealing money possibly wasn't why Jesse had ridden to the Daviess County bank in the first place. Jesse was likely there to avenge the death of his hero, Bloody Bill Anderson.

Anderson's killer, Samuel Cox, had returned to his hometown after the war, and Jesse by all accounts knew it. And, tragically, Sheets happened to bear a close resemblance to Cox. Whether or not Jesse pointedly sought out Cox or just mistook Sheets for Cox when he entered the bank, he was fully convinced that he had killed his sworn enemy in cold blood, telling everyone who would listen afterward that he had avenged the death of the great bushwhacker.

Jesse James was a warrior to the core, but the stories of his being a "good" bad guy are exaggerations of true tales or complete fabrications. It is true that

A NINETEENTH-CENTURY LITHOGRAPH DEPICTS WILLIAM "BLOODY BILL" ANDERSON. IN CENTRALIA, MISSOURI, HE ORDERED THE EXECUTION OF MORE THAN TWENTY UNARMED UNION SOLDIERS CAPTURED ON THEIR WAY HOME ON FURLOUGH. HIS BOASTS OF OFFERING NO QUARTER TO THE ENEMY MADE MANY THINK OF HIM MORE AS A HOMICIDAL MANIAC THAN A SOLDIER. YOUNG JESSE JAMES, HOWEVER, LOOKED UP TO ANDERSON AND ARGUABLY CONSIDERED HIM A FATHER FIGURE.

"Bloody Bill" Anderson (litho), American School, (19th century)

he didn't rob banks *only* for the money, that he most likely felt passionately that his deeds were as political in nature as the were profitable, and that he is known to have robbed train passengers only twice during his many train robberies (although that's twice more than the mythmakers mention). But his goal certainly wasn't to share his newly gained wealth with the poor.

Jesse was, in essence, fighting an old war, at a time when most other former Confederates were moving on with their lives. Jesse was bold, for sure, but he was also angry and impetuous—a dangerous combination that is not mentioned in any known ballads.

## CONTEMPORARY MYTHMAKING

On the afternoon of September 26, 1872, three men approached the ticket gate at the Kansas City Exposition where a large crowd of attendees was exiting. One of the men strutted up to the window and grabbed a tin box filled with approximately $1,000.

The shocked ticket taker reached out and attempted to take it back. A slight scuffle ensued, but when one of the men fired his revolver, the ticket taker backed off. The crowd froze, trying to make sense of what had just happened, and the trio made a quick getaway on their horses. The James brothers are usually credited with the audacious robbery; however, a few historians question their involvement, emphasizing a lack of hard evidence proving such.

Whether or not Jesse and Frank were the actual perpetrators, the robbery secured them a place in frontier mythology. *Kansas City Times* editor John Newman Edwards was particularly taken with the brazen act. Although he had known about Jesse James and his exploits (the young man was quickly gaining fame around the country), this was the robbery that inspired Edwards to begin a body of writing dedicated to heaping praise on the former Confederate guerilla and contributing more than any other writer to the myth of Jesse James.

Originally from Virginia, Edwards himself had served in the Confederacy, fighting Union troops in Texas and, like Jesse and his comrades, refused to surrender when the war ended. Rather than lay down their weapons, he and his comrades crossed the border into Mexico, where the unit's commander, General Jo Shelby, attempted to hire his unit out in the fight between Juaristas and the French, but to no avail.

In 1866, the Confederates decided life in the Union was preferable to Mexico, and they trudged back north. Eventually landing a job at the Kansas newspaper, Edwards decided to promote the South's cause with his pen. By all signs, he was better at soldiering than writing, but his influence on building Jesse James up into a folk hero is inarguable.

After the Kansas City Exposition raid, Edwards penned an article entitled "The Most Desperate and Daring Robbery of the Age," in which he praises his heroes' "cold-blooded nerve and stupendously daring villainy" and claimed the robbery "surpasse[d] anything in the criminal history of this country, at least if it does not overtop the exploits of Claude Duval or Jack Shepherd [famous English highway bandits]." (Another newspaper, the *Kansas City Daily Journal of Commerce,* took a more sober view of the heist. The perpetrators, it said, were "deserving of hanging to a limb.") Later, in a piece called "The Chivalry of Crime," Edwards wrote:

> These are not bad citizens, but they are bad because they live out of their time. The nineteenth century is not the social soil for men who might have sat with Arthur at the round table, ridden at tourney with Launcelot … What they did we condemn. But the way they did it we cannot help admiring. It was as though three bandits had come to us from the storied [and medieval German village of] Odenwald … and shown us how the things were done that poets sing of.

The obsession of the Confederate aristocracy with all things medieval is well documented. Even by nineteenth century standards, though, Edwards' prose is over the top. Yet his readers loved it, buying completely into the sanitized and romanticized version of medieval Europe transported to the American frontier. And Jesse James himself was one of Edwards' biggest fans. He began leaving letters at the scenes of his crimes, seemingly aware that they would somehow land up in the hands of Edwards or another supporter in the press. (Some historians believe that the letters were fakes, possibly penned by Edwards himself.) In them, Jesse would rail against Yankee corruption and portray himself as a stout fighter for the poor and oppressed. In one letter, he actually claimed to "rob from the rich and give to the poor"; in another, he compared himself to Napoleon and Alexander the Great.

Edwards later claimed to have conducted a lengthy personal interview with Jesse James, in which the bandit again stated his innocence in certain crimes. Jesse presented detailed evidence expunging himself of robberies, train heists, and murders; dared his enemies to confront him; and painted himself as a victim of conspiracies and Yankee animosity. The interview is at best a "purple patch" exaggeration of a real conversation or a complete fabrication on the part of Edwards.

## END OF THE ROAD

In 1877, Jesse James and his gang decided to strike the Union where they believed it would hurt most—in the north. They settled on the town of Northfield, Minnesota, most likely because it was the hometown of former "carpetbag" governor of Mississippi, Adelbert Ames, who had served in the Civil War under Union General Benjamin Butler, a man particularly despised by Southerners for his draconian security measures in New Orleans.

The now-wealthy Ames later married Butler's daughter and, it was believed, kept his fortune deposited in the town's bank. The James gang rode for days to reach their destination—a huge effort for what began as a sadly conceived objective and ended up a resounding fiasco.

Late in the morning of September 7, the James brothers and three members of their gang rode into Northfield. Over a breakfast of ham and eggs in a tavern, they discussed politics and tried to bet the tavern owner that the Democrats would win the next election. (The owner didn't take them up on it.) They left the restaurant, took a quick look around the town, split up into two groups, and rode out of town.

At about 2 PM, the group of five rendezvoused near the bank in town. Two stayed with the horses outside while the three others, including Jesse and Frank, entered the bank. Jesse pulled out his gun, approached the counter, and demanded cash. Within moments, word of the robbery spread from the bank to the streets. Chaos ensued.

Outside, Northfield's citizens began shooting at the two strangers outside the bank. Others, who carried no weapons, threw rocks at them. Inside, the robbers argued with the bank employees. Waving their guns menacingly, the James brothers and their partner screamed at the bankmen to open the safe.

The safe, though, was on a time lock and could not be opened. The robbers threatened to kill everyone in the bank if the safe weren't opened. At some point, a Swedish immigrant named Nicholas Gustavson who didn't speak English and was understandably confused, was told to get out the way. When he didn't move, he was shot in the head.

With bullets flying in the street, the robbers abandoned the idea of gaining access to the safe. They grabbed any money lying within sight and left the bank to make their getaway. On their way out, one of them, believed to have been Jesse, put his gun to the head of cashier Joseph Heywood and pulled the trigger, killing him instantly. In the gunfight outside, two members of the James gang were killed. Jesse, Frank, and four other gang members (three of whom had been guarding a nearby bridge) escaped. They made off with $26.70, or $4.45 each.

## IN THE GUNFIGHT OUTSIDE, TWO MEMBERS OF THE JAMES GANG WERE KILLED. JESSE, FRANK, AND FOUR OTHER GANG MEMBERS ESCAPED. THEY MADE OFF WITH $26.70, OR $4.45 EACH.

To Frank James, Northfield marked the beginning of the end of his career. He soon became exhausted from living on the run and moved east with his family, eventually earning a living as a livestock importer. He was arrested, arraigned, and/or tried for various crimes between the years 1882 and 1884, beating the rap every time.

Jesse, though, wouldn't give up the ghost. After the departure of Frank, he went to work forming a new crew and hatched new schemes to lash out as his old enemy, the Union, and make a lot of money while doing it. But by this time, it just wasn't the same. There were a number of bounties on Jesse's head, and even those who made a hero out of him in the '70s began considering him more of a problem than an asset. Reconstruction had ended, and most ex-Confederate soldiers and Southern sympathizers had begun adapting to life in the Union. Even John Newman Edwards stopped answering Jesse's correspondences. Other than penning his erstwhile hero's obituary in 1882, Edwards was done with him.

# MURDERED BY A "DIRTY LITTLE COWARD"

Jesse James sat in the parlor of his new home in St. Joseph, Missouri, with two new members of his gang. It was April 3, 1882, and almost all the others had been arrested or killed. A number of bounties had been offered for the capture of Jesse over the years, but recently the governor of Missouri himself issued a $10,000 reward—and now Jesse was worried. With the state itself officially turning against him, it finally began to dawn on Jesse that he had been living in the past. Clearly, there was little room in the future of the United States for a gun-toting Confederate outlaw.

As the three men discussed the details of a new robbery they were planning, Jesse looked up at a picture on the wall. Noticing that it was covered with dust or perhaps cobwebs, he stood up to brush it clean. He turned his back to his new partners: Charles Ford, who had taken part in Jesse's last train robbery, and Charles's twenty-year-old brother Robert, an inexperienced but eager hanger-on of the now much-diminished gang. As the brothers watched Jesse cleaning the picture, Robert quietly drew his gun. Jesse's last action in his brief but exciting life was uncharacteristically domestic. Robert pulled the trigger. The bullet tore through the back of Jesse's head. The loud crack of Robert's gun was punctuated by the thud of the outlaw's body hitting the floor.

In all, Jesse James is believed to have taken part in twenty-six robberies of banks and trains, netting more than $260,000 by very conservative estimates, and killing at least ten people, including a Pinkerton detective investigating the James brothers, innocent bystanders, and bank and train employees. The majority of victims were unarmed.

His assassination is called a "betrayal" by the Jesse James mythmakers, but what exactly Ford *owed* Jesse is never mentioned. Sure, he was living in Jesse's house, but they were there to plan another robbery. In a time when horses were the quickest modes of transportation, it wasn't uncommon to have long-term guests.

Jesse James and Robert Ford were partners in crime, and their relationship was one of convenience. Jesse and his gang members weren't friends in the traditional sense of the word. In fact, Jesse had murdered a member of his own gang, Ed Miller. As rewards for his capture began piling up, Jesse was becoming more and more paranoid of getting caught, and he believed Miller was going to contact the authorities to collect the reward. They argued about it, and Jesse killed Miller in an ensuing duel. (Miller was the one who introduced Jesse to Robert Ford.)

In another moment of extreme suspicion, Jesse had asked certain members of the gang to kill Jim Cummins, another member of whom Jesse was suspicious. They refused, but Cummins disappeared soon afterward, probably murdered by Jesse.

Rarely is Ford's name mentioned in popular history without the qualifying adjective "coward" because he didn't look into Jesse's eyes when he pulled the trigger. He may well have been a coward, but that's beside the point. His murder of Jesse James was a gang-style hit. Ford wanted the reward money, plain and simple, and he killed the one man who stood in his way. Most of Jesse James' victims, too, held no weapon and posed no threat to their murderer. John Sheets was killed as he was filling out a bank slip; Jesse shot the Northfield bank clerk Joseph Heywood in the side of the head. If such actions can be called those of a coward, Jesse James and Robert Ford were not that different.

## NOTHING MORE THAN A CRIMINAL

Ford's betrayal was the perfect (and final) element in the making of the Jesse James myth. Despite the Robin Hood comparison, no evidence exists that he ever gave his money to the poor. His first heists fit perfectly into the mold of Robin Hood, however. In the traditional folklore approach of portraying good and evil in simplistic, black-and-white terms, the English outlaw was the ultimate force of "good" fighting against the utterly "bad" Sheriff of Nottingham.

During the morality play of Reconstruction, the Union was the definition of "bad," and Jesse James, a powerful symbol who fought the faceless institutions of an evil empire, was the manifestation of "good." Problem is, real people work for institutions such as banks, and Jesse James' legend wasn't helped by the men he shot point blank. Many of the people who Jesse James killed had courageously refused to give the outlaw what he wanted, even though they knew their lives were in danger.

They were, in many cases, ordinary citizens who didn't have much to lose by emptying a safe, yet nevertheless resisted Jesse James—out of strong convictions of what is right and wrong, out of contempt for someone who flouts the law, or out of down-home personal feistiness. If a morality play *must* be made from the story of Jesse James, it is his victims who are the heroes.

It is true that sympathy for Jesse James and his gang ran throughout the region, but the extent of it has been exaggerated—as have the reasons for it. As in the present day, police in the nineteenth century relied heavily on witnesses and informants to catch their man; without first-hand information, an investigation would usually hit a dead end.

Jesse James well understood the critical importance of the cooperation of those who could identify him. (No wonder he began getting paranoid when it became clear that his support was running thin.) No doubt, many people who might have stepped forward in the beginning of his career refused to do so because of Jesse's reputation as a courageous opposer of Reconstruction. It's probable, however, that many, if not most, remained silent because they understood the violent, vengeful nature of the man who had run with Bloody Bill.

In his masterful biography of the outlaw, T. J. Stiles goes so far as to introduce the concept of terrorism to the Jesse James story.

> Terrorist? The term hardly fits with the traditional image of [Jesse James] as a Wild West outlaw yippin' and yellin' and shooting it out with the county sheriff. But he saw himself as a Southerner, a Confederate, a vindicator of the rebel cause, and so he must be seen in the context of Southern "outlaws"—particularly the Klan and other highly political paramilitary forces. . . . He cannot be confused with the Red Brigades, the Tamil Tigers, Osama bin Laden, or other groups that now shape our image of terrorism. But he was a political partisan in a hotly partisan era, and he eagerly offered himself up as a polarizing symbol of the Confederate project for postwar Missouri.

If Osama bin Laden's purpose on September 11, 2001 was, as many political commentators claim, to spark a worldwide uprising of Muslims against Western ways, a parallel view of Jesse James, whose goal was to get the "South to rise again," is at least arguable.

What is more than just arguable is the view of the James gang as a smaller, less effective version of Cosa Nostra, Hell's Angels, or MS 13. They take money where they can get it and use it to fund their next crime.

Reporters in the days of modern criminal enterprises would never get away with such aggrandizing, openly supportive screeds in the style of John Newman Edwards. But that's not to say a certain gangland mythos doesn't exist. Outlaw biker gangs are often depicted in film and literature as freedom-loving good ol' boys who will only hurt you if you're dumb enough to stand in the way of their road-warrior lifestyle. In reality, they rob and kill with the best of them.

And the Italian Mafia has long been viewed by many as a renegade agency against mainstream corruption. Mario Puzo's *The Godfather* series of books, along with the subsequent movies, surely attests to this, as did the daily public show of support outside the New York City courthouse every day that Gambino crime boss John Gotti stood trial for racketeering—when, in reality, if any one of those supporters were to be in the wrong place at the wrong time or possess something of value, he or she would experience the same fate as the victims of Jesse James.

# CHAPTER 10

# THE EARP GANG: LAWMEN OR LAWLESS?

## (1881)

S AY "O.K. CORRAL" AND THE SAME PICTURE POPS INTO THE minds of millions of people. It's a cold, blustery day in the high desert town of Tombstone, Arizona. Three tall, broad-shouldered men whose long frock coats do not hide their holstered six-guns slowly walk down the dusty street. With them is a skinny man with a shotgun. Waiting for them are four grubby men in cowboy outfits. They, too, have holstered six-guns.

The head of the frock-coated crew, U.S. Marshal Wyatt Earp, leading his brothers, Virgil and Morgan, and their friend, Doc Holliday, tells the cowboys to throw up their hands. Instead, the cowboys draw their guns, and both sides begin shooting. When the smoke clears, the evil Clanton-McLaury Gang, which had been terrorizing Tombstone, is kaput, and the lawmen led by Wyatt Earp have established law and order.

In reality, Wyatt Earp was wearing a mackinaw instead of a frock coat, and he carried his revolver in a coat pocket instead of a holster. The truth is that the "Shootout at the O.K. Corral" was the climax of a feud between two crooked factions, and the victors fled from Arizona after they'd committed murder.

## WYATT EARP AND HIS GANG

Wyatt Earp was once a city policeman in Wichita, Kansas, from April 1875, until he was fired for disturbing the peace a year later. Later, he became number two man in the four-man police force of Dodge City, Kansas. At the time of the gunfight at the O.K. Corral, he was merely a citizen deputized temporarily by

WYATT BARRY STAPP EARP POSED FOR THIS 1883 PHOTO WHEN HE WAS THE NUMBER TWO MAN ON THE FOUR-MAN POLICE FORCE OF DODGE CITY, KANSAS. EARP, A GAMBLER AND CON MAN, FOUND IT HELPFUL TO HAVE A LAW-ENFORCEMENT BADGE. HIS ATTEMPT TO BECOME A SHERIFF IN ARIZONA LED TO ONE OF THE AMERICAN WEST'S MOST CELEBRATED GUNFIGHTS.

Wyatt Earp (1848-1929) June, 1883 (b/w photo), American Photographer, (19th century)

## MYTH

LAWMAN WYATT EARP AND HIS FRIENDS WIPED OUT THE CLANTON-MCLAURY GANG OF CATTLE RUSTLERS WHO HAD BEEN TERRORIZING THE TOWN OF TOMBSTONE, ARIZONA, IN 1881.

## REALITY

AT LEAST TWO OF THE EARP GANG—WYATT EARP AND DOC HOLLIDAY—WERE CROOKS THEMSELVES. THE TWO CLANTONS WERE BUT A TINY PART OF THE RUSTLER COMMUNITY OF COCHISE COUNTY, AND THE TWO MCLAURYS WERE MERELY CLANTON NEIGHBORS. THE SHOOTOUT WAS THE CLIMAX OF A FEUD BETWEEN TWO CROOKED FACTIONS.

his brother Virgil, Tombstone's city marshal, and the nominal leader of his group. Wyatt claimed to have been appointed a deputy U.S. marshal after the fight, but the U.S. Marshal Service has no record of such an appointment.

Wyatt did not specialize in law enforcement. He had been a buffalo hunter and was always a professional gambler. He was also a con man. In 1879, he was run out of Mobeetie, Texas, for selling gold bricks.

Allie Earp, Virgil's wife, once raged to Mattie Blaylock, Wyatt's common-law wife, about "that sneaking, con-man husband of yours" when Doc Holliday's paramour, "Big Nose Kate" Elder, accidentally opened a closet door. Paula Mitchell Marks, in *And Die in the West,* quotes Allie's description of what happened: "Out of the closet came a big suitcase, spewing out on the floor . . . Wigs and beards made of unraveled rope and sewn on black cloth masks, some false mustaches, a church deacon's black frock coat, a checkered suit like drummers wear, a little bamboo cane. Lots of things like that!"

"Wyatt's disguises," Big Nose Kate said. She explained that Doc had let Wyatt keep them in her house, but she demanded that he move them. She told Allie that Wyatt would soon have "that stupid Virge under his thumb like Morgan."

Early in his career, Wyatt was a horse thief in the Cherokee Nation. He was arrested and indicted but jumped bail and fled the Indian Territory. When the big cattle herds bypassed Dodge City for rail terminals farther west, Wyatt Earp moved in 1879 to another boom town—Tombstone, Arizona, where silver mining attracted—besides miners—card sharks, prostitutes, merchants, and thieves. Wyatt, thirty-one, was joined by his brothers, Jim, thirty-eight,

Virgil, thirty-six, and Morgan, twenty-eight. Jim, a wounded Civil War veteran, took no part in any of the gunfights.

Wyatt expected to make money not by digging silver ore but by gambling and staking out mining claims and selling them. He also hoped to be appointed sheriff when Cochise County, which includes Tombstone, was created. He became a deputy sheriff in Pima County, but later resigned and was replaced by Johnny Behan. The reason for his resignation has never been explained. It may have been because Pima County Sheriff Charlie Shibell was a Democrat, and being associated with him might hurt Wyatt's chances for sheriff when Cochise County was created.

Sheriffs in newly created Arizona counties were appointed by the territorial governor, Republican John C. Fremont. The sheriff collected taxes as well as enforcing the law, and he was allowed to keep 10 percent of what he collected. In Cochise County, the job would bring in about $40,000 a year, a fortune in the 1880s. But instead of Earp, Fremont appointed Democrat John Behan, possibly because the majority of voters in the new county were Democrats.

Among other things, Wyatt coveted Behan's mistress, Josie Marcus, sometimes called Sadie Marcus. She was an actress and an heiress to a San Francisco department store fortune. She soon left the dull Behan for the dashing gambler. Wyatt happily squired the pretty actress around while he forbade his common-law-wife, Mattie, from going downtown or associating with the townspeople.

Wyatt obtained a quarter interest in the faro—a card-and-board gambling game—franchise at the Long Branch Saloon. Wyatt had already established a reputation as a tough gunman, through his tall tales of how he tamed the Kansas cow towns and his demonstrated expertise with a revolver. It seems he got his share of the franchise because he could provide protection for his associates. He also got a job with Wells Fargo. Often described as a stage coach guard, it was more of a company detective—someone to investigate robberies and run down the robbers. The other Earp brothers found jobs in Tombstone: Jim became a faro dealer, and Morgan went to work for Wells Fargo.

Virgil became a policeman in Tombstone, reporting to City Marshal Fred White. Being a police officer was important to Virgil, Wyatt, and Morgan. A lawman could carry a gun openly. (In 1881, many Tombstone citizens carried guns, but they were concealed, because "packing heat" was illegal.) And if you were in law enforcement, there were numerous ways to intimidate opponents. That's another reason why Wyatt yearned to be sheriff and Virgil to be city marshal. Morgan, too, became a city policeman.

## DOC HOLLIDAY

Soon after the Earps settled in Tombstone, they were joined by an old friend, John Henry "Doc" Holliday.

Holliday was different from the Earps and their other friends. He was not a poorly educated, rough-hewn frontiersman, but a highly educated, southern gentleman from Georgia. He had graduated from the Pennsylvania College of Dental Surgery in Philadelphia, but he learned that he had tuberculosis, a disease that killed his mother when he was fifteen. A doctor advised him to move to a drier climate. Holliday moved west, where he practiced dentistry. He learned, however, that he could make more money pulling hidden aces than pulling teeth, so he abandoned dentistry.

Gambling in the Wild West was a dangerous profession. Players who felt they had been cheated seldom complained to authorities, although Doc was once arrested on a charge of "unequal gambling." Instead of the law, they resorted to fists, knives, or guns. Wasted by TB, Holliday would have been beaten in a fist fight by the average fifteen-year-old boy, according to his friend and Earp gang member Bat Masterson. So he usually carried two revolvers, one in a shoulder holster and one in a hip holster. As additional insurance, he also carried a long knife under his coat tails.

"Doc Holliday was afraid of nothing on earth," Masterson said. And quite unlike the cool and calculating Wyatt Earp, he had a hot temper. TB may have had something to do with Holliday's daring. He often said he'd rather die from a bullet or a knife than "consumption," as the disease was then called.

"He was the nerviest, speediest, deadliest man with a six-gun I ever saw," said Wyatt Earp. His draw was phenomenally fast, but there was nothing phenomenal about his accuracy. He missed many opponents and hit others in places like a hand or foot, even at point-blank range.

Many of the shootings took place when Doc was drunk. Nevertheless, he managed to fill a number of graves. He was utterly unpredictable and the most feared member of the Earp Gang. But this smooth-talking multiple murderer

JOHN HENRY HOLLIDAY, KNOWN AS DOC, WAS A DENTIST BUT WAS MORE FAMOUS FOR PULLING A GUN THAN PULLING TEETH. HE WAS DYING FROM TUBERCULOSIS, BUT SAID HE'D PREFER TO DIE IN A GUN OR KNIFE FIGHT. HOT-TEMPERED AND HOMICIDAL, HE KILLED AT LEAST EIGHT MEN AND WOUNDED MANY MORE. BUT IN THE END, TUBERCULOSIS, NOT A BULLET OR A BLADE, BROUGHT HIM DOWN.

Doc Holliday, c.1882 (b/w photo), American Photographer, (19th century)

was also the author of many affectionate—not romantic—and philosophic letters to his cousin, Melanie Holliday, a Catholic nun. Melanie Holliday, author Margaret Mitchell said, was the inspiration for the saintly Melanie Wilkes in *Gone With the Wind*.

## THE COWBOYS

Many of the ranchers in the county sold cattle they hadn't raised. The herds came from Mexico, and they were supplied by a large and active rustler community, known locally as the Cowboys.

The rustlers did not constitute a gang. They were a loosely organized group who tended to follow a couple of proficient gunfighters named Curly Bill Brocius and John Ringo. One of the groups within the rustler community was the Clanton brothers, who followed their family patriarch, Newman "Old Man" Clanton. After Old Man was killed by Mexican soldiers while driving a herd of stolen Mexican cattle, the Clantons continued in the family business.

The McLaury brothers, friends of the Clantons, were customers of the rustlers, rather than rustlers themselves—as were most of the ranchers in Cochise County. One of them explained that giving the rustlers a cold shoulder was a good way to get your cattle stolen. Nevertheless, to the Earps, being friendly with the Clantons made you as bad as them.

Rustling cattle was not the Cowboys' biggest sin in the eyes of Tombstone's residents. Few of the citizens raised cattle, and anyway, the cows mostly came from Mexico. The Civil War was still a vivid memory in the 1880s, and most of the Tombstone citizens came from Union territory and belonged to the Republican Party. Most of the Cowboys were Southerners and Democrats. The two groups just didn't like each other.

## THE LAW AND ORDER LEAGUE

The Earps, who were strong Union men, quickly became popular with the citizens of Tombstone. The fact that Doc Holliday's father had been a Confederate major didn't seem to detract from the Earp Gang's popularity. Wyatt especially made powerful friends, such as John P. Clum, editor of the *Tombstone Epitaph*, who became mayor of Tombstone.

Clum backed the Earp brothers when they organized what they called "the Law and Order League," a political party. Wyatt planned to run for sheriff at the next election. In addition to cattle rustling, there were stagecoach robberies. The Law and Order people claimed that the Cowboys were responsible; the Cowboys blamed other citizens of Tombstone. The evidence indicates that both groups were right. Two stage robbers, Frank Stillwell and Pete Spencer, arrested

## WHO WAS WHO AT THE O.K. CORRAL

Few retellings of the O.K. Corral tale hint at how complicated the situation was. Parables about good versus evil are seldom complicated. Consequently, the traditional cast of characters is limited to the Earp brothers and Doc Holliday on one side and the Clanton and McLaury brothers on the other, with Johnny Behan as a kind of evil presence lurking in the background.

The cast of major characters was more numerous, though. It included the following:

**The Earp Gang**

Wyatt Earp

His brothers: Jim, Virgil, Morgan, and Warren

Doc Holliday

Bat Masterson (very briefly in Tombstone)

**The Cowboys**

Newman "Old Man" Clanton

His sons: Ike (Joseph Isaac), Phin (Phineas Fay), and Billy (William Harrison)

Frank McLaury

His younger brother: Tom

Curly Bill Brocius

Johnny Ringo

**Alleged Stagecoach Robbers**

Billy Leonard, a Cowboy and a close friend of Doc Holliday

Harry Head, a Cowboy

Jim Crane, a Cowboy

Luther King, a member of the Cowboy faction

**Others Connected with the Stagecoach Robbery**

Bob Paul, a candidate for sheriff in adjoining Pima County

Frank Stillwell, Tombstone businessman

Pete Spencer, Frank Stillwell's partner in business and crime

Marshall Williams, Wells Fargo's special agent in Tombstone and alleged "inside man"

**The Earp Women**

Big Nose Kate Elder (or Fisher), Doc Holliday's paramour

Allie Earp, Virgil Earp's wife

Mattie Blaylock, Wyatt's common-law wife

Josie Marcus, whom Wyatt later married after abandoning Mattie

Lou Earp, Morgan Earp's common-law wife

Bessie Earp, Jim Earp's wife

**Arizona Lawmen and Officials**

Fred White, Tombstone city marshal

Johnny Behan, Cochise County sheriff

Billy "Breck" Breakenridge, Behan's deputy

Cawley Dake, the U.S. Marshal for Arizona

John P. Clum, mayor of Tombstone and editor of the *Tombstone Epitaph*

for stage robbery about this time, were also Tombstone businessmen. They were tracked down and arrested by two posses, one led by Johnny Behan and composed of Cowboy sympathizers, the other organized by Virgil and Wyatt Earp.

The Earps and the Cowboys were not always deadly enemies. They could cooperate when each side saw an advantage. One such instance made an Earp a top law enforcer: Virgil became city marshal (police chief) of Tombstone in 1880.

Tombstone City Marshal Fred White was disarming Curly Bill Brocius. The young Cowboy leader was celebrating something or other by shooting his Colt .45 in a city street. White demanded Curly Bill's gun. The cowboy handed it over, but the gun went off, fatally wounding White.

Virgil Earp claimed he had grabbed Brocius from behind just as he was handing over the gun, and the gun accidentally fired. The best explanation is that the rustler used a trick known ever after as the "Curly Bill spin." The gunman hands the officer his revolver butt first, but with his trigger finger in the trigger guard. As the officer reaches for the gun, the gunman with a quick flip of his wrist reverses the muzzle's direction and fires.

Fred White agreed that the shooting was accidental, but he was in severe shock, and Curly Bill performed his trick so fast White couldn't really see what happened.

The outcome was advantageous to both Brocius and Earp. Curly Bill got rid of an annoying lawman, and Virgil replaced the missing marshal until an election could be held. Virgil expected to win easily, but he was defeated by Ben Sippy in a special election and then in the regular municipal election in January 1881. But six months later, Sippy took a leave of absence and disappeared. He never returned to Tombstone. Virgil again became city marshal. But relations between the Earps and the Cowboys had taken a strange turn well before that.

## THE FATAL STAGE ROBBERY

On March 15, 1881, an attempt was made to hold up the stagecoach traveling from Tombstone to Benson, Arizona, shortly after it left Tombstone. The robbery was botched. The driver and a passenger were killed, but the coach got away.

Sheriff Johnny Behan organized a posse, including his deputy, Billy Breakenridge, Wyatt Earp, Virgil Earp, Morgan Earp, Doc Holliday, Wells Fargo special agent Marshall Williams, and Bat Masterson, who was visiting his friend Wyatt. The fact that the posse included the Earp Gang and their friends, like Masterson and Williams, shows that Behan had no great animosity toward Wyatt Earp—at least not enough to preclude him from enlisting first-class fighting men.

The posse didn't catch the robbers, but they found a man named Luther King, who confessed that he had held the bandits' horses. King didn't want to talk until his captors told him (mendaciously) that a woman who was a friend of Doc Holliday had been killed. King, like many others, was absolutely terrified of the scrawny little dentist. He identified the holdup men as Harry Head and Jim Crane, a couple of Cowboys not well known in Tombstone, and Billy Leonard, a former watchmaker from New York, who was a close personal friend of Doc Holliday. Leonard, like Holliday, had a good education, and the two had been close ever since Doc ran a saloon in Las Vegas, New Mexico.

There was a rumor that Doc himself was one of the robbers. A telegraph worker said he and a companion were stringing wires when they heard a shot and saw Doc Holliday racing for Tombstone—and away from the shots. It has been pointed out that King did not identify Holliday as one of the robbers. But with the hot-headed and homicidal Holliday on the posse, could he be expected to?

## THERE WAS A RUMOR THAT DOC HIMSELF WAS ONE OF THE ROBBERS. A TELEGRAPH WORKER SAID HE AND A COMPANION WERE STRINGING WIRES WHEN THEY HEARD A SHOT AND SAW DOC HOLLIDAY RACING FOR TOMBSTONE— AND AWAY FROM THE SHOTS.

There were other rumors. One was that Marshall Williams, who was later fired from Wells Fargo after it was proved that he had been stealing from the company for years, had tipped off Wyatt and Morgan Earp that the stage was carrying $20,000 worth of silver. At any rate, many in Tombstone and Cochise County said the hunters were hunting themselves. Behan and Breakenridge brought King back to Tombstone, left him in the care of Undersheriff Harry Woods. Minutes later, King walked out of the unlocked rear door of the jail and disappeared.

Doc's on-again-off-again lover, Big Nose Kate, added to the rumors. After one of her spats with Holliday (he wanted her to stop being a freelance prostitute and she didn't want to), Kate got drunk and told Johnny Behan that Doc had helped rob the stage and committed the two murders. Behan arrested Holliday,

but when Kate sobered up, she recanted her statement, and Justice Wells Spicer ordered the charges dropped.

## WYATT'S PUBLICITY PROPOSAL

None of this activity distracted Wyatt Earp from his main goal—the sheriff's badge. He decided that the stagecoach robbery offered an opportunity in his campaign for sheriff. He approached Ike Clanton and Frank McLaury, who either knew Leonard, Head, and Crane or knew how to reach them.

"I told them I wanted the glory of capturing Leonard, Head, and Crane, and if I could do it, it would help me make the race for sheriff at the next election," Wyatt said. "I told them that if they would put me on the track of Leonard, Head, and Crane and tell me where those men were hid, I would give them all the reward and would never let anyone know where I got the information."

Ike corroborated the story—sort of. He said Wyatt offered, in addition to the reward money, $6,000 from his own pocket. And, Ike added, Wyatt said "he would have to kill them or else have to leave the country. He said he and his brother, Morg, had piped off to Doc Holliday and Billy Leonard the money that was going off on the stage, and he said he could not afford to capture them."

Wyatt said Ike responded favorably to the offer, saying he wanted to get Billy Leonard "out of the way," because Leonard owned some land Ike was trying to claim.

Circumstances made Wyatt's scheme moot. Leonard and Head got themselves killed a short time later. Jim Crane got a gang together and killed the killers. Then Crane went traveling with Old Man Clanton and his stolen Mexican steers. Mexican troops stole across the border and hit Clanton's party where they were camped. Crane, like Old Man Clanton, died.

But that didn't stop Wyatt. He proposed a new scheme to Clanton: Clanton, his brothers, and their friends would pretend to hold up a stage, then the Earp brothers and Holliday would appear and drive them off. Nobody would be hurt, and Wyatt would get good publicity for his campaign for sheriff.

Ike Clanton was not a man who would make a major scientific breakthrough or write a classic novel, but he wasn't that dumb. He knew that in Wyatt's case there could be no stage robber like a dead stage robber. He rejected the proposal and tension between the Clantons and McLaurys, and the Earp gang increased tremendously.

The Law and Order League in Tombstone began talking about forming a vigilance committee to rid Chochise County of the Cowboys. On the other side, Marshall Williams, the Wells Fargo agent, had gotten drunk and said enough to Ike Clanton to make him think that Wyatt Earp had talked about his deal with Clanton. Ike was furious and terrified that his rustler friends would learn that he had agreed to double-cross some of them.

## THE ROAD TO THE O.K. CORRAL

On October 25, 1881, Tom McLaury planned to come into Tombstone to complete a cattle sale to a local butcher. Ike Clanton decided to accompany him, with the main purpose of getting drunk.

While 18-year-old Tom McLaury was conducting family business, Ike Clanton checked his guns as the law required, had a few drinks, and entered a lunchroom at around midnight. Doc Holliday and Wyatt and Morgan Earp were also in the lunchroom. The Clanton and Earp accounts differ, but both agree that Holliday and Clanton had words concerning the robbery of the Benson stage coach. Holliday and Morgan Earp, with their hands under their coats, told Clanton to go and get his gun. Virgil Earp showed up with his deputy, Jim Flynn. Virgil told Morgan and Doc to leave Ike alone, adding, according to Ike, "While Jim is here."

According to Wyatt Earp, Ike Clanton left, threatening Holliday and all three Earps. "You must not think I won't be after you all in the morning," Wyatt quoted Ike. If Ike said that, he was not only drunk but insane. He was alone and no gunfighter, but all three Earps were highly proficient, and Holliday was perhaps the most dangerous man in Arizona.

About half an hour later, Ike got into a poker game. At the same table were Tom McLaury, Johnny Behan, and Virgil Earp. The next morning, he retrieved his revolver and rifle and staggered around Tombstone muttering threats against the Earp brothers and Holliday. Virgil and Morgan Earp sneaked up behind him, bashed him on the head, took his guns, and dragged him off to the courtroom, where the judge fined him $25 and confiscated the guns.

A little later, Wyatt encountered teenaged Tom McLaury. "Are you heeled or not?" Earp asked the boy. McLaury said he had no gun. Earp slapped him with his left hand and hit him on the head with his gun. The kid fell down and struggled to his feet. Wyatt pistol-whipped him again. A witness recalled that McLaury protested that "he had never done anything against him [Earp] and was a friend of his," but Wyatt hit Tom McLaury "four or five times" with the revolver.

Around 2 PM, Billy Clanton and Frank McLaury rode into Tombstone. They knew Ike would be drunk and expected that Tom would have trouble getting him into the wagon. The citizens of Tombstone expected a lot more trouble than that.

THE O.K. CORRAL, SCENE OF THE LEGENDARY GUNFIGHT BETWEEN THE EARP GANG AND THE CLANTONS AND MCLAURYS. THE SHOOTOUT WAS THE CLIMAX OF A FEUD BETWEEN TWO CROOKED FACTIONS, NOT A VICTORY FOR LAW AND ORDER, IN SPITE OF THE MANY REENACTMENTS IN THE MOVIES AND ON TELEVISION.

OK Corral (b/w photo), Arizona Historical Society

## SHOOTOUT AT THE O.K. CORRAL

One citizen, B. E. Fallehy, later testified, "I heard some stranger ask Ike Clanton what was the trouble; he said there would be no trouble. . . . Then saw the marshal [Virgil Earp] and the sheriff [Johnny Behan] talking. The sheriff says, 'What's the trouble?' the marshal says, 'Those men have been making threats. I will not arrest them but will kill them on sight.' "

Behan found the cowboys lined up on Fremont Street behind the O.K. Corral. Ike Clanton and Tom McLaury said they had no guns. Behan searched them to make sure. Billy Clanton and Frank McLaury said they were just about to leave. In a minute they'd take both their guns and themselves out of Tombstone. Behan looked up the street and saw the Earp Gang approaching.

For some reason, Virgil Earp had given Doc Holliday his shotgun. It was a weapon not likely to be mistaken for a hunting arm. Its ten-gauge barrels were sawed off to about fourteen inches, and its stock was sawed off just behind the pistol grip. Holliday carried it in his hand under his long gray overcoat. Behan ran up to the Earp Gang and asked for time to disarm the two armed cowboys. They brushed by him as if he weren't there.

It should be noted that the Earps and Holliday were not facing all the rustlers in Cochise County—only two of them and two of their neighbors. And of the four, only two were armed.

## TOM McLAURY THREW OPEN HIS COAT TO SHOW HE WASN'T ARMED, AND DOC HOLLIDAY BLASTED HIM WITH A BARREL FULL OF BUCKSHOT, KILLING HIM INSTANTLY.

Martha King was shopping at the butcher shop as the Tombstone gunmen marched down Fremont Street. She saw Holliday's coat blow open, revealing the shotgun. "I heard this man on the outside," she said. "[He] looked at Holliday, and I heard him say, 'Let them have it.' And Doc Holliday said, 'All right.' "

Tom McLaury threw open his coat to show he wasn't armed, and Doc Holliday blasted him with a barrel full of buckshot, killing him instantly. Morgan Earp, the "man on the outside," fired at almost the same time and hit Billy Clanton. Ike Clanton ran for dear life and hid in a photographer's studio. Doc Holliday, perhaps shaken by the recoil of his hand cannon, missed him. Wyatt

Earp shot Frank McLaury. He said he drew his gun after McLaury but "beat the drop," as they said in those days.

What he testified to is impossible. In the 1930s, Ed McGivern, a trick shooter and a pioneer in the electrical timing of shooting stunts, proved that to beat a man to the draw who started first, you would have to be twice as fast as him. Nobody is twice as fast as an experienced gunman, and Frank McLaury was, according to Wyatt Earp, "a good shot and a dangerous man."

Although hit, Frank McLaury was still standing. He tried unsuccessfully to get his rifle from the saddle scabbard on his horse, then drew his revolver and gave Doc Holliday a slight wound. Morgan Earp fired again, hitting Frank McLaury in the head. Billy Clanton, down but not out, fired from the ground and hit Morgan in the shoulder and Virgil in the leg. Both wounded Earp brothers shot Billy Clanton again. A bystander ran up to him, and Billy's last words were a request for more cartridges.

## DENOUEMENT

The "trial" that followed the shootings was merely a preliminary hearing to decide if the case should go to a grand jury, and even that was a farce. The judge was Wells Spicer, a close friend of Wyatt Earp. Virgil and Morgan Earp, being seriously wounded, were excused from testifying. Wyatt Earp's "testimony" consisted of reading a written statement, and no one was allowed to cross-examine him. Spicer ignored the testimony of all disinterested witnesses. Although the defense could produce no one to say the cowboys fired first, Spicer decided that the Earp Gang was doing its duty as officers of the law.

Wyatt Earp then gathered a "posse" of hard cases from all over the Southwest and shot up the town of Charleston where the rustlers met to drink, but they didn't get any rustlers.

Somebody got Virgil Earp, though. They ambushed him and shot him, leaving him crippled for life. A little later, someone shot Morgan Earp in the back as he was making a pool shot. A second bullet just missed Wyatt. Virgil took Morgan's body to their parents in California, and Wyatt took his posse out to hunt for the killers. They apparently lured Frank Stillwell, who, they suspected, killed Morgan, to a train station in Tucson and riddled him with bullets before he could draw his gun.

Unfortunately for the Earps, Tucson was in Pima County. The sheriff of Pima swore out a warrant charging Wyatt Earp; Warren Earp, Wyatt's youngest brother, who had just joined him; Doc Holliday, and Sherman McMasters, a stage robber friend of Wyatt's, with murder. The Earps and their friends managed to elude posses from Pima and Cochise counties while hunting others on their black list.

## WYATT'S STEEL VEST WAS ONE OF THE REASONS DOC HOLLIDAY EVENTUALLY BROKE UP WITH HIM. DOC SAID HE WAS TIRED OF TAKING RISKS WYATT DID NOT TAKE BECAUSE OF HIS BULLETPROOF UNDERSHIRT.

They killed a Mexican suspected, with little reason, of being an accomplice in the murder of Morgan, and they claimed to have had a fight with nine Cowboys during which Wyatt killed Curly Bill Brocius. Most people at the time did not believe the last claim, because Curly Bill's body was never found and the Earps were not known for burying their victims. One of the Cowboys involved in the fight said he had a clear shot at Wyatt but did not kill him because of Wyatt's steel vest. Wyatt's steel vest was one of the reasons Doc Holliday eventually broke up with him. Doc said he was tired of taking risks Wyatt did not take because of his bulletproof undershirt.

Wyatt and company eventually surfaced in Colorado, where Bat Masterson had powerful connections, and Colorado rejected an extradition request by Arizona. Memories of the murders gradually faded. Wyatt married Josie Marcus and abandoned Mattie Blaylock, who became a prostitute and then committed suicide.

Wyatt outlived all his contemporaries. Doc Holliday, in spite of everything, died of tuberculosis. Wyatt found an author, Stuart Lake, who listened to all his lies and wrote a book, *Wyatt Earp, Frontier Marshal,* which turned the old thug into the Sir Galahad of the frontier.

# LIES FROM JUST YESTERDAY

THE BATTLE OF MANILA. U.S
WARSHIPS STEAM INTO MANILA
BAY TO ENGAGE THE SPANISH
FLEET ON MAY 1, 1898. THE
RESULT WAS ONE OF THE MOST
ONE-SIDED BATTLES IN HISTORY.
THE AMERICANS, COMMANDED
BY COMMODORE GEORGE DEWEY,
SANK THE ENTIRE SPANISH FLEET
WITHOUT LOSING ONE MAN.

A painting called the 'Battle of Manila' /
Hulton Archive / Getty Images

# CHAPTER 11

# THE PHILIPPINE INSURRECTION: AGAINST WHAT GOVERNMENT?

## (1898–1902)

F OR MORE THAN A CENTURY, AMERICAN SCHOOLCHILDREN have had to study the Philippine Insurrection, which followed the Spanish-American War. What they learned was that the United States won the islands from Spain, but the barbarous natives, called Moros, revolted against American rule.

There are a few things wrong with this hazy history. The most important is that there was never an insurrection against the United States. When the fighting began on February 4, 1899, the United States had under neither international nor U.S. law possession of the Philippines. There was a Philippine Insurrection, but it was against Spain. Second, the first fighting and the heaviest fighting was not against the Muslim Moros, but against Christian Filipinos. The Philippines were about 90 percent Christian, about the same percentage as in the United States. Newspapers in the United States, whether they supported or opposed the war, however, invariably cartooned the Filipinos as grass-skirted savages, whether noble or ignoble.

Public ignorance about the islands was huge. All that most people in 1898 knew about the 7,100 islands between Taiwan and Borneo was that they were among the "South Sea Islands"—that vague and storied home of hula dancers and cannibals. Few Americans could have found the archipelago on a map, in spite of its distinctive shape.

It looks something like an octopus trying to eat a giant clam, with the octopus body being Luzon, the largest island and location of the capital, Manila;

UNITED STATES SOLDIERS FIRE ON FILIPINO POSITIONS DURING THE PHILIPPINE WAR, CIRCA 1899. THESE TROOPS WERE VOLUNTEERS RATHER THAN REGULARS, AS CAN BE SEEN BY THEIR RIFLES. VOLUNTEERS WERE EQUIPPED WITH THE OLDER SINGLE-SHOT SPRINGFIELD, WHILE REGULARS HAD THE REPEATING KING-JORGENSEN.

Getty Images

strings of smaller islands stretching south being the tentacles; and Mindanao, the second largest island, the giant clam. Surely few would have guessed that there were Filipino doctors, lawyers, and railroad engineers, that the islands contained millions of people—a population many times the combined populations of all the rest of Spain's colonies, and that the inhabitants had spent 300 years absorbing European culture.

That ignorance did not completely extend to high government officials; they knew where the Philippines were, at least. But it gave them an opportunity to do things that many people would have strongly opposed.

For example, getting rid of European colonies in the Americas had been a popular cause in the United States since before the Monroe Doctrine. The Spanish-American War was popular because it was fought to free Spain's colony, Cuba. Many, perhaps most, people who wanted to get rid of colonies did not want the United States to acquire any. When the bill authorizing American intervention in Cuba was put before the Senate in April 1898, Senator Henry M. Teller of Colorado proposed an amendment forbidding the United States from exercising "sovereignty, jurisdiction, or control" over Cuba. The amendment passed. Cuba was on everybody's mind because the war was going on there, and Hearst and Pulitzer made sure everyone knew the gory details in their newspapers. Nobody thought about Spain's other colonies. Puerto Rico appeared to be happy with Spanish rule, and nobody had a clue as to what, if anything, was going on in the Philippines or Guam.

Some people did want colonies. The "economic imperialists" like Mark Hanna, chairman of the Republican National Committee, wanted colonies so the United States' rapidly expanding industry would have markets. This group would have preferred to get the colonies without war. After all, war is wasteful. But as long as the United States had a war, they wanted to take advantage of it.

## TEDDY ROOSEVELT—SUPER HAWK

Then there were the real imperialists. The most prominent was the assistant secretary of the navy, Theodore Roosevelt. Roosevelt wanted colonies more for strategic than for economic reasons. Britain, Germany, France, and the Netherlands all had colonies in the Far East. Unlike any of them, the United States was a Pacific power, but it had no bases on the far side of the Pacific.

Roosevelt had another motive, too. He believed, like historian Frederick Jackson Turner, that the frontier, which had confronted Americans from the end of the sixteenth to the beginning of the twentieth centuries, had shaped the national character. Overcoming primitive conditions and primitive people had developed American ideals and given them the energy they had demonstrated in other fields. Turner had decided that the frontier had closed in 1900. Roosevelt thought there was an acute need for a new frontier with primitive people to overcome.

In a speech at the Naval War College, Roosevelt explained why: "All the great masterful races have been fighting races. No triumph of peace is quite as great as the supreme triumph of war. The diplomat is the servant, not the master, of the soldier."

Roosevelt's contemporary, Kaiser Wilhelm II of Germany, could not have topped that. Roosevelt was a hawk, but not a chicken hawk (the term for a pro-war politician who is personally afraid to fight). When war with Spain broke out, Roosevelt and his personal physician, Dr. Leonard Wood, organized a volunteer cavalry regiment, the "Rough Riders," composed of cowboys and Ivy League college boys. They went to Cuba, but Wood was promoted out of the regiment, and Roosevelt became its commander. A darling of the press, Roosevelt became a national hero, even though the 10th Cavalry, an all-black (except its officers) regular army regiment, had to rescue the Rough Riders from a trap at a place called Las Guasimas, and black troops, not the Rough Riders, captured the blockhouse on San Juan Hill, on July 2, 1898, the climax of the ground war. Nevertheless, the Rough Riders got credit for "taking San Juan Hill"—credit that propelled Roosevelt into the vice presidency.

## "MEIN GOTT, MEIN GOTT!"

Commodore George Dewey was a member of the circle of hawks who followed Roosevelt. Dewey was fifty-nine years old, about six years from retirement, but

he was a man after Roosevelt's heart. In Roosevelt's autobiography, he recalled a time when the United States and Chile were having trouble. Dewey's ship was in Argentina and would need to take on coal before it could get to Chile. Dewey ignored regulations and bought coal himself without consulting headquarters so he could hurry to Chile and be ready for war. Instead of an old man, Roosevelt saw a red-hot warrior—just the man to lead the navy's asiatic squadron. And the assistant secretary got him that job.

In case of war with Spain, Dewey was to proceed to Manila and attack the Spanish fleet there. Dewey's "China squadron" wasn't much. He had nine ships. Three were cruisers, but one was only a Coast Guard cutter. The Spanish had forty ships, but many had wooden hulls and most needed repairs. Just before the Americans left Hong Kong, a British regiment threw a party for them.

"A fine set of fellows," one of their hosts said, "but unhappily we shall never see them again."

In spite of the U.S. Civil War, when the United States created the world's most powerful army and navy, Europeans did not consider the United States a great power. That view was about to change. Dewey sailed past the fortress of Corregidor, across the supposedly mined harbor of Manila, and sank the entire Spanish fleet on May 1, 1898, without losing a man.

Europeans began to look at the United States in a new light, but the prince of Prussia apparently was not convinced that the United States was a major power.

Prince Henry of Prussia, the Kaiser's brother, commander of the German naval squadron at Hong Kong, reported to Berlin that "The [Filipino] natives would gladly place themselves under the protection of a European power, especially Germany." And so Henry sent some German ships to Manila Bay to look for an opportunity. The German ships ignored Dewey's fleet and the international rules for the behavior of neutrals in a blockaded port. Finally, one of Dewey's ships fired a shot across the bow of a German cruiser that refused to stop. The German admiral sent an officer to Dewey to protest.

One of Dewey's officers later reported, "The admiral [Dewey had been promoted immediately after his victory in Manila Bay] has a way of working himself up to a state of great earnestness as he thinks out a question." Beginning quietly, Dewey became more and more "earnest" as well as louder and louder. Finally, he yelled, "If the German government has decided to make war on the United States, or has any intention of making war, and has so informed your admiral, it is his duty to let me know." He hesitated a moment and then continued: "But whether he intends to fight or not, I am ready!"

The German officer left muttering, "Mein Gott, mein Gott!"

There were no more German provocations.

## A COLONY FULL OF "NATIVES"?

Back in the United States, the end of the Spanish War left people undecided about what to do, if anything, about Spain's colonies. Cuba, guaranteed independence, was already organizing a republic. The United States was occupying Puerto Rico, and it looked as if it intended to stay there. McKinley was in the habit of writing memos to himself. Right after Manila Bay, he scribbled a note

VICE PRESIDENT THEODORE ROOSEVELT, LEFT, AND PRESIDENTIAL ADVISOR MARK HANNA CONFER WHILE PRESIDENT WILLIAM MCKINLEY LIES DYING FROM AN ASSASSIN'S BULLET. SECRETARY OF WAR ELIHU ROOT IS AT THE RIGHT. ALTHOUGH BOTH ROOSEVELT AND HANNA FAVORED ANNEXING THE PHILIPPINES, THEY DISLIKED EACH OTHER. HANNA ONCE SAID OF ROOSEVELT, "THAT COWBOY IS JUST ONE HEARTBEAT FROM THE WHITE HOUSE."

Library of Congress—digital version copyright Science Faction

to himself, "While we are conducting war and until its conclusion, we must keep all we get; when the war is over, we must keep what we want."

Puerto Rico was a nearby island; its people, like the Americans, were heirs to Western European culture. Keeping it would be no problem.

The Philippines were something else. They consisted of 7,100 islands, containing millions of people, on the other side of the world. The Filipinos were a different race, and their culture—if any—was totally unknown to the average American.

The political situation in the Philippines was equally unknown. While the revolt in Cuba against Spain was going on, another revolt was in progress in the Philippines. Both began in 1896. The Philippine *Insurrectos*, as the Spanish called them, had adopted a constitution modeled after that of the United States. They elected congressmen, senators, and a president, a lawyer named Emilio Aguinaldo. The revolt began as a guerrilla war, but the Filipinos formed a regular army with a military hierarchy, uniforms, modern rifles, and a few machine guns. The fighting went back and forth for some time.

On December 27, 1897, as American pressure on Spain was increasing, the Spanish agreed to a truce. Spain promised a host of reforms and agreed to pay the Insurrectos if Aguinaldo would go into exile. So his people could get the reforms and the money, Aguinaldo went to Hong Kong. The Spanish quickly reneged on their promises, and the fighting became more intense. According to Oscar F. Williams, U.S. consul in Manila, "Insurgents are being armed and drilled and are rapidly increasing in numbers and efficiency." By the time Dewey entered Manila Bay, the Filipinos had almost pushed the Spanish into the sea. Dewey brought Aguinaldo home and spoke to "Don Emilio" of an American-Filipino alliance.

## MCKINLEY'S MESSAGE FROM GOD

After Manila Bay, McKinley sent troops to the Philippines. Officially, they were to help the Filipinos in their siege of Manila. Aguinaldo protested, saying his people didn't need any help. The troops themselves were told they were an army of occupation. The Spanish could not bear to surrender to the people of their former colony, so they agreed to surrender to the Americans alone.

And so U.S. troops stayed in the Philippines in spite of the objections of their "allies." Instead of allies, the Americans treated the Filipinos like a

EMILIO AGUINALDO, ONCE PRESIDENT OF THE PHILIPPINES, STANDS ON THE BALCONY WHERE, MANY YEARS EARLIER, HE FIRST PROCLAIMED PHILIPPINE INDEPENDENCE. AGUINALDO LED THE FIGHT AGAINST SPAIN AND LATER AGAINST THE UNITED STATES. WHEN HE FAILED TO DEFEAT THE AMERICANS IN REGULAR WARFARE, HE SWITCHED TO GUERRILLA FIGHTING.

Photo by Jack Birns / Time Life Pictures / Getty Images

conquered people. They searched Filipino houses without warrants, knocked down any Filipino who didn't show them enough "respect," and showed no respect at all for the Filipina women they searched. The officers called the Filipinos "Indians;" the soldiers called them "niggers."

"We have to kill one or two every night," a private wrote home.

Back across the Pacific, President McKinley explained the decision he had made about the islands.

> I walked the floor of the White House night after night until midnight, and I am not ashamed to tell you, gentlemen, that I went down on my knees and prayed to Almighty God for light and guidance more than one night.

> And one night it came to me this way—I don't know how it was but it came: (1) that we could not give them back to Spain—that would be cowardly and dishonorable; (2) that we could not turn them over to France or Germany—our commercial rivals in the Orient—that would be bad business and discreditable (3) that we could not leave them to themselves—they were unfit for self government—and they would soon have anarchy and misrule over there worse than Spain's was; and (4) there was nothing left for us to do but take them all, and educate the Filipinos, and uplift and civilize and Christianize them.

McKinley was proposing to "Christianize" the only Christian country in the Far East. He was going to "civilize" Manila, which had electric lights and electric street cars before most American cities. At the time he was talking about "giving" the Philippines to some other country, the United States didn't even have Manila. He did not explain why the Filipinos were "unfit for self government." Admiral Dewey, who certainly knew more about the Philippines than McKinley, said, "In my opinion, these people are far superior in their intelligence and more capable of self government than the natives of Cuba, and I am familiar with both races."

But McKinley had his way, and Spain agreed to sell the Philippines and its other island colonies to the United States for $20 million.

When Aguinaldo's people heard of the treaty, they wanted to declare war on the United States, but *el presidente* advised them to wait. He didn't think the treaty would be ratified by the U.S. Senate.

But thirty-six hours before the treaty was to go before the Senate, some drunken Filipinos and a trigger-happy U.S. soldier made Senate ratification moot.

## "FIGHTING . . . MUST GO ON TO THE GRIM END"

On the night of February 4, 1899, a group of Filipinos, who appeared to have been drinking, approached a U.S. Army checkpoint. Private William Grayson called "Halt!" One of the Filipinos mimicked him, calling "Halto!"

"Well, I thought the best thing to do was shoot him," Grayson testified later.

Another sentry shot a second Filipino, and then firing became general between Americans and Filipinos. American warships in the harbor joined in. When the shooting was over, sixty Americans and 3,000 Filipinos were dead.

The next morning, Aguinaldo proposed to General Ewell S. Otis, commander of the American troops, that they establish a neutral zone between the two armies.

---

## THE BOOGEY MEN OF THE SOUTH

Back in the nineteenth century, sailors' wives used to warn naughty children that "the boogey man will get you if you don't watch out." The term "boogey man" is supposed to come from Malay pirates called Bugi. Among the Moros, like the Sea Dyaks of Borneo, piracy was an honorable profession.

To young Americans shipped to the strange islands, the Moros of Mindanao and the Sulu archipelago were by far the strangest inhabitants. They were Muslims—Moro means Moor in Spanish, the Muslims most familiar to the sixteenth century Spanish. They were the first Muslims most Americans had ever seen. While the Christian Filipinos had a European culture, the culture of the Moros was pure Malay, with a veneer of Islam.

The Moros wore different clothing, and they were always armed with a variety of exotic swords and knives. Their version of Islam was different, too. It bred fanaticism. An individual Moro would occasionally take an oath to die trying to kill as many Christians as he could. Then he would take a hefty dose of drugs and go on a rampage. Such a man was extremely hard to stop.

The late Joseph E. Smith of the Army Materiel Command, whose father served in Moroland before the First World War, told of a Moro who began to shoot American and Filipino Christians and was hit thirty times with bullets from a .30-06 rifle, a .45-70 rifle and blasts from a 12-gauge shotgun before he was stopped.

The Moro War followed the first Philippine War and was a piddling affair compared to the so-called "Insurrection." The Moros constituted less than a tenth of the Philippine population, and their feudal chiefs, the datus, would not cooperate with each other. The war was marked with two notable massacres, one in 1906 and in 1913, in which hundreds of Moro men, women, and children were slain by U.S. troops.

The Moros, though, were so exotic and so scary that troops returning from the Philippines talked of little else. And so the Moros came to be regarded as our sole enemy in the Philippine War.

Otis rejected the idea. "The fighting having begun must go on to the grim end," he said.

The war had begun before the United States had any legal title to the islands, even by the standards of the colonial era, when governments traded millions of colonial people as if they were poker chips. It was not, therefore, an insurgency.

The first news the Western World got of the war was a statement the day after the fight by U.S. Secretary of War Elihu Root:

> On the night of February 4, two days before the U.S. Senate approved the treaty, an army of Tagalogs, a tribe inhabiting the central part of Luzon, under the leadership of Aguinaldo, a Chinese half-breed, attacked in vastly superior numbers, our little army in possession of Manila, and after a desperate and bloody fight, was repulsed in every direction.

Root managed to cram an astonishing amount of misinformation in that one sentence. There was no organized attack. The Filipinos did not fire first. The Insurrecto numbers were hardly overwhelming. There were 80,000 Insurrectos in the 7,100 islands, and about 30,000 spread over Luzon, the largest island. Only half of them had rifles, and many of those did not know how to aim a rifle. The 16,000 Americans were all in Manila, and the American fleet was in the bay.

Further, Emilio Aguinaldo was not a "Chinese half-breed." How Root got that idea is unknown, unless he thought a pure Filipino wasn't smart enough to lead a revolutionary movement. Finally, the Tagalogs (tah-GAH-logs) were not and are not a tribe but the largest ethnic group in the islands, and their language became Pilipino, one of the two national languages of the Philippines (the other is English). A tribe is a social organization with a chief or governing body—something entirely lacking among Tagalogs in 1899.

## FREDDIE'S FAST EXPRESS

Most of the troops sent to the Philippines were in Volunteer units, participants in a system no longer used to raise American troops. In time of emergency, the president would call on the governors to raise Volunteer regiments to serve for the duration. The governor would appoint regimental commanders and begin recruiting. One of those regiments was the 20th Kansas Volunteer Infantry, commanded by Colonel Frederick W. Funston, a man who began his army career near the top.

Funston had no regular military experience, but he had fought with the Cuban guerrillas in the revolt that preceded the Spanish-American War. Wounded, he had returned to the United States and was recuperating when the America went to war. The governor of Kansas appointed him commander of one of the state's Volunteer regiments, and he went to the Philippines. His unit spearheaded the American drive up Luzon against Aguinaldo's regulars.

He captured some disassembled locomotives, had his men put them together again, and created "Freddie's Fast Express," an armored car with mounted cannons and machine guns that was pushed by a locomotive. It routed the Filipino troops from position after position. Funston won the Medal of Honor and was promoted to brigadier general for leading an assault across the widest river in Luzon. He crossed the river under fire on an improvised raft with the first of many raft-loads of assault troops.

With the Spanish-American War over, all Volunteers were returned to the United States to be mustered out. Major General Arthur MacArthur (Douglas' father) was impressed with the daring Funston. He got the War Department to ask Funston to stay in the army and return to the Philippines.

When Funston returned, however, he found a new kind of war.

## THE EX-GUERRILLA AND THE GUERRILLAS

Aguinaldo had decided that his poorly equipped troops could not cope with the Americans in regular warfare. He told them to doff their uniforms, scatter across Luzon in small groups, and fight the Americans as guerrillas. The Filipinos doffed their chivalry with their uniforms. A favorite method of attack was to approach American soldiers with hidden bolos (Philippine Spanish for a heavy work knife, like the Cuban machete). Suddenly, they would produce the bolos and chop up the Americans.

GENERAL FREDERICK FUNSTON, WHO, IN ONE OF THE MOST DARING ACTIONS BY A GENERAL OFFICER IN ANY WAR, CAPTURED EMILIO AGUINALDO IN HIS HEADQUARTERS. FUNSTON, WHO ACTUALLY DID "WIN THE HEARTS AND MINDS" OF THE FILIPINOS, WAS ONE OF THE UNITED STATES' MOST SUCCESSFUL ANTI-GUERRILLAS— NOT SURPRISING, BECAUSE HE HIMSELF HAD BEEN AN INSURGENT GUERRILLA IN CUBA.

Library of Congress.
(Herbert E. French Collection)

The Americans countered with various kinds of torture to make Filipinos identify the guerrillas. Some were dragged behind galloping horses. Some were hanged until they passed out and then hanged again. Others were tied to a tree, shot in the legs, and left overnight. If they didn't talk the next day, they were shot again. Then there was the infamous "water cure." A hose was inserted into a subject's mouth and a tank of water poured into him. When his body was distended to the bursting point, the water was forced out of him with kicks. One returning soldier told of the cure being given to a village priest. After the water had been kicked out of him, the priest was asked again to name names. He was silent.

## THE AMERICANS COUNTERED WITH VARIOUS KINDS OF TORTURE TO MAKE FILIPINOS IDENTIFY THE GUERRILLAS. SOME WERE DRAGGED BEHIND GALLOPING HORSES. SOME WERE HANGED UNTIL THEY PASSED OUT AND THEN HANGED AGAIN. OTHERS WERE TIED TO A TREE, SHOT IN THE LEGS, AND LEFT OVERNIGHT.

"Give the nigger another dose," an officer said. The troops said it wouldn't do any good. The priest was dead.

And there were reprisals. A favorite was burning down an entire village where there was "insurgent" activity.

Funston talked tough to American reporters, but he took an entirely different approach with the Filipinos. He believed friendship worked better than torture, and he was to prove that spectacularly.

Funston's experience in Cuba was an enormous help. He spoke fluent Spanish, and he understood the Spanish colonial social structure. In every area, there were *principales*, community leaders. He cultivated them and developed contacts with the Insurrectos. Historian Brian McAllister Linn, in his *The U.S. Army and Counterinsurgency in the Philippine War, 1899–1902*, writes "Although a vocal advocate of repression, [Funston's] actual conduct was characterized by lenient surrender terms, rewards for collaboration, and personal friendship."

Funston developed his own intelligence network, which included U.S. soldiers, Filipino principales, Filipino villagers, and former Insurrectos. One of the latter was Lazaro Segovia y Gutierrez, a brilliant Spaniard who joined Aguinaldo's army when Spain refused to let him take his Filipina wife back to Spain.

When he heard about Funston, Segovia arranged to surrender personally to the U.S. general and former Cuban guerrilla.

Funston's policies paid off February 4, 1901. A courier from Aguinaldo escaped an ambush and sought shelter with the mayor of a village. The mayor was one of Funston's prinicipale friends, and he convinced the courier to surrender. He and the letters he was carrying were sent to Funston. The letters were in Tagalog, which Sergovia could read. Some were also in cipher. Funston and the Spaniard worked all night and eventually broke the cipher. One was from Aguinaldo to his cousin asking for reinforcements. It said the courier could guide them to his hidden headquarters in the mountains.

Funston got a detachment of Macabebe Scouts, U.S. Army auxiliaries recruited from an ethnic group that had long been hostile to Tagalogs. Legend had it that they were descended from Mexican Indians recruited by the Spanish centuries before to help them run the Philippines. The Macabebes would pose as Insurrectos, and they would be commanded by Sergovia. Funston and four other Americans would pose as prisoners of war. They would take an almost impossibly difficult trail to the village of Palinan, where the Filipino president had his headquarters. Arthur MacArthur reluctantly gave his consent to Funston's plan.

"Funston," he said, "this is a desperate undertaking. I fear I shall never see you again."

But he did. Funston captured Aguinaldo March 23, 1901, and brought him back to Manila. In spite of cries in the United States to hang Aguinaldo, MacArthur treated the ex-president as an honored guest. Aguinaldo formally surrendered April 19, 1901. Most of the Insurrecto leaders followed suit. The war did not end totally. Funston, desperately ill, had been sent back to the States, and there was scattered fighting—with atrocities on both sides—for several years. But in 1902, the Philippines were quiet enough for President Theodore Roosevelt to declare the war was over.

# CHAPTER 12

# *THE PROTOCOLS OF THE ELDERS OF ZION:* A DEADLY KIND OF LIE

## (1800s–1940s)

CONCOCTED IN THE LAST YEARS OF THE NINETEENTH century by Tsarist Russia's secret service, and plagiarizing from a number of fictional sources, *The Protocols of the Elders of Zion* arguably became the most destructive lie of the twentieth century. Designed to take the heat off the Romanov family's ineffectual government of Russia by painting the agitators for political change as stooges of a Jewish conspiracy to rule the world, it was a tool used to incite pogroms against Russia's Jewish communities.

When many anti-Communist White Russians fled Russia in the years following the Bolshevik Revolution of 1917, Russia's particular brand of anti-Semitism traveled with them and *The Protocols* began to be translated into the languages of Western Europe and beyond.

One of their most notable supporters included car industry pioneer Henry Ford. However, their most disastrous use was as a philosophical underpinning for Adolf Hitler's *Mein Kampf*, which metastasized into the persecution of the Jews in Germany and culminated in the genocidal madness of the Final Solution. *The Protocols'* influence on Hitler's sloppy philosophy was such that some commentators have described the document as "a warrant for genocide."

Although known to be a lie in Russian circles from the outset and publicly outed as fraudulent from the 1920s on, anti-Semitic groups the world over continued to publish *The Protocols*. In a remarkable instance of the truth being of peripheral import, the conspiracy theory of *The Protocols* is frequently used to incite religious hatred today and millions believe it, from far-right

**MYTH**
*THE PROTOCOLS* OUTLINE A JEWISH CONSPIRACY TO TAKE OVER THE WORLD.

**REALITY**
NINETEENTH CENTURY RUSSIA'S TSARIST POLICE CREATED *THE PROTOCOLS* TO TAKE THE HEAT OFF THE ROMANOV FAMILY'S INEFFECTUAL GOVERNMENT, ENCOURAGE ANTI-SEMITISM, AND PAINT POTENTIAL REVOLUTIONARIES AS STOOGES OF THE ALLEGED JEWISH CONSPIRACY.

American Christians to fundamental Islamists. In some Middle Eastern countries, they can even be found on the school syllabus. They are, quite clearly, a lie that will not die.

## CONCOCTING THE CONSPIRACY

*The Protocols of the Elders of Zion* consists of twenty-four protocols supposed to be the minutes of a secret meeting of a council of Jewish leaders toward the end of the nineteenth century at which they made plans to achieve world domination. The number of the Elders of Zion is usually given as 300 and the text is framed as advice from the presiding Elders to an initiate.

Each of the twenty-four protocols (see "The Twenty-Four Protocols" on page 207 for a list) is divided into a series of aphorisms that discuss tactics for taking over a world defined by goyim—the Yiddish word for non-Jew—laxity, and decadence. The plan is to use the weakness of goyim against themselves.

The socialist movements sweeping Europe in the eighteenth and nineteenth centuries are presented as a plot the Jews have hatched to kill off the non-Jewish population.

"We appear on the scene as alleged saviors of the worker from this oppression when we propose to him to enter the ranks of our fighting forces—socialists, anarchists, communists—to whom we always give support in accordance with an alleged brotherly rule (of the solidarity of all humanity) of our social masonry. The aristocracy, which enjoyed by law the labor of the workers, was interested in seeing that the workers were well fed, healthy, and strong. We are interested in just the opposite—in the diminution, the killing out of the goyim. Our power is in the chronic shortness of food and physical weakness of the worker because by all that this implies he is made the slave of our will, and he will not find in his own authorities either strength or energy to set against our will. Hunger creates the right of capital to rule the worker more surely than it was given to the aristocracy by the legal authority of kings."

In this schema the liberals and revolutionaries who are fighting to overthrow governments in the apparent interest of the people are recast as mere pawns of the Elders of Zion, who will usurp them once the old order has been dispatched with. There are sections that deal with the financial systems of the world, usually the cornerstone for those interested in peddling Jewish conspiracies, while other sections evoke other famous anti-Semitic myths such as the blood libel whereby Jews were accused of using the fresh blood of Christian children in their Passover feasts.

## RUSSIAN ORIGINS

*The Protocols* first appeared publicly in a right-wing St. Petersburg newspaper, *Znamya (*the *Banner),* in serial form between August 28 and September 7, 1903. The editor and publisher, Pavel Krushevan, was a member of the Black Hundredists, a group of anti-Semitic, ultra-nationalist right-wingers who were working to preserve the authority of the Orthodox Church and the tsar. Four months prior to their publication, another Krushevan newspaper, *Besserabetz,* had helped incite a pogrom against the Jews in Kishinev (now Chisinau, the capital of Moldavia), where 49 Jews were killed, more than 500 injured, and 700 houses and stores destroyed.

## THE TWENTY-FOUR PROTOCOLS

The twenty-four Protocols of the Elders of Zion outline the means by which the Jews will dominate the world. They are:

Protocol I The Basic Doctrine
Protocol II Economic Wars
Protocol III Methods of Conquest
Protocol IV Materialism Replaces Religion
Protocol V Despotism and Modern Progress
Protocol VI Take-Over Technique
Protocol VII World-Wide Wars
Protocol VIII Provisional Government
Protocol IX Re-Education
Protocol X Preparing for Power
Protocol XI The Totalitarian State
Protocol XII Control of the Press
Protocol XIII Distractions
Protocol XIV Assault on Religion

Protocol XV Ruthless Suppression
Protocol XVI Brainwashing
Protocol XVII Abuse of Authority
Protocol XVIII Arrest of Opponents
Protocol XIX Rulers and People
Protocol XX Financial Program
Protocol XXI Loans and Credit
Protocol XXII Power of Gold
Protocol XXIII Instilling Obedience
Protocol XXIV Qualities of the Ruler

*The Protocols* were subsequently published in full in 1905, as the final chapter to religious fanatic Sergei Nilus' apocalyptic tome *The Great Within the Small: Antichrist Considered as an Imminent Political Possibility, Notes of an Orthodox Believer.* Nilus saw the world in religious terms. For him, the socialist revolution was analogous to the predictions in the Bible's *Book of Revelations* that before the second coming of Christ, the anti-Christ would come, be celebrated by the Jews as the Messiah, and take over the world. He claimed to have seen secret documents whereby King Solomon the Wise as long ago as 929 B.C. had met with his council of elders at the citadel in Jerusalem to concoct a plan to conquer the world without bloodshed. Over the intervening centuries, this plan had been fine-tuned by successive generations of Jewish Elders to the point where it was now on the cusp (according to Nilus) of being successfully implemented. The copy of *The Protocols* he was publishing, he further claimed, had been stolen from the Jewish Elders and leaked to him.

In the 1911 edition introduction to his book, Nilus wrote:

> In 1901, I succeeded through an acquaintance of mine (the late Court Marshal Alexei Nicolayevitch Sukotin of Tchernigov) in getting a manuscript that exposed with unusual perfection and clarity the course and development of the secret Jewish Freemasonic conspiracy, which would bring this wicked world to its inevitable end. The person who gave me this manuscript guaranteed it to be a faithful translation of the original documents that were stolen by a woman from one of the highest and most influential leaders of the Freemasons at a secret meeting somewhere in France—the beloved nest of Freemasonic conspiracy.

Yet in his 1905 edition, Nilus claimed that *The Protocols* had been written at a meeting of the Elders of Zion held in 1902–1903. By the time of his 1917 edition, the source had changed again. This time it was allegedly the first Zionist conference, which took place in 1897 at Basel in Switzerland. He claimed it was Circular 18 of the conference. Yet this document was never found, and it is highly unlikely it ever existed. In an epilogue to the first English edition published in 1920, Nilus changed his mind again, claiming that "My friend found them in the safes at the headquarters of the Society of Zion, which are at present situated in France."

A LAWYER AND MYSTIC, SERGEI NILUS PROFITED FROM THE SUPERSTITIONS AND INTRIGUES OF THE RUSSIAN COURT TOWARD THE TURN OF THE TWENTIETH CENTURY. HIS WIFE HAD INFLUENCE WITH THE TSARINA AND HER SISTER, AND IT WAS THROUGH THIS THAT NILUS GOT PERMISSION TO PUBLISH *THE PROTOCOLS*, OVERTURNING THE PREVIOUS BAN OF NICHOLAS II. OVER NUMEROUS SUBSEQUENT EDITIONS, HIS STORY OF HOW HE CAME TO GET HIS HANDS ON THEM CHANGED ON MORE THAN ONE OCCASION.

## A DIVERSION FROM INCOMPETENCE

It might seem ludicrous that such a poorly verified work of second-rate philosophy should gain significant traction in Russia's political debate. However, Russia at the time was a fairly ludicrous place. Both the tsar and his wife were heavily under the influence of mystics and charismatic charlatans such as Rasputin. Tsar Nicholas had adopted his father's autocratic persona but lacked the intellectual capacity to rule effectively, leaving him susceptible both to the views of religious fanatics such as Nilus, who romanticized the tsar, as well as to more able ultranational forces such as the Black Hundredists.

Like his father, Alexander III, Nicholas was a committed anti-Semite. *The Protocols* were introduced into the royal household by Grand Prince Sergei Alexandrovich, who was also governor of Moscow, had close connections to the Black Hundredists, and was personally involved in discrimination against the Jews. Not only was Sergei the uncle of the tsar, he was also married to Elizaveta, the sister of the tsarina, Alexandra.

It's not known exactly when Nicholas got to read *The Protocols,* though it preceded their publication. His initial reaction was enthusiastic: They were a pleasant, causal diversion from the effects of his own incompetence and helped to confirm his belief that "everywhere one can recognize the directing and destroying hand of Judaism." Like Hitler, he was planned on incorporating *The Protocols* as a linchpin of his politics. However, his interior minister, Pyotr Stolypin, had several people look into *The Protocols* to see whether they could be deployed as the foundation for a major anti-Semitic campaign, only to discover they were a fraud. In response to hearing this, Nicholas, who, although incompetent, maintained a sense of honor, ordered "Drop *The Protocols*. One cannot defend a pure cause by dirty methods." As a consequence *The Protocols* were banned.

## THE PUBLICATION OF THE PROTOCOLS

Just because the tsar had washed his hands of this dodgy document didn't mean it was finished. Many in the ultra-nationalist side of politics were concerned about the tsar's ability to resist the tide of Liberalism, while politicians such as Stolypin, who proposed to stabilize Russian society by creating a class of wealthy peasants, were perceived by the left and right alike as a danger to their agendas.

THE LAST RUSSIAN TSAR, NICHOLAS II, WHO WAS KILLED BY THE BOLSHEVIKS DURING THE RUSSIAN REVOLUTION. TO DEFLECT ATTENTION FROM ITS OWN PROBLEMS, THE RUSSIAN GOVERNMENT ENCOURAGED ANTI-SEMITIC CONSPIRACY THEORIES. WHEN HE FIRST READ *THE PROTOCOLS*, HE WAS ENTHUSIASTIC. HOWEVER, ON DISCOVERING THAT THEY WERE MOST LIKELY A FORGERY, HIS SENSE OF HONOR PREVENTED HIM FROM ALLOWING THEM TO BE USED OFFICIALLY TO STIR UP ANTI-SEMITIC SENTIMENT.

Associated Press

Princess Elizaveta was concerned about a cooling in the relationship between her tsarina sister and herself. One of the reasons for this she thought was the influence French occultist and hypnotist Pierre Vachet had at court. Elizaveta contrived to have the Frenchmen replaced by a more Russian mystic. Her thoughts turned to Sergei Nilus. The attempt was not successful, yet in introducing Nilus to the court, Elizaveta managed to get him married to one of the tsarina's ladies-in-waiting, Elena Ozerova, whose uncle, Philip Stepanov, had first introduced *The Protocols* to Grand Prince Sergei. On behalf of her husband Nilus who, although qualified as a lawyer, was too much of mystic to make much of a living, Ozerova petitioned the government's censorship committee to overturn the ban on *The Protocols,* so her husband could use them in his book.

Against the backdrop of the chaotic 1905 Revolution (which saw the assassination of Grand Prince Sergei, who was known for his ultra-conservatism and cruelty), Nilus received permission to publish *The Protocols* in September 1905. Given that every edition and translation the world over can be traced back to this edition, it was the moment when the future of one of history's greatest lies became assured.

## THE LIE MIGRATES TO WESTERN EUROPE

As the political crisis in Russia developed into the Bolshevik Revolution of 1917, the ultra-nationalists increasingly tried to garner the support of the peasants by associating the Bolshevik revolutionaries with a Jewish conspiracy to rule the world. They were helped in this by the fact there were quite a few Jewish Bolsheviks, most notably revolutionary leader Leon Trotsky.

As the Red Army gained ascendancy in the Revolution, many White Russians fled en masse to Europe and America. For many of these displaced Russians who had lost their land, social status, and possessions, the 1917 Revolution was evidence *The Protocols* were true. Some took copies of Nilus' text containing *The Protocols* with them, and it was from these that *The Protocols* came to be translated into other European languages.

The association of the Bolshevik Revolution with a Jewish Conspiracy peddled by the White Russians caught the attention of anti-Semites all over the world. Interestingly, in the first English language edition, published in the

*Philadelphia Public Ledger* by journalist Carl Ackerman, references to the Jews were replaced directly with references to the Bolsheviks.

The first explicitly anti-Semitic English language edition appeared in Britain in the *Morning Post* in 1920. It was followed with an anonymous translation titled *The Jewish Peril* by a racist publishing outfit, the Britons, in the same year. Other editions were not long in coming.

Perhaps the most powerful man to grab hold of *The Protocols* and run with them was Henry Ford, who had purchased the *Dearborn Independent* primarily as a vehicle for exercising his anti-Semitic beliefs. Whereas many people identified the Jewish Peril with the Bolsheviks, others in America such as Ford were concerned with the perceived Jewish hegemony over the finance industry and the emerging motion picture business. The neat thing about *The Protocols*, at least for the conspiracy minded anti-Semite, was that it provided a theory that could be deployed against the perceived influence of the Jews whether they were left wing or right wing, pillars of society or revolutionaries.

## THE LIE AS A LITERARY THEFT

As *The Protocols* spread into the major European languages and were read by millions, evidence increasingly began to build that they were a forgery. Nilus was probably enough of a zealot to actually believe the story he was fed was the truth. Yet as Nicholas' initial decision not to permit the publication of *The Protocols* showed, there were many in Russia who believed them to be a fraud from the outset.

However, the extent of the fraud only became apparent as translations proliferated and more and more people became curious as to the origins of this strange document. Perhaps the major breakthrough came in 1921, when the Constantinople correspondent for the English *Times*, Phillip Graves, was approached by a Russian émigré in dire financial straits with a manuscript. Although the title page was missing, it had been printed in Geneva in 1864. Graves wrote in the *Times*:

> Before receiving the book from Mr. X, I was, as I have said, incredulous. I did not believe that Sergei Nilus' *Protocols* were authentic; they explained too much by the theory of a vast Jewish conspiracy. Professor Nilus' account of how they were obtained was too melodramatic to be credible, and it was hard to believe that real 'Learned Elders of

Zion' would not have produced a more intelligent political scheme than the crude and theatrical subtitles of *The Protocols*. But I could not have believed, had I not seen, that the writer who supplied Nilus with his originals was a careless and shameless plagiarist.

Unbeknownst to him, Graves had been given by his Mr. X a copy of a pamphlet that had been written in French by Maurice Joly to satirize the ambition of France's Louis Napoleon, the ambitious, authoritarian, and ultimately disastrous nephew of Napoleon who ruled France from 1852–1870. On the missing title page was *Dialogue aux enfers entre Machiavel et Montesquieu (A Dialogue in Hell between Machiavelli and Montesquieu)*.

In the text the two philosophers meet on a deserted beach in hell and enjoy a Socratic dialogue. Montesquieu, the French essayist and enlightenment philosopher, advocates the liberal cause while Machiavelli is there as a thinly disguised reference to the behavior of Louis Napoleon. Machiavelli-Napoleon's defense of competent ruthless dictatorship as an effective mode of government is undercut by references to the Hausmannisation of Paris, which saw many of the old neighborhoods of Paris demolished to make way for the grand boulevards today, Louis Napoleon's financial extravagance, and his use of secret societies as an agent of foreign policy.

Joly was arrested and jailed when he tried to smuggle copies of the pamphlet into France and eventually committed suicide in 1879. He could never have imagined that he would have posthumously become the author of large chunks of *The Protocols of Zion*. Although the French police destroyed most of the copies of his *Geneva Dialogues,* one surviving copy found its way into the hands of the Tsarist Secret Service, the Okhrana, in Geneva. Grave's article showed that entire slabs of Joly's book had been translated into Russian and then copied into *The Protocols*. For example:

> You do not know the unbounded meanness of the peoples… groveling before force, pitiless towards the weak, implacable to faults, indulgent to crimes, incapable of supporting the contradictions of a free régime, and patient to the point of martyrdom under the violence of an audacious despotism… giving themselves masters whom they pardon for deeds for the least of which they would have beheaded twenty constitutional kings.
>
> — Machiavelli, in *The Geneva Dialogues,* p. 43

In their intense meanness the Christian peoples help our independence—when kneeling they crouch before power; when they are pitiless towards the weak; merciless in dealing with faults, and lenient to crimes; when they refuse to recognize the contradictions of freedom; when they are patient to the degree of martyrdom in bearing with the violence of an audacious despotism. At the hands of their present dictators, Premiers, and ministers, they endure abuses for the smallest of which they would have murdered twenty kings.

—*The Protocols of the Elders of Zion,* p. 15

*The Geneva Dialogues* was not the only text used in the creation of *The Protocols*. The idea of a meeting of the Elders of Zion has been traced to a novel called *Biarritz* by Sir John Retcliffe. Retcliffe was not a Sir at all. Rather he was Herman Goedsche, a Prussian postal worker and reactionary who was fired from the Prussian postal service for forging letters implicating the democratic leader, Benedic Waldeck, in a plot against the Prussian regime. Finding himself without an income, Goedsche began to write sensationalist romance novels. He was also an avowed anti-Semite.

*Biarritz* was published in 1868. In one chapter, "At the Jewish Cemetery in Prague," Goedsche, ignorant of the fact that ten of the twelve tribes of Israel no longer existed, wrote a scene where twelve Jewish leaders meet Satan in a graveyard, report on the status of their conspiracy toward world domination, and come away with the intention of being kings of the world within the century. Many of the strategies discussed to achieve this domination seem to have been copied from Joly's *Dialogues*. Given that the Jewish Cemetery chapter of Goesdche's novel was translated into Russian and circulated independently as a pamphlet, it's quite likely it was the catalyst for the eventual fusing of the two texts in the Protocols.

## ARISTOCRATIC AUTHOR

So if it wasn't the Elders of Zion who wrote the document, then who wrote it? It remains uncertain as to exactly who wrote *The Protocols,* but it's likely the forgery was created at the direction of the Paris head of the Okhrana at the time, Pyotr Rachovsky, to try and link the opponents of the tsar to a worldwide Jewish conspiracy.

# Mein Kampf

To the Huntington Library
from
G S Patton
April 14 1945

The man most commonly identified with its writing is Mathieu Golovinski, a Russian aristocrat whose father had been a friend of novelist Fyodor Dostoevsky. At university, Golovinski joined the Holy Brotherhood, an ultra-nationalist anti-Semitic secret society that used forged documents to discredit revolutionaries. From there he went to work for the tsar's government press department as a spin doctor and briber of journalists. Eventually, his scheming got the better of him, and he was denounced as an informer by novelist Maxim Gorky and dismissed.

Golovinski became a freelancer of sorts and worked with the son of Maurice Joly at a Paris newspaper, where he probably discovered the *Geneva Dialogues*. He was hired by Rachovsky to write *The Protocols* as a piece of propaganda. Showing himself to be a man of intrigue and opportunism rather than ideals, Golovinski went on to scheme for the Bolsheviks after the 1917 Revolution until his death in 1920. It was during this same period that his fraud began to extend its influence in the world.

## THE SIGNIFICANCE OF THE LIE

...To what extent the whole existence of this people is based on a continuous lie is shown incomparably by *The Protocols of the Wise Men of Zion,* so infinitely hated by the Jews. They are based on a forgery, the *Frankfurter Zeitung* moans and screams once every week: the best proof that they are authentic. What many Jews may do unconsciously is here consciously exposed. And that is what matters.

It is completely indifferent from what Jewish brain these disclosures originate; the important thing is that with positively terrifying certainty they reveal the nature and activity of the Jewish people and expose their inner contexts as well as their ultimate final aims. The best criticism applied to them, however, is reality. Anyone who examines the historical development of the last hundred years from the standpoint of this book will at once understand the screaming of the Jewish press. For once this book has become the common property of a people, the Jewish menace may be considered as broken.

—*Mein Kampf* by Adolf Hitler

More than anything else, the significance of *The Protocols* can be found in Hitler's use of them as a foundation for his anti-Semitism. The devastation caused to Germany by the conditions of surrender under the Treaty of Versailles created

THE FRONT COVER OF HITLER'S *MEIN KAMPF.* WRITTEN WHILE HE WAS IN PRISON AND PUBLISHED IN 1926, *MEIN KAMPF* WAS A TURGID AMALGAM OF AUTOBIOGRAPHY AND POLITICAL PHILOSOPHY. ITS ANTI-SEMITISM LEANED HEAVILY ON A FERVENT BELIEF IN *THE PROTOCOLS OF THE ELDERS OF ZION.*
Associated Press

conditions extremely conducive for conspiracy theory. *The Protocols* emerged at just the right time and immediately found an eager German audience.

Although books and articles had shown *The Protocols* to be a lie since 1920, Hitler, as have many since, had no trouble in asserting their truth. Although it's unlikely that the absence of *The Protocols* would have prevented the ascendancy of Hitler and his rabid anti-Semitism, they were useful, and as such can be considered a contributing factor to the rise of the Nazis, and also of the Final Solution.

Other notable adherents to *The Protocols* of that era included Henry Ford, who said:

> The only statement I care to make about *The Protocols* is that they fit in with what is going on. They are sixteen years old, and they have fitted the world situation up to this time. They fit it now.

Despite all the evidence to the contrary, Ford maintained the truth of *The Protocols* until 1927, when he was forced to make a public recantation, which he did by passing the buck onto his staff, arguing unconvincingly that they had misled him into believing their authenticity. Given Ford's central role in the American military-industrial complex and his admiration of Hitler, it's possible *The Protocols* played a (small) part in the political atmosphere that caused the United States' tardy entry into World War II.

One could be forgiven for thinking that after the Holocaust, *The Protocols* would have been consigned to history as one of the world's ugliest lies. Yet they have continued to prosper, particularly in the Middle East, where they help fuel the long-running conflict between the Israelis and the Arab world. In some countries such as Saudi Arabia, *The Protocols* can even be found on school syllabuses. The oppressive ruling elites of these countries see the same opportunity that Tsar Nicholas did: *The Protocols* are a convenient way of finding scapegoats for the poor living conditions most inhabitants of the Arab world continue to live in. Paradoxically, one of the other major proponents of *The Protocols* as truth tend to be conservative Christian groups. The rise of Neo-Nazism, particularly among the many disaffected inhabitants of the former Soviet bloc, is another domain where *The Protocols* are enjoying resurgence in the hands of people who couldn't care less about their authenticity.

CHAPTER 13

# HAROLD LASSETER: FINDER OF A REEF OF GOLD?

### (1930s)

T HE CAMELS WERE AGITATED. HARRY LASSETER WAS HAVING a hard time controlling them. The animals kicked at the dusty ground and refused to follow his lead. The smaller one hissed and spat at him when he tried to adjust its harness. Lasseter and the two camels had been traveling for miles, making their way through the Australian wilderness. At times, the heat was unbearable.

Insects, high temperatures, difficult terrain, and the constant threat of attack by aborigines dampened his spirits but not his resolve. He was a man on a mission, intent on rediscovering the reef of gold he claimed he'd stumbled upon years ago. Weeks earlier, Lasseter had served as the guide on an organized expedition to find the valuable reef. Led by bushman Fred Blakely, the party included an engineer, a prospector, a pilot, and several explorers.

They set out in July 1930. From the start, the expedition was beset by difficulties. The plane hired to do aerial reconnaissance on the site crashed, injuring the pilot. The trucks used in the expedition got stuck in the sand. Then the party got lost in the outback. Food and water reserves ran out. Lasseter's behavior grew increasingly bizarre, leading the others to wonder whether the reef actually existed. Numerous arguments broke out. Blakely called off the expedition.

An angry but determined Lasseter trudged on, this time accompanied by a dingo hunter named Paul Johns. The new alliance was short-lived. While Johns was resting at their makeshift camp, Lasseter wandered off on his own.

HARRY LASSETER MARRIED FLOR-ENCE SCOTT IN 1903. TOGETHER THEY HAD THREE CHILDREN. DESPITE HIS MARITAL STATUS, LASSETER ENGAGED IN A NUMBER OF AFFAIRS AND TOOK A SECOND WIFE WHILE STILL WED TO SCOTT.

State Library of South Australia

He returned with the exciting news that he had found the gold reef. In his hand he clutched a bag full of what he said was freshly collected gold. He refused to let Johns inspect it. Johns, naturally, was suspicious. The two men got into a fistfight. Johns left Lasseter with two of his five camels and abandoned the expedition.

Camels in tow, Lasseter braved the blistering Australian heat. The outback was a desert with no water in sight. He took pains to ration his water and food; both were preserved in packs on the camels. Lasseter set up camp and spent the evenings writing in his diary and composing letters to his wife. One night while he was sleeping, the camels ran off, leaving him stranded in the outback without food or water.

Lasseter walked until he collapsed onto the dusty earth. He was dehydrated and starving. His lips cracked from the heat. The lack of nourishment added to his delirium. Aborigines discovered him passed out in the sun and moved him to a nearby cave. For several weeks, the Aborigines tended to him. An older woman and an elderly man Lasseter dubbed Old Warts because of the blemishes on his back brought him food and water. They shared what little food they had. But resources were scarce, and the Aborigines barely had enough to feed themselves. Eventually, they moved on, because Lasseter had become a burden and was too weak to accompany them.

Lasseter took shelter in the cave. He penned letters and waited to be rescued. Starving and parched, he scribbled in his diary, "Have shrunk still further and flies and ants have nearly eaten my face away ... Beaten by sandy blight. What an epitaph. [A]gony of starvation may drive me to shoot myself. What good a reef worth millions? I would give it all for a loaf of bread."

Realizing that help was not imminent, Lasseter left the cave and attempted to walk back to civilization. He never made it. He died alone in the outback. He was fifty years old.

## DELUSIONS OF GOLD AND GRANDEUR

Harry Lasseter was nothing if not colorful. Friends and colleagues consistently described him as eccentric, grandiose, unhinged, and erratic. He was known to be a difficult man and prone to belligerence. His early military record lists him as being mentally unstable and unfit for service.

Many people cling to the idea that he did find a reef of gold. But it is doubtful that such a treasure exists, more so that Lasseter managed to repeatedly locate and then forget its location. It is more likely that Lasseter, a storyteller by nature, made the whole thing up.

The idea that there was a reef made of gold hidden in the Australian outback was tantalizing but improbable. Such fanciful ideas are the stuff of legend. The search for hidden treasure has formed the basis of many a book and Hollywood movie. Inspired by the enduring legend of El Dorado, dozens of European explorers, including Sir Walter Raleigh, mounted expeditions to search for the mythical jewel-studded city. Of course, their searches were in vain. El Dorado did not exist.

Lasseter was fascinated by such stories. He was also entranced by the novels of Harold Bell Wright—so much so that he adopted the author's name. An American, Wright was best known for *The Mine with the Iron Door*. Published in 1923, the novel chronicled the search for a stash of gold and silver buried inside an Arizonian cave. While Lasseter took his name from Wright, he appeared to lift his story from English author Simpson Newland. Lasseter's tale of found—and lost—gold is suspiciously similar to the plot of Newland's 1900 novel *Blood on the Tracks*.

A logical assumption would be that Lasseter adopted these stories as his own. With his history of mental instability and tendency to spin yarns, Lasseter was especially prone to fantasy. After telling the story of the gold reef for so many years, the unbalanced man may well have convinced himself of its veracity. For Lasseter, the lie was more attractive than the truth.

## BIRTH OF THE MAN—AND THE LEGEND

Lasseter was born in Meredith, Victoria, in Australia, on September 27, 1880. His given name was Lewis but friends called him "Possum." Later, he added Harold Bell to his name in honor of the American novelist.

Lasseter was a stocky, barrel-chested man fond of telling tales far taller than his small stature of 5-foot 3-inches (160 centimeters). He told people he drew up the original plans for the Sidney Harbor Bridge (a lie) and that he invented a battleship that could withstand the impact of torpedoes. Lasseter also claimed to have served as a pilot in the air force during World War I. In fact, he was found unfit; his military file notes Lasseter "has marked hallucinations, wants to join flying corps as a friend is going to present him with an aeroplane."

Lasseter spent some time in the United States as a young man. There he met and married Florence Scott. He also developed a keen interest in the Mormon Church; he found the church's policy on polygamy especially

appealing. Later in life he took a second and third wife and engaged in a number of extramarital affairs. His daughter Ruby would later write in her diary, "My mother was continually hearing of his numerous infidelities, which he took little trouble to hide. For some reason, women who had been quite respectable became fascinated by him."

In Australia, Lasseter eked out a living as a carpenter and then as a miner and prospector. In 1929, he began telling a fantastic story about a gold-bearing quartz reef he discovered thirty-two years earlier while prospecting for rubies near the MacDonnell ranges, west of Alice Springs. His brown eyes twinkled when he described the seven-mile wide reef he swore was lined with gold as "thick as plums in pudding." Lasseter said he chipped away at the reef and obtained a few gold-bearing nuggets that he stashed inside an oatmeal bag.

Gold in pocket, Lasseter headed for town. He planned to have the nuggets assessed and then return with the proper equipment and stake his claim to the

AFTER THE OFFICIAL
EXPEDITION WAS CUT SHORT,
LASSETER JOINED FORCES WITH
DINGO HUNTER PAUL JOHNS.
WITH A CONVOY OF FIVE CAMELS,
LASSETER AND JOHNS CONTINUED
TO SEARCH FOR THE REEF
OF GOLD.
National Archives of Australia

reef. Along the way, things went awry. Both of his horses died, leaving him stranded. Desperately lost and dehydrated, Lasseter was rescued by an Afghan camel driver who was passing through the area. The camel driver brought him to the camp of a man named Harding. There, Lasseter recuperated. When he was well enough to travel, he told Harding, a former government miner, about his incredible discovery.

According to Lasseter, the nuggets he'd collected from the reef were assayed at the highest quality. Ecstatic, he and Harding's men used them to raise money to buy supplies, equipment, and camels, and they set out to find the reef. The mission was a success. The men set their watches to fix the reef's location but later found that their watches were off. The glittering gold reef was once again lost. Harding left for the United States and was never heard from again.

## PROPOSITIONS BORN OF PIPEDREAMS

In 1929, Lasseter first approached the government with an "out of the ordinary" proposition to fund an expedition to find the gold reef. "For the past eighteen years I have known of a vast gold-bearing reef in Central Australia," he wrote. (Lasseter contradicted his previous statements of discovering the reef thirty-two years earlier.) "Assays taken over fourteen miles of reef show values of three ounces to the ton."

Two months later, Herbert Gepp, chairman of the Development and Migration Commission, and Dr. Keith Ward, the South Australian government geologist, met with Lasseter in Sydney. The eccentric Lasseter immediately struck the men as being unstable. They were skeptical of his story about the gold reef. A later search for the mysterious Harding proved unsuccessful. No record of such a man existed.

Nevertheless, Gepp realized that a highly publicized expedition for gold might be good for the country. Australia was in the midst of a great depression. A treasure hunt could motivate the unemployed—of which there were many—to get out into the fields to prospect for gold and valuable minerals. Such activity would lift the spirits of an otherwise depressed and restless population.

In 1851, Australia experienced gold rush fever after the precious metal was discovered in Victoria. Newcomers hoping to make a fortune in the mines

flooded the dry country. Boomtowns such as Ballarat and Bendigo grew in size and popularity as miners struck pay dirt there. At one point, Australia's gold output was the highest in the world. But those times had passed. Alluvial gold grew scarce and ran out. The remaining untapped mines were too deep and too costly to plumb. The gold rush had ended by the time Lasseter finally caught the government's attention.

Despite Gepp's initial enthusiasm, he was unable to convince his colleagues to back Lasseter's expedition. In his official report he concluded that, "the evidence is too meager to provide proof that there exists a profitable gold field of material size in the area reported by Mr. Lasseter, and the despatch of a party, based on Mr. Lasseter's information, should be regarded only in the form of a

AFTER FAILING TO OBTAIN GOVERNMENT SUPPORT FOR AN EXPEDITION, LASSETER, FRONT, CONVINCED THE AUSTRALIAN WORKERS' UNION TO FUND AND MOUNT A SEARCH FOR HIS FABLED GOLD REEF.

Central Australian Gold Expedition, MacDonnell Ranges, 1930 [picture] / National Library of Australia

gamble. We therefore cannot recommend it except as a portion of an organized prospecting of certain areas throughout the interior of Australia."

Lasseter's request for government funding was denied.

## A PROPER EXPEDITION

Turned down by the government, Lasseter next approached the Australian's Worker's Union (AWU). He regaled the members with his story of the glittering gold reef. They heard all about his fateful discovery and rescue by a camel driver, and the kindness of a government prospector named Harding who gave him shelter in his time of need. Lasseter bragged that he was a ship's captain, had been a pilot, and invented a torpedo-proof submarine. Lasseter's tall tales raised quite a few eyebrows. Still, the union was seduced by the prospect of seven miles of gold.

AWU president John Bailey approved Lasseter's proposal. The union and the Central Australian Gold Exploration Company (CAGE) raised £5,000 to finance the expedition. A party of eight men was assembled. Fred Blakeley, a bushman of limited experience, was chosen to lead the expedition. Lasseter was hired as a guide and paid a salary of £5 per week. The expedition included two six-wheeled Thornycroft trucks and a small plane named, appropriately enough, the Golden Quest.

The county was abuzz with news of the expedition. Bailey was interviewed by the *Melbourne Press* and inadvertently caused an uproar over race relations with the Aborigines. Questioned about safety from certain hostile Aborigine tribes that resided in the outback, Bailey bragged that his team will be "armed to the teeth." The newspaper was bombarded with angry letters from readers protesting the use of arms against the natives. In an attempt at damage control, Lasseter wrote to the paper explaining (unconvincingly) that the firearms were needed because "wild dogs are reliably reported to have killed two injured and helpless men" in the outback.

The expedition embarked in mid-July 1930. From the start there were problems. Blakeley was a poor leader and unfamiliar with the region that allegedly housed the gold reef. There was an experienced and accomplished explorer in the party, but Blakeley refused to take advice from him. As a consequence, the leader led the party into one logistical jam after another. Blake-

AN EXPERT BUSHMAN, BOB BUCK ASSISTED MANY LOST TRAVELERS IN HIS LIFETIME. WHEN HARRY LASSETER WENT MISSING IN THE OUTBACK, THE CENTRAL AUSTRALIAN GOLD EXPLORATION COMPANY HIRED BUCK TO LOCATE HIM.

Portrait of Bob Buck (picture) / National Library of Australia

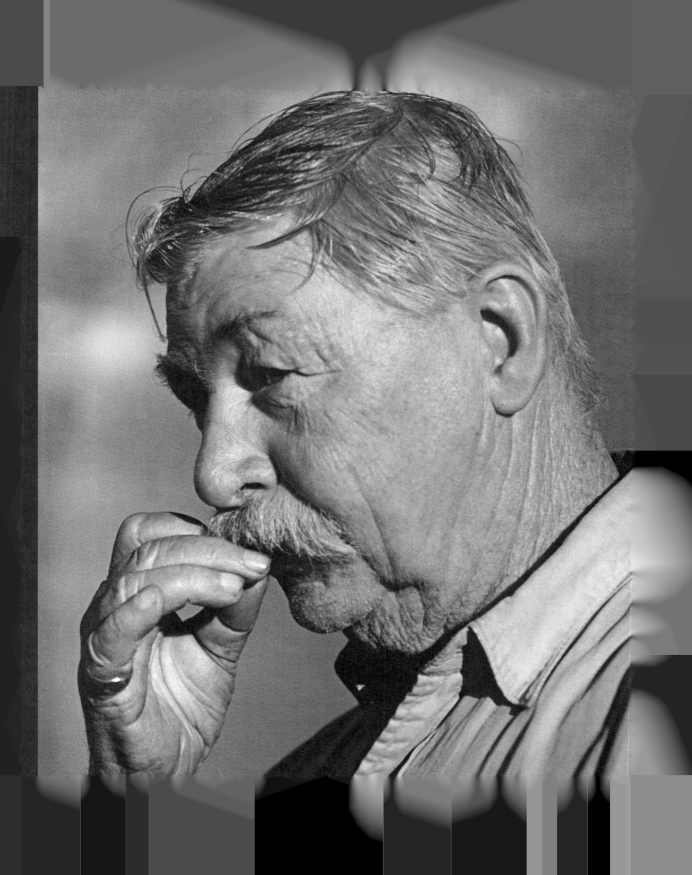

ley failed to obtain the proper maps, mismanaged the water and food supplies, got the party lost, and was unable to keep the men focused on the mission.

Lasseter and Blakeley argued about which direction to take. Golden Quest crashed, injuring the pilot and damaging a propeller, rendering the plane inoperable. The area was beset by imposing sand dunes. The trucks got stuck in the sand, causing delays as the men worked to dig the vehicles out. The party grew increasingly frustrated by the constant setbacks.

Lasseter made matters worse with his bragging and obnoxious behavior. He spun outrageous yarns about his accomplishments in the war and as a prospector and bushman. He gave conflicting stories about the gold reef and was unable to find the landmarks he claimed to have seen years earlier. He was also paranoid and suspected the men were intent on swindling him. At night, Lasseter commandeered the firearms and piled them into the truck that served as his bed. He wrote to his wife, Florence, that the expedition was not going as planned.

The men began to openly doubt Lasseter's sincerity—and his sanity. The consensus was that he was a fraud, his gold reef a fairytale. Lasseter appeared to have scant knowledge of the outback, leading the other men to believe that he had only read about the region, never actually traversed it. Blakeley called him a charlatan. "If Lasseter's story is true, he was thus the first explorer to cross the continent from east to west," commented one explorer. As the weeks passed, tensions mounted, and tempers flared. To the relief of everyone but Lasseter, the expedition was aborted at the end of August 1930.

## ALONE IN THE OUTBACK

After his camels ran off, Lasseter holed up in a cave and spent sixteen weeks waiting to be rescued. A passing tribe of Aborigines took pity on the strange white man. The man whom Lasseter had dubbed Old Warts did his best to communicate with him. They did not speak the same language and spent most of their time together pointing at things and drawing pictures in the dirt to express themselves. An older Aborigine woman visited Lasseter often. The tribe was nomadic, however, and after two months, moved on. Lasseter was too weak to travel, and it is unlikely that they would have allowed an outsider to join them.

Help from C.A.G.E. was not immediately forthcoming. It was not until February 1931 that renowned bushman Bob Buck was hired to search for

Lasseter. Buck set out with a small party and several camels. After searching for a month, Buck and his companions found Lasseter. He had been dead for some time. Lasseter's diary and several letters to his wife were found nearby. Buck and the men buried the body in the outback in Winter Glen country.

## LASSETER'S LEGACY LIVES ON

Lasseter died in 1931. But his legend lives on in Australian folklore. His elusive gold reef—Australia's own Holy Grail—has never been found. The prospect of unclaimed treasures out in the wilderness continues to capture the imagination of modern explorers and daydreamers alike. Since Lasseter's death, more than a dozen expeditions have been mounted to search for his fabled reef.

### SINCE LASSETER'S DEATH, MORE THAN A DOZEN EXPEDITIONS HAVE BEEN MOUNTED TO SEARCH FOR HIS FABLED REEF.

The most recent expedition, commissioned by Lutz Frankenfeld, took place in May 2007. Frankenfeld claimed he had discovered Lasseter's gold reef. A businessman and founder of Darwin's Beer Car Regatta, Frankenfeld secured a twenty-five year lease for the land on which the reef allegedly stands. He is currently making plans to mine it. Frankenfeld has not revealed the reef's location.

Australian historian Peter Forrest is skeptical about Frankenfeld's claim. He believes the gold-bearing quartz reef was a figment of Lasseter's imagination. "I haven't been given any information to make me change my mind," Forrest told reporters. "But," he added, giving hope to treasure hunters everywhere, "I have been wrong before."

# CHAPTER 14

# JOHN DILLINGER: DEAD OR ALIVE?

## (1934)

T HE NIGHT OF JULY 22, 1934, WAS STEAMING HOT IN CHICAGO. Many people had left their houses and apartments and were strolling along the streets trying to keep cool.

One group of about twenty men was not moving. The suspicious men were standing along Lincoln Avenue on the sidewalk outside the Biograph Theater. They worried the manager, Charles Shapiro, who thought they might be planning to rob his theater. Or maybe they were members of a gang contemplating something worse than robbery. The wars between Al Capone and his rivals were still fresh in everyone's memory. Capone was now the big man in Chicago's underworld, but gang murders hadn't quite stopped. Shapiro called the police.

When the Chicago cops arrived, James Metcalfe showed them his identification. He said he was a special agent of the FBI, and he and those suspicious-looking men outside the theater were part of a top secret FBI operation. The cops drove away. Melvin Purvis, FBI special agent in charge of the Chicago office, had been told that the Chicago police were corrupt and would tip off John Dillinger.

Purvis had received a hot tip from an out-of-state cop, Martin Zarkovich of the nearby Indiana city of East Chicago. A friend of his, Anna Cumpanas, better known in Chicago as Anna Sage, who ran bordellos in Indiana and Chicago, said she knew the most-wanted criminal in America, John Dillinger, and could set the stage for his capture. Zarkovich introduced her to Purvis. In return for Dillinger, Cumpanas wanted the cancellation of the order deporting her to her native Romania. Purvis agreed.

> **MYTH**
> NOTORIOUS GANGSTER
> JOHN DILLINGER WAS SHOT
> AND KILLED OUTSIDE
> THE BIOGRAPH THEATER
> IN CHICAGO ON JULY 22, 1934.
>
> **REALITY**
> MANY PEOPLE NO LONGER
> BELIEVE IT WAS DILLINGER
> WHO WAS KILLED,
> BUT A SMALL-TIME CRIMINAL
> NAMED JIMMY LAWRENCE.

Martin Zarkovich also had a request. He and his captain, Tim O'Neill, and three Indiana detectives wanted to be in on the capture. Purvis agreed to that, too. Purvis did not know that two days before this night, two out-of-state cops, probably Zarkovich and O'Neill, had approached John Stege, chief of the Chicago Police Department's "Dillinger squad." They said Dillinger was in Chicago, and they could set up an ambush. There was only one condition: Dillinger could not be captured. He had to be killed. Stege threw them out of his office, saying he was not a murderer.

## THE LADY IN RED

On the infamous night, Cumpanas had called Purvis and told him that Dillinger and his current girlfriend, one of her employees, would be going to the movies and that she would accompany them. So that there would be no mistake, she said she would wear a burnt orange skirt.

Cumpanas was a key person because neither Purvis nor any of the FBI men had ever seen Dillinger. The agents had been warned that he had probably undergone plastic surgery, something that was quite fashionable for Midwestern gangsters at that time, both to avoid recognition and foil fingerprint identification. Indeed, Purvis was the only G-man who had ever seen Cumpanas.

Dillinger and the two women would go to either the Marlbro Theater on the west side of Chicago or the Biograph on the north side. Purvis and Special Agent Ralph Brown drove to the Biograph, and Purvis sent Zarkovich to check out the Marlbro. Zarkovich knew Anna Cumpanas well; he was her lover. Purvis, nicknamed "Nervous Purvis" by the other agents, sat in a parked car and chain smoked during the four-hour wait for Dillinger.

Finally, he saw Anna Cumpanas with a young woman and a man wearing glasses. The man—plastic surgery or no plastic surgery—looked remarkably like the pictures of John Dillinger. Under the marquee lights, Cumpanas' orange skirt looked blood red. Purvis decided that the best way to capture Dillinger was when he left the theater. He called his headquarters and asked for all available agents as well as Zarkovich and the other East Chicago cops. It was when the rest of the Dillinger hunters had deployed outside the theater that Shapiro had called the police.

Purvis was supposed to light a cigar as a signal for the agents to move in. "Nervous" Purvis reportedly struck ten matches. By the time he had lit the cigar, the agents' quarry was dead. Purvis later stated that he had yelled, "Stick 'em up, Johnny! We have you surrounded." Others reported that Purvis had said nothing. But he had ripped every button off his sport jacket trying to reach his gun.

The official FBI report said that someone had shouted something, and Dillinger drew a pistol and started to run. The agents opened fire, and Dillinger fell dead. The report did not identify who had actually fired the fatal shot. FBI Director J. Edgar Hoover said the Dillinger operation was a team effort; he wanted no individual heroes.

## THE REPORT OF DILLINGER'S DEATH GOT A MIXED RECEPTION IN DEPRESSION-STRICKEN AMERICA. MANY REJOICED THAT "PUBLIC ENEMY NUMBER ONE" WAS NO LONGER ROBBING BANKS. BUT OTHERS MOURNED BECAUSE THEY SAW DILLINGER AS A KIND OF ROBIN HOOD.

## BUT WAS IT DILLINGER?

The report of Dillinger's death got a mixed reception in Depression-stricken America. Many rejoiced that the man Hoover called "public enemy number one" was no longer robbing banks. But others mourned because they saw Dillinger as a kind of Robin Hood. He robbed the rich banks, even if he gave nothing to the poor. But whether they were happy or sad about it, nobody doubted that Dillinger had been killed.

In the public mind of 1934, FBI agents were supercops, perfect in every way. They could not have been mistaken about the man shot in front of the Biograph Theater. Not for another generation would anyone question what happened.

The death of Dillinger was the cause of celebration at the "Seat of Government," as Hoover and his agents called FBI headquarters in Washington. Hoover frequently said that the elimination of Dillinger was the high point of his career. He had a death mask of the outlaw in his office. In the outer office, he put Dillinger's gun and broken glasses on display in a glass case.

There was a good reason for both Hoover and Purvis to celebrate. Before the coup at the Biograph, their jobs were in danger, and John Dillinger was responsible.

Dillinger, a good-looking, athletic man, had the sort of flair that interested the press. He would do things like leap over bank counters to get the money in tellers' cages or tell would-be depositors to keep their money, because he only wanted the bank's cash. So Dillinger made headlines, and Hoover fretted because robbing banks was not a federal crime at that time. It wasn't until Dillinger broke out of the Crown Point, Indiana, jail on March 3, 1934, that the FBI were able to go after him. To add insult to injury, Dillinger most likely accomplished this feat with a wooden gun, although the FBI maintains the weapon was real. When Dillinger stole a sheriff's car and drove it across the state line to Illinois, the FBI had the green light to go after him.

## THE LITTLE BOHEMIA FIASCO

After the jail break, Dillinger began recruiting a new gang because most of his old colleagues were in prison. He needed some quiet time to make plans, so he and his gang moved into the Little Bohemia Lodge, a resort deep in the woods of northern Wisconsin.

On April 20, Purvis, special agent in charge of the FBI Chicago office, got a tip that Dillinger and his crew were at the lodge. Purvis led a small army of FBI agents into the North Woods. As they approached the lodge, nervously holding submachine guns and revolvers, three men left the building and got into a car. About the same time, the lodge owner's watchdogs began to bark, prompting two bartenders to come out and see what was the matter.

Purvis yelled at the men getting into the car, "We're government agents!" and motioned for his men to move in. The men apparently did not hear him and started the car.

"Don't shoot! Don't shoot! Those are customers of ours!" the bartenders shouted. As the car backed up, Purvis and his men opened fire, riddling the car with bullets. When the firing stopped, John Hoffman, a gas station attendant from nearby Mercer, Wisconsin, jumped out of the car, clutching his wound, and ran screaming into the woods.

John Morris, a cook at a Civilian Conservation Corps (CCC) camp, who had been hit four times, staggered into the lodge looking for a telephone and then passed out. The third man, Gene Boiseneau, another CCC man, had been killed instantly.

Purvis and his men then began firing indiscriminately into the lodge. They fired at the building, but hit nobody. The lodge owner, Emil Wanatka, the bartenders, and three women who were wives and girlfriends of the gang members

FBI AGENTS MAY OR MAY NOT HAVE FATALLY SHOT JOHN DILLINGER OUTSIDE THE BIOGRAPH THEATER IN CHICAGO ON THE NIGHT OF JULY 22, 1934. PRIOR TO THE SHOOTING, THE AGENTS HAD BEEN WARNED THAT DILLINGER MAY HAVE UNDERGONE PLASTIC SURGERY, WHICH WAS FASHIONABLE FOR MIDWESTERN GANGSTERS AT THE TIME, TO BOTH AVOID DETECTION AND FOIL FINGERPRINT IDENTIFICATION.
Associated Press

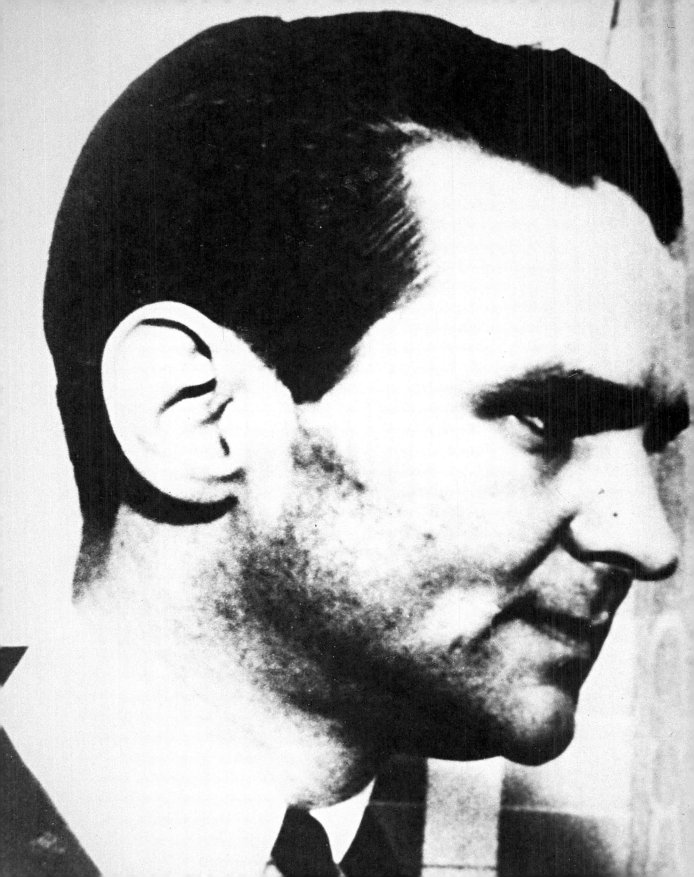

hid in the cellar. When Dillinger first heard the shooting, he and his men fled to their rooms on the second floor, squeezed through a rear window, dropped to a first floor roof, and then jumped to the ground. They left all their belongings except their guns and disappeared into the woods.

Another member of the gang, Lester Gillis, alias Baby-face Nelson, was staying with his wife at a nearby cabin. Nelson was a new member of the gang, unstable and homicidal. He was the opposite of the violence-avoiding Dillinger, but good help had been hard to get. After taking a shot at Purvis, Nelson ran to a neighboring resort operated by Alvin Koerner and demanded a car.

Meanwhile, Wanatka had managed to leave his resort while Purvis and his agents were firing at the first floor. He ran into Nelson at Koerner's. Fortunately for the innkeeper, two FBI agents, J. C. Newman and W. C. Baum, and deputy sheriff Carl C. Christiansen, drove up at that moment. Nelson shot all three— one FBI agent fatally—and took the FBI car.

Wanatka returned to his own lodge and told Purvis all his men at Koerner's had been shot. Purvis was writing a report and didn't seem interested in what the innkeeper told him. All he wanted to know was how Wanatka spelled his name.

## "OUST HOOVER AND PURVIS!"

Purvis may not have been interested, but the national newspapers were. They demanded that both Purvis and Hoover be fired. U.S. Senator Kenneth McKellar conducted hearings that were highly critical of the FBI. And highly influential members of the Roosevelt administration were seriously considering replacing the FBI director.

Wanatka received generous compensation for the damage that Purvis and his men had inflicted on his lodge. And he took advantage of the fact that the Dillinger gang had left all their clothing and other property behind. He used those belongings to set up a Dillinger "museum." And that led to the first serious questions about the identity of the man gunned down July 22, 1934.

## LETTER OF INTENT

Long after the shootings at Little Bohemia and the Biograph Theater, in the spring of 1968, *Chicago Land Magazine* editor Jay Robert Nash dropped by the

MELVIN PURVIS WAS ONCE THE GOLDEN BOY OF THE FBI. BUT IN ADDITION TO PROBABLY KILLING THE WRONG MAN IN FRONT OF THE BIOGRAPH THEATER, HE WAS ACCUSED OF THE COLD-BLOODED MURDER OF "PRETTY BOY" FLOYD, AND WAS A BLATANT PUBLICITY HOUND. J. EDGAR HOOVER WOULD NOT BE UPSTAGED, AND HE PROB-ABLY BELIEVED (CORRECTLY) THAT PURVIS WAS A PUBLIC MENACE. PURVIS LEFT THE BUREAU AND BECAME THE LEADER OF THE POST TOASTIES JUNIOR G-MEN.

Melvin Purvis (1903-60) (b/w photo), American Photographer, (20th century)

Dillinger Museum. Emil Wanatka, Jr., son of Dillinger's unwilling host, showed him a mysterious letter he had received. It read:

Emile Wanatka, Jr.
Little Bohemia Lodge
Manitowish Waters, Wisconsin

Dear Sir:

Am sending a letter and photo of Dillinger as he looks today for you to place on exhibit in your museum. The man shot was James Lawrence who told the woman in red, Anna Compana, [sic] that he was Dillinger.

After the shooting Dillinger moved to Hollywood where he has worked ever since under an assumed name.

J.E. Hoover stated, "There is every indication that the man shown was Dillinger except the proof. It's customary to send into headquarters the fingerprints of every man shot by the FBI, but no fingerprints have come in spite of a regulation burial."

The fingerprints were taken of the man shot, but they did not match those of Dillinger, therefore they were not sent in, because if they were the FBI would have to admit that the wrong man was killed.

Dillinger's sister Audrey said she could positively identify her brother by a scar on his leg.

After viewing the body, she said, "There is no question in my mind. Bury him." But what she was really looking for was a birthmark, which was not there. But naturally by saying this she protected both Dillinger and the FBI.

The man shot had black hair and brown eyes, to [sic] large for Dillinger.

Yours Sincerely,
John H. Dillinger

With the letter was a picture of a man who might have been Dillinger thirty-four years after he was supposedly killed.

ANNA SAGE, ALSO KNOWN AS ANNA CUMPANAS, IS PICTURED HERE AT THE CHICAGO POLICE STATION WHILE BEING QUESTIONED BY AUTHORITIES ON JULY 24, 1934, TWO DAYS AFTER DILLINGER WAS ALLEGEDLY KILLED. SAGE, WHO RAN BORDELLOS IN INDIANA AND CHICAGO, HELPED POLICE SET THE STAGE FOR DILLINGER'S CAPTURE IN EXCHANGE FOR THE CANCELLATION OF THE ORDER DEPORTING HER BACK TO HER NATIVE ROMANIA.

Associated Press

## DIGGING UP THE PAST

The letter and picture started Nash on a series of inquiries and interviews.

Among other things, Nash checked with the Colt factory and learned that the .380 automatic displayed in Hoover's office as the gun Dillinger was carrying had not left the factory until five months after the outlaw was reported to be dead. That discovery raised the suspicion that the man shot outside the Biograph had been unarmed, despite the FBI report to the contrary.

The other item displayed with the pistol was the eyeglass frames the man had been wearing when he was shot. Dillinger had perfect eyesight, according to naval (he had been a sailor for a short time, but had deserted) and prison records. The FBI said the spectacles were sunglasses. However, Nash learned frames of that type were used only for prescription glasses in the 1930s.

The Dillinger autopsy was not in the coroner's office. One elderly employee believed it had never been filed. But Nash learned that Dr. J. J. Kearns, the chief pathologist as the time, had a copy. The autopsy showed that the supposed Dillinger had brown eyes. In addition, because the body had black hair, the FBI said the brown-haired Dillinger had dyed his hair.

---

## THE MYSTERIOUS MAN WHO SHOT "DILLINGER"

According to FBI folklore, the man who killed Dillinger was Charlie Winstead, a former Texas cowboy and deputy sheriff. Winstead had joined the Bureau in 1926, before J. Edgar Hoover got there. He was one of several tough gunfighters Hoover had placed on the "Dillinger squad" because he thought the lawyers and public accountants he had hired might need help with motorized bank robbers such as Dillinger.

Winstead is something of a mystery. Jay Robert Nash, in his book *The Dillinger Dossier,* reports that Joseph Pinkston, a collector of Dillinger memorabilia, inquired about Winstead and was told that the FBI never had an agent named Charles Winstead. However, William C. Sullivan, later number two man in the Bureau, worked for Winstead as a young agent.

Winstead was special agent in charge of the El Paso office, which covered all of New Mexico. Other agents told Sullivan his new boss was sour, eccentric, disagreeable, and impossible to work with—all of which Sullivan found to be true. Winstead especially disliked "big city boys from the East." But when he learned that Sullivan was a farm boy from the East who said, "I worked around cattle and horses all my life, and I think I made a big mistake leaving the farm," they became fast friends and often rode horseback through Winstead's desert jurisdiction.

In 1942, after sixteen years in the Bureau, Winstead had had enough. He told J. Edgar Hoover to "go to hell," and took a commission in the army. Sullivan inherited Winstead's Stetson, boots, saddle, lasso, and revolver, a .357 Magnum, when Winstead died in 1974.

Although you can change your hair color, you can't change the color of your eyes. Nash checked his interview notes and old records for the color of Dillinger's eyes. According to the navy, in 1923, they were blue. According to the FBI, in 1934, they were gray. His long-time girlfriend, Evelyn Frechette, said they were bluish-gray. A boyhood neighbor, May Jeffers, said they were "kind of blue." William L. Tubbs, a reporter who knew him, said, "They were about the color of this [indicating a bluish-gray metal ashtray]." Some attempts to explain the change of eye color have attributed it to trauma to the head or to the 100-degree temperature that night, both of which are ridiculous.

The autopsy also showed that the dead man had a rheumatic heart condition and arteriosclerosis. There is no record of Dillinger having either condition. He had been an outstanding baseball player as a semi-pro and was noted for his speed and agility in prison games. He had also joined the navy when that service was small and highly selective. And his athleticism as a bank robber had earned him the attention of the press. None of these things would have been possible for the subject of the autopsy.

The scars on the body did not correspond with those Dillinger was known to have, including one from a bullet wound in the shoulder. The recent wounds on the body refuted the FBI report of how Dillinger was shot while running away. The angles of entry and exit showed that the dead man had been shot while lying prone on the street.

Nash found eyewitnesses to the shooting who said that a "big man" had grabbed "Dillinger" and threw him on the ground after which he had been shot. Charlie Winstead, the reputed gunman, was short and wiry. The description of the big man did fit the appearance of Martin Zarkovich, the cop from East Chicago, Indiana.

The body had been identified as Dillinger's by an older sister who had practically raised him after his mother died. As the letter-writer said, she had protected Dillinger. The FBI said that Dillinger had been living in Chicago using the alias Jimmy Lawrence. But there was a real Jimmy Lawrence, a small-time crook who had moved to Chicago from Wisconsin. He was never seen in Chicago or anywhere else after the day of the murder.

## DILLINGER'S TOMB

The body might have been exhumed to double-check these points—if someone was willing to spend a vast amount of money.

Howard T. Wood, executive vice president of the Crown Hill Cemetery in Indianapolis, where "Dillinger" is buried, said the outlaw's father, John W. Dillinger, came back the day after the burial and requested changes in the grave.

He had them dig down again and cover the coffin with a mass of concrete mixed with scrap iron. Then four huge slabs of concrete reinforced with chicken wire were placed at staggered intervals over the concrete-covered casket. According to Wood, anyone wishing to dig up the body would need one of the biggest cranes in the world to get the coffin up. And then the only way to open it would be to blast.

"There wouldn't be enough left [of the remains] to put in a cookie jar," he said.

## IS THE FAMOUS BANK ROBBER BURIED IN INDIANAPOLIS? THE FBI AND OTHERS SAY YES. BUT MANY NO LONGER BELIEVE IT.

The grave-sealing project cost thousands of dollars, money the retired John Wilson Dillinger just didn't have. John Herbert Dillinger, however, had stolen somewhere between $500,000 and $1 million—a sum that could go a long way in the Depression.

Is the famous bank robber buried in Indianapolis? The FBI and others say yes. But many no longer believe it.

# CHAPTER 15

# THE UNCONQUERABLE AFGHANISTAN?

**A**FTER CENTURIES OF BLOODY CONTENTION FOR WHAT BOTH sides considered world supremacy, the Macedonians defeated the Persians in the Battle of Gaugamela and delivered a symbolic final blow to the Persian Empire with the destruction of the great palace of Persepolis in 331 B.C.

The Macedonian commander, Alexander the Great, had finished what his forebears had begun, and now marched his army east, searching for his Persian rival, Darius III, who had fled the battle with what was left of his military. He caught up with Darius, in 331 B.C., but it was too late to exact revenge on the man whose predecessors had destroyed so much of the Greek homeland: Darius was dead, killed by his own people, his corpse riddled with stab wounds and bound in gold chains.

This was no way for Alexander, who considered himself a direct descendant of the god Zeus, to inherit an empire. He needed to conquer.

So he went after Darius' murderer, a Persian named Bessus, who had retreated to the province of Bactria in what is now northern Afghanistan. In the sixth century, the Persian leader Cyrus the Great had conquered the territory that composes modern Afghanistan, and the Persians had ruled it ever since. That would soon change.

When Alexander learned that Bessus had crowned himself king of Persia, he knew what he had to do to satisfy his hunger for glory. The Macedonian marched his army eastward. Bessus bided his time in Bactria, well aware of the extraordinarily difficult terrain and climate that Alexander's army would have to

GENGHIS KHAN AND HIS TROOPS ENGAGE THE ENEMY IN A STEEP MOUNTAIN PASS. JUST ONE OF MANY CONQUERORS OF AFGHANISTAN, THE MONGOL LEADER RAMPAGED THROUGH THE LAND DURING THE TWELTH CENTURY, DESTROYING BUILD-INGS AND HOMES, MURDERING ENTIRE POPULATIONS, AND THEN LEAVING—A WISE MOVE, GIVEN THE LONG STREAM OF POWERS INEVITABLY OUSTED FROM AFGHANISTAN AFTER CONQUERING THE NATION WITH RELATIVE EASE.

Genghis Khan (c.1162-1227) Fighting a Battle in a Mountain Pass (ink on vellum). Chinese School

**MYTH**
AFGHANISTAN HAS
ALWAYS BEEN A COUNTRY
IMPOSSIBLE TO CONQUER.

**REALITY**
AFGHANISTAN HAS BEEN
CONQUERED MANY TIMES
THROUGHOUT HISTORY,
BUT FOREIGN INVADERS
HAVE NOT BEEN ABLE
TO UNIFY OR CONTROL
THE COUNTRY FOR LONG.

contend with before they could reach him. Like so many leaders after him, Bessus likely hoped that his rival would be forced to give up long before reaching Bactria.

## GHOSTS IN THE MOUNTAINS

When the Soviet Union withdrew from Afghanistan in 1989, much was made of the Afghan warriors—the mujahideen (soldiers of God)—who had resisted the puppet government put in place by the Soviets after their invasion a decade earlier. Afghan fighters were raised to a level of world-class warriors.

Due mainly to the fierce resistance of insurgents, the Communists had, in fact, been unable to create a long-term puppet regime in Afghanistan, as they had in other nations around the world. Soviet veterans returned home from the battlefield with blood-chilling stories about the fighting prowess of the mujahideen in the Hindu Kush mountain range, the Pansjir Valley, and the villages bordering Pakistan.

Soviet units ascending seemingly barren hills, for example, would suddenly see mujahideen all around them, popping out of the shadows between rocks and boulders, unloading their Russian-made AK-47s at them. By the time the Soviets could respond with a coordinated counterattack or artillery strike, the Afghans would have disappeared back into the shadows. Many Russian soldiers referred to their enemy as *dukhi* (ghosts).

Afghans decimated Russian transport trucks trekking through valleys or over bridges with crude yet effective remote-controlled bombs crafted from, among other things, unexploded Soviet ordnance. The Afghans used makeshift weaponry, especially in the beginning of the war, yet they were creative, resilient, and determined. That they were able to expel one of the two most advanced military powers on the planet contributed to the myth that Afghanistan was and always has been an unconquerable nation.

## CONQUERED, THEN LEFT BEHIND

Conquering Afghanistan, however, has never proved particularly difficult. Instead, the challenge for invaders has been the subsequent control of the country, due largely to the many diverse groups of people that make up the nation.

At least twenty ethnic groups inhabit the mountains and deserts, speaking as many as thirty different languages. Pashtuns, Tajiks, Hazaras, Turkmen, and others can trace their roots back hundreds, even thousands, of years. These groups, simply put, live by their own rules. As a result, Afghanistan is not and never has been a fully unified nation.

Indeed, the Hindu Kush ("Hindu Killer") and surrounding territory are Afghanistan in name only. Its people are called Afghan only for convenience sake. The nation basically consists of a ring of cities around the Hindu Kush—the mountain range at the southern end of the Himalayas—which dominate much of Afghanistan.

The closest the country ever came to unification was around the turn of the century, under the rule of Abdur Rahman, but it did not last long. The nation's borders were determined during Rahman's reign, but they were based solely on the interests of the British, Russians, and Indians. Abdur Rahman agreed to the borders only because he had no leverage against these great powers, yet the borders remain meaningless to many Afghans.

The eastern border with Pakistan—the Durand Line, named after the Englishman who created it in 1893—is particularly problematic, because it runs right through the territory traditionally held by the Pashtuns, many of whom, to this day, don't recognize it. This situation has been a great help to Osama bin Laden, who is believed to have been hiding out in this region since 9/11. It's a lawless land, with each village operating as its own entity. Intelligence gathering in such an area depends largely on information from the local population. The problem for the Americans hunting members of al Qaeda's leadership is that within this isolated world, the leader of each small village wields an inordinate amount of power. A single person can often derail investigations into the enemy's whereabouts.

Another problem Afghanistan's conquerors face is the country's terrrain, which consists of valleys that are impassable most of the year due to heavy snowfall, vast deserts separating fertile regions, and two-thirds of the land 5,000 feet above sea level. The Afghan people live in relative isolation from one another, resulting in vastly different ways of life.

For example, the urban lifestyle of inhabitants of the main cities, such as Kabul, which has a population of about three million, differs vastly from that of the Kuchis, a Pashtun tribe of nomadic herders on a perpetual search for new grazing land—something they have been doing for 3,000 years.

## A PATTERN OF VIOLENCE

Although ancient conquerors did not attempt to unify the nation (their modus operandi tended to be a bit more savage) the modern powers since the nineteenth century, for political and economic purposes, have consistently tried—and failed—to bring the different peoples together.

One reason is that, logistically speaking, Afghanistan is a nightmare. Foreign powers have never been able to maintain a ruling presence in enough of its isolated areas at once and inevitably withdraw with their goals unmet.

The problem invaders face in Afghanistan is not a military one. Everyone from Alexander the Great to the Soviet Union was able to achieve their tactical goals during the initial invasion. And after conquering the nation, they have been able to quell isolated uprisings with relative ease. The problem with Afghanistan is political in nature. Fighting guerilla-style warfare, Afghans have historically been successful in grinding down the morale of both the soldiers and the people back home (and, hence, the wills of the politicians), forcing the enemy to withdraw before strategic aims, whatever they may be, are achieved. This, of course, does not bode well for the United States, whose leaders seem to invariably confuse tactical triumphs with strategic victory, both in Afghanistan and Iraq.

And so goes the story of Afghanistan—a never-ending pattern of being overrun by foreign powers, experiencing a long-term guerilla insurgency, seeing the withdrawal of the invader, and awaiting the arrival of a new one.

To be sure, Afghanistan's history is one of supreme violence, and fighting great powers is a way of life for a large portion of its people. The country has experienced few periods of peace during the past 2,500 years. When kings, emperors, khans, or superpowers weren't invading the country, smaller, internal factions were killing one another in conflicts the rest of the world knew nothing about.

Afghanistan also has the misfortune of being situated among the empires of India, Central Asia, and the Middle East, each of which, at some point in time, had found the land either an important route between civilizations, a strategically critical area for security purposes, or simply a convenient neighbor to ransack. Often referred to as a "crossroads of empires," Afghanistan has hosted some of history's most ruthless conquerors, such as Alexander the Great, who took over all of its major cities in the fourth century B.C., and Genghis Khan, who decimated much of the country during the Middle Ages.

## SO GOES THE STORY OF AFGHANISTAN—A NEVER-ENDING PATTERN OF BEING OVERRUN BY FOREIGN POWERS, EXPERIENCING A LONG-TERM GUERILLA INSURGENCY, SEEING THE WITHDRAWAL OF THE INVADER, AND AWAITING THE ARRIVAL OF A NEW ONE.

The eventual collapse of these empires provided only a relatively brief interlude in Afghanistan's violent history. Globalization, which was begun in earnest by the British in the nineteenth century, didn't change Afghanistan's plight. The country was merely put in the crosshairs of far-flung nations, including Great Britain, the Soviet Union, and the United States, for various different reasons.

## ALEXANDER THE GREAT AT THE END OF THE WORLD

By the time of Alexander, Greek mapmakers had charted land beyond the Persian Empire, but the western empires had no firsthand experience with that part of the world. It was believed, however, that the territory beyond the Persians marked the farthest limit of world—and that those who ventured beyond present-day India would disintegrate.

And so, in his search for Bessus, the Macedonian commander marched his army of 40,000 men farther east than any western leader before him, into no-man's-land.

One can imagine that when Alexander the Great looked east across the flat desert of western Afghanistan and saw the very end of the Hindu Kush mountain range emerging suddenly and starkly from the ground, he truly believed he was on his way to the world's end.

As he began marching his army south, toward the city of Herat, Bessus was counting on his fellow satraps (governors) and conspirators—one ruling the area around the city of Herat, the other governing the region south of the Hindu Kush, around Kandahar—to delay Alexander's army. He probably did not expect them to defeat Alexander, but if they could delay him long enough to make his journey arduous, perhaps the country itself—its harsh terrain and unpredictable weather—would destroy the advancing army or at least force it to turn back west.

Bessus understood his allies about as poorly as he understood his enemy. Upon learning of Alexander's approach, the satrap (governor) of Areia, Satibarzanes, promptly prepared himself for surrender. Alexander rewarded such fealty by letting the satrap keep his position, with the understanding that he now worked for the Macedonians. Knowledge of his limits in such cases was one of Alexander's greatest assets. Here in Herat, he knew he couldn't run the city with his own leaders and defend it with a standing army, so he characteristically extended his power by proxy, renamed the city after himself (in this case, Herat became Alexander-in-Areia), and marched on toward his next conquest.

The Macedonian force took the well-worn route that past and future conquerors of Afghanistan would take. It naturally marched south, hugging the mountains, toward Kandahar, seat of power of the then-fertile Arachosia province. When the Macedonians reached the city, in 329 B.C., they discovered that the Persian satrap Barsaentes had fled to India, in essence leaving the city as a gift to the conqueror from the west. Alexander promptly renamed the city and settled down for the winter before taking the expedition north into the narrow passes of the Hindu Kush, to Bactria, where he would continue his hunt for Bessus.

It was on the march north that the Macedonians got their first real taste of Afghanistan's punishing and extreme weather. Setting out in the beginning of April, Alexander believed he had timed his march perfectly. In any given year, this might have been true, but in 329 B.C. winter made one final strike before giving way to spring, devastating the army as it marched between Kandahar and Kabul. Coming from the mellow climes of the Aegean, they had never experienced cold and ice in such aggressive and unrelenting ferocity. Food stores ran out and none could be found in the desolate and suddenly deadly mountains. Soldiers lucky enough to avoid freezing to death suffered from frostbite, some losing fingers and toes to it. Morale sunk to new lows.

Alexander entered another city, south of present-day Kabul, and renamed it Alexandria-in-the-Caucuses (the Macedonians mistakenly believed this mountain range to be an extension of the Caucuses), and continued their hard trudge north, leaving the deadweight—soldiers suffering from frostbite, injuries, disease, and severe exhaustion—to recover in the conqueror's newest city.

The Macedonians resupplied their stores of food by plundering any village or city they happened to march through on the way to Bactria. They took advantage of the lush areas that seemed to pop up from the moon-like landscape here and there, vegetation growing due to the presence of small streams and rivers.

When the Macedonians reached Balkh, the main city of Bactria, Bessus fled. Although Alexander was thirsting for Bessus' blood, he was probably happy to enter the city without a fight, given his army's torturous journey. And they were pleased with another surprise: Balkh was as fertile and green as anyplace they had thus far seen in Afghanistan. It was a pleasant surprise after completing four-fifths of the journey around Afghanistan's Hindu Kush.

But Alexander would not wait long and soon led his army north to find Bessus, who had crossed the Oxus River (the present-day Amu Darya, the river dividing Afghanistan and Uzbekistan). The soldiers experienced yet another radical change in climate and terrain, because the land between Balkh and the Oxus was a scorching desert. Running out of water during the days-long march, many soldiers succumbed to the heat. Others, suffering from severe dehydration, compounded the problem by desperately drinking the only liquid on hand—wine—and experiencing a sort of death by hangover.

Even though terrain and climate had beaten Alexander's army down, it was nevertheless a force to be contended with, and Spitamenes, a Persian leader north of the Oxus, wanted to avoid a fight. In a clear display of the conditional nature of alliances in Afghanistan and its surroundings, Spitamenes handed his fellow Persian over to Alexander with the hope that the powerful Macedonian would bypass his realm. Alexander had Bessus' ears and nose removed before executing him. Unfortunately for Spitamanes, the Macedonians continued north, propelled by Alexander's desire to go down in the history books as having ruled more land than the Persians.

Behind him, though, the Afghan cities in which he had left garrison forces were in rebellion against Macedonian rule. Upon learning this, Alexander sent parts of his army back to suppress the unruly tribes. In one military engagement, the Macedonians fell victim to an enemy maneuver that is still favored in that part of the world. Overwhelmed by Alexander's infantry, the cavalry beat a hasty retreat—and led the fast-pursuing Macedonians into an ambush, killing almost every single one.

Furious, Alexander turned his entire army south to take back control of Balkh, which had descended into chaos. Tensions ran high within the Macedonian command, and Alexander began to lose control over his top commanders. One night, during a drunken bacchanalia—a common occurrence in the Macedonian high command—Alexander got into an argument with his cavalry commander, Cleitus, a man who had saved Alexander's life during a battle with the Persians. As tempers flared, weapons were drawn, and Alexander stabbed Cleitus in the chest, killing him. After sobering up, he reportedly fell into a state of extreme guilt and depression.

In the summer of 327 B.C., Alexander led his army into India (which included present-day Pakistan), where it fought a great battle at the Jhelum River. Some of the enemy rode into the fight on elephants, which must have been an exceedingly strange and fearsome sight to the Macedonians, who probably had never seen such strange-looking beasts.

Reconnaissance parties that had ventured east reported that the world, in fact, did not end beyond India, and that they had only scraped a small part of its surface. A leader can convince thousands of men to march and fight for undefined goals for only so long, and Alexander knew it. If he continued marching his forces toward world's end, they would eventually mutiny. It was a certainty. After five long years, Alexander did what he had never done before; he gave up and marched his Macedonians west.

## INVASION OF THE MONGOLS

By the early thirteenth century, having been the victim of numerous smaller empires, much of Afghanistan was firmly in the hands of Shah Allah al-Din Muhammad II of the Khwarezm empire, which stretched west to cover all of Iran.

To the northeast was the vast Mongol empire, whose army was composed of aggressive horsemen commanded by a man named Timujin, later known as Genghis Khan. Muhammad II had received delegates from the Great Khan, and had sent others in return, and the two empires agreed to remain peaceful trading partners. It was tense peace, however. In Afghanistan, the Mongols' reputation preceded them. Led by Genghis Khan, they had swept through northeast Asia, seemingly unconcerned with the traditional practice of subduing and ruling people. They simply wanted to conquer, and to the Mongols, conquering meant death and destruction.

In 1218, a group of Mongolian merchants stopped in a Khwarezm border province run by a Khwarezm named Inalchuq, a brash governor of the city of Otrar (in present-day Kazakhstan). He decided to help himself to all the goods in the caravan free of charge and hold the Mongol traders prisoner. He sent Muhammad a message that he had in custody a group of Mongol spies (he was probably right) and requested permission to execute them.

Why Muhammad gave the go-ahead is not exactly known. A blizzard had recently decimated his army during a failed march to seize Baghdad, leaving it in no shape to take on the Mongols. Historians theorize that he probably knew the Mongols were going to invade anyway and perhaps hoped that such a bold statement might make them think twice. Inalchuq quickly carried out the order, sending Genghis Khan the message to keep his spies at home.

Genghis Khan did not respond with thousands of horsemen looking for blood, as one might expect. Instead he sent a small delegation directly to Muhammad to politely request the head of Inalchuq. Even the Great Khan, this move said, can be a reasonable man. Perhaps spooked by such a surprisingly calm but direct response, Muhammad rashly killed one of the diplomats and burned the beards off the others. He sent them back to tell their leader what to do with his request—a message that would have lasting consequences for Afghanistan that can be seen even today.

The Mongol leader delivered his response personally, expressing his disappointment by leading a force of 100,000 to 200,000 warriors armed to the teeth and hell-bent for destruction through the gates of the Khwarzmed Empire. It wasn't even a contest. Genghis Khan had at his disposal the raw power of the planet's greatest army, the maneuverability of a world-class cavalry, an officer staff to rival any of history's greatest, an incredible talent for logistics and organization, and the ruthlessness of history's greatest tyrants.

The Mongols tore through the empire, razing every city in their path and killing the inhabitants by the thousands. When they reached Otrar, Genghis

Khan executed Inalchuk by having molten silver poured into his ears and eyes. Muhammad, terrified, fled to Balkh and, later, to an island in the Caspian Sea where he died of disease.

On their rampage though Persia and northern Afghanistan, the Mongols left the calling card that had made them famous in their conquests to the north—pyramids of the heads of their victims. In the city of Merv, north of Herat, it has been reported, Genghis Khan ordered each soldier to behead at least 300. This was after they had surrendered.

## ON THEIR RAMPAGE THOUGH PERSIA AND NORTHERN AFGHANISTAN, THE MONGOLS LEFT THE CALLING CARD THAT HAD MADE THEM FAMOUS IN THEIR CONQUESTS TO THE NORTH—PYRAMIDS OF THE HEADS OF THEIR VICTIMS.

With columns of his army ravaging the land and cities west of Afghanistan—the heart of the former Persian empire—Genghis Khan moved deeper into Afghanistan. There, he briefly met his match in the battle at Parwan, a small village near Gazni, suffering the only decisive defeat of the entire campaign at the hands of Afghan mountain warriors. Still, all it really accomplished for the Khwarazems was to further enrage Genghis, who began moving his army of 70,000 south.

Meanwhile, the Afghans, who had been defending their local territory, and weren't fond of fighting other peoples' wars, simply returned home when they saw the Mongols departing. The battle had achieved nothing more than creating a temporary delay of the monstrous army.

Within three years of Genghis Khan's invasion, the better part of Afghanistan was flattened, and the Mongol army had vanished, leaving the wrecked land for future generations to attend to. Genghis Khan had even destroyed the vast irrigation systems of the Bamyan Valley, in central Afghanistan, reducing a fertile farming and grazing area into the desert that exists to this day.

It has always been assumed that he destroyed the irrigation system simply because he could—an assumption not at odds with his history. But recent historians have theorized that this might have been a tactical move. The Afghans, who have always displayed a penchant for guerilla-style warfare, might have used the network of irrigation tunnels as a means for sneak attacks and ambushes.

The Mongols left a wide swath of destruction in Afghanistan, but that is not their only legacy. Among the diverse ethnicities living in the mountains today are the Hazaras, a staunchly independent group residing in the Hindu Kush that has refused over the centuries to fall under the rule of any government. Hazaras' physical features contain clear signs of Mongolian descent, and DNA tests have proved this to be so. Eight hundred years after the departure of Genghis Khan, his people still fight on.

Another isolated group of people—the Nuristanis, who live in the northeastern section of the Hindu Kush—are perhaps descendants of a past conqueror. Many of these people have red hair and light skin and look more like European tourists than Afghan mountain people. Until only 100 years ago, the Nuristanis worshipped a group of nature gods similar to the idols of the ancient Greeks. While many Nuristanis passionately argue their direct line to Alexander the Great, the subject remains debatable among scholars.

## DRAGGED INTO THE MODERN AGE

The modern era would be no kinder to Afghanistan. As merchant ships began replacing land caravans, world trade became truly global for the first time in history, and, as a result, Afghanistan's role would change from a subcontinental invasion route to transcontinental buffer state. England's East India Company had by then expanded greatly, and its interests had become inseparably connected to Great Britain's national security—largely due to India's role as saltpeter supplier—and, therefore, Britain's military presence in the region was heavy.

England's direct competitor in Asia was the burgeoning Russian empire. Peter the Great had pulled his nation out of its relative isolation during the previous century and began paving a path of openness and exchange with its Asian neighbors and Western powers. The nation remained on that path, gaining territory further south and developing relations with the Persians, who displayed a keen interest in Herat, the control over which they had fought on and off with native Afghans for years.

Concerned that the emerging superpower would use Afghanistan as a base to invade India, the British moved in to protect their so-called "jewel of the crown"—and, thus, Afghanistan was once again dragged into war.

In 1838, British and Indian troops invaded Afghanistan under the pretense that the Crown was attempting to install the country's "rightful ruler," Shuja Shah Durrani, a Pashtun friend of England, who had earlier proclaimed himself king of Afghanistan but was soon after ousted and sent packing to India. What England clearly wanted was a puppet regime with which to fend off Russian incursions.

As most other great powers had experienced in Afghanistan, the English found the conquering of Afghanistan to go relatively smoothly, but the managing of its people proved to be an impossible task. They had marched into Kandahar untouched and took Ghazni with few casualties. Shuja was easily placed in power. But the Afghans who had stepped aside when the British entered the country now began to revolt against Shuja's rule and the English military presence, killing soldiers and officers in the streets. The British, making a rare choice in their long history of imperialism, decided to evacuate Afghanistan, leaving Shuja to fend for himself. (He was assassinated within three months.)

## AS MOST OTHER GREAT POWERS HAD EXPERIENCED IN AFGHANISTAN, THE ENGLISH FOUND THE CONQUERING OF AFGHANISTAN TO GO RELATIVELY SMOOTHLY, BUT THE MANAGING OF ITS PEOPLE PROVED TO BE AN IMPOSSIBLE TASK.

As the English army trekked through the snow-covered mountains from Kabul on New Year's Day 1842, it was attacked by a large unit of Pashtun warriors. Fighting in knee-deep snow, the Pashtuns annihilated almost the entire force of 16,000 British and Indian troops. The approximately fifty soldiers who escaped to a garrison in Jalalabad languished without food, water, or ammunition. Like Alexander the Great's troops 2,000 years before, most succumbed to the harsh Afghanistan winter. Only a handful survived. Succeeding decades would see the Russians advancing ever farther toward Afghanistan, and in 1878, the British invaded once again, with the same result—an inglorious retreat from Kabul.

Two years later, in 1880, Abdur Rahman, grandson of Dost Mohammad Khan, Afghanistan's leader during the first Anglo-Afghan War, took the throne. Possessing equal parts political savvy and ruthless opportunism, he was a man with whom the British could work. He agreed that England would handle his foreign affairs, while he would handle matters within Afghanistan.

The British, having learned the hard way about the futility of enacting political solutions by force in Afghanistan, turned to diplomacy. They entered into talks with the Russians to establish Afghanistan's western and northern boundaries, both sides tacitly agreeing to keep one another at bay.

The British also facilitated an agreement (albeit, a tense one) between Indian leaders and Abdur Rahman to create the "Durand Line"—the eastern border of Afghanistan, which bisected the Pashtun tribes, placing them in different countries. (Today, this is the line between Afghanistan and Pakistan; the border area is often referred to as "Pashtunistan.")

For his part, Abdur Rahman went to work modernizing his country and dragging the Afghan people—*all* Afghan people—into the nineteenth century. Using an iron fist to suppress rebellions and weaken ethnic groups vying for power, he used tactics not unlike those of Saddam Hussein in Iraq. Abdur Rahman began deporting difficult Pashtuns—especially the Ghilzais (the people who slaughtered the British and Indian troops during their first retreat from Kabul)—and forcing Hindus to convert to Islam. He established a central government, the *loya jirga,* and developed a wide intelligence network to act as his eyes and ears around the country.

It ultimately took a combination of brute force, open cooperation with a foreign power, and advanced communications to do it, but it can be safely said that Abdur Rahman was the first person in history to create some semblance of centralized power in Afghanistan.

## THE RED TIDE HITS AFGHANISTAN

Russia was able to avoid a conflict with Britain in the nineteenth century. No doubt its leaders were pleased to see the world's most feared military chased out of Afghanistan twice in a matter of thirty years. A century and a half later, though, they would find themselves in even worse straits than the English had been in.

In 1978, Afghan president Nur Muhammad Taraki, a Marxist and friend of the Soviet Union, began a bloody campaign to turn his Islamist nation Marxist. The country revolted; cities everywhere saw thousands of furious people demonstrating against Taraki's Marxist reforms, which included the seizure of property

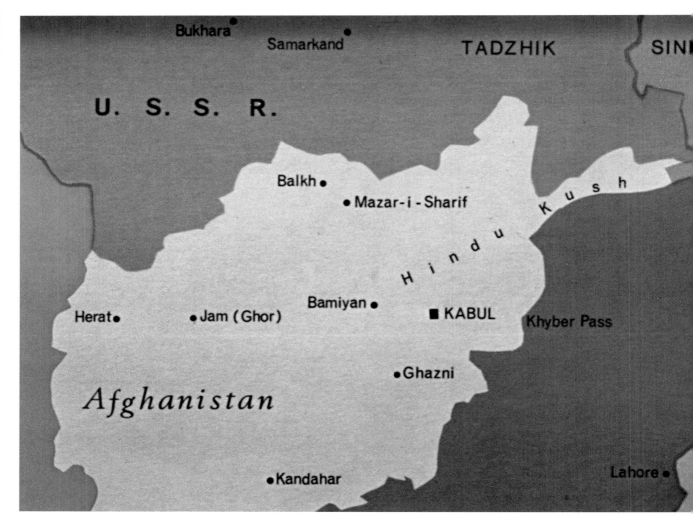

from landowners and redistribution of it to the peasantry, setting an age limit on all marriages, and creating an educational system for both boys and girls.

Taraki took his cue on how to enforce these reforms from his Bolshevik friends: Ram them down the throats of the populace and kill those who don't swallow—in this case, religious leaders, intellectuals, and political rivals. This method, of course, served only to stoke the blaze.

In September of 1979, Taraki was overthrown by a rival in his own political party, Hafizullah Amin. The Soviets, believing that Amin was in secret talks with American intelligence, supplied greater amounts of weapons and military support to Amin to stabilize the Communist party in Afghanistan against the Islamic rebels—but secretly planned to assassinate him.

Amin and the Russian military were successful in wiping out small bands of insurgents across the countryside and maintaining a hold on the central government, but by now the Russians, feeling their new ally had destabilized the nation, had had enough of him. On December 27, 1979, a unit of elite Soviet forces dressed in Afghan military uniforms raided Amin's compound and killed him, along with his 200 bodyguards. Within minutes, the Russians were in control of the Afghan government and military. (Officially, they announced that they had acted in accordance with the "Treaty of Friendship" they had signed with Taraki; Amin, they claimed, was an enemy of Afghanistan, and it was their responsibility to protect the nation by assassinating him.)

The Russians put a new leader in place, Afghanistan's ambassador to Czechoslovakia, Babrak Karmal, and began a years-long military campaign to quell the rebellions and bring Afghanistan into the family of Communist bloc nations. Officially, U.S. President Jimmy Carter responded with forceful words, a trade embargo on grain to the Soviet Union (Argentina immediately began exporting grain to the Russians, at a lower price), and a boycott of the summer Olympics. Unofficially, he took the more effective action of sending arms, ammo, and equipment to the mujahideen, along with military trainers.

The Russians quickly seized Afghanistan's major cities, but within a short time found themselves knee-deep in a quagmire, fighting against tribal warriors

## THE COMMUNISTS' BLOODY RISE

With its characteristic unsubtle flair for pronouncements, the Communist party chose New Year's Day 1965 as its day of "birth" in Afghanistan, the festivities being held at the home of Noor Taraki.

The party was officially named the People's Democratic Party of Afghanistan (PDPA) and was, of course, closely allied with the Soviet Union. Before long, the party succumbed to the tendencies typical of Communist organizations: Members began bickering about just how left-wing the party should be and

eventually splintered into two groups—the more mainstream, Persian-speaking Parcham (Banner) group, led by Babrak Karmal, and the radical, Pashtun-speaking Khalq (People) group, headed by Taraki.

In 1973, General Mohammed Daoud, with the help of the PDPA, seized the government from the country's leader, King Mohammed Zahir Shah. Soon, though, he dumped PDPA members from the government and made it clear to Soviet leader Leonid Brezhnev that Afghanistan was no pawn of Russia. In April

1978, he and his family were killed during a violent rebellion launched by the Communists. The PDPA took the country over, naming Taraki president and Karmal deputy minister; Taraki immediately removed any Parcham-aligned officials from their posts and, to keep the government to himself, sent Karmal packing to Czechoslovakia as official ambassador. The Soviets' man was now firmly in charge of the nation.

OFTEN REFERRED TO AS A "CROSSROADS OF EMPIRES," AFGHANISTAN HAS THE BAD LUCK OF BEING SITUATED DIRECTLY IN THE PATH OF NUMEROUS CONQUERORS THROUGH HISTORY. IT IS A NATION IN NAME ONLY. ITS BORDERS ARE ESSENTIALLY MEANINGLESS TO MOST OF AFGHANISTAN'S INHABITANTS, ESPECIALLY THOSE IN RURAL AREAS, WHO PREFER TO LIVE IN ISOLATION FROM ONE ANOTHER. THIS FRAGMENTATION MAKES AFGHANISTAN RELATIVELY EASY TO CONQUER, BUT NEARLY IMPOSSIBLE TO RULE.

Map of Central Asia (colour litho), English School, (20th century)

in the hills, rebel factions inside the cities, and sections of the remaining Afghan army that had risen up against the new occupier. They launched major offensives in the hotly contested Panjshir Valley and the border areas with Pakistan, but even after five years, the situation remained the same. The Russians responded by increasing their deployments to Afghanistan, building up a force of more than 100,000 troops by 1985. It didn't work. The buildup just seemed to attract more mujihadeen from the hills.

By 1989, the Soviets had propped up the Afghan military enough to at least pretend they were leaving a stable country behind. More than 14,000 Russian soldiers had been killed and about 50,000 wounded. Hundreds of thousands more succumbed to illness and disease, and millions of Afghan soldiers and civilians were killed, wounded, or displaced.

## THE TWENTY-FIRST CENTURY AND "TALIBANISTAN"

Jimmy Carter's national security advisor, Zbigniew Brzezinski, once boasted that his department had predicted the main Soviet invasion six months before it happened. That is why, he claimed, the Carter administration had begun supplying the mujahideen with training and weaponry—not so much because it believed in the insurgents' cause, but because it wanted to *provoke* an invasion.

Brzezinski went on to point out that the plan worked perfectly; the Carter administration had dished out to the communists their own Vietnam, which had caused permanent damage to their military. Within a few years of the Russians' withdrawal, the Berlin Wall would be torn down, and the Soviet Union would be no more. Brzezinski might have exaggerated his accomplishments, but in the game of global politics, America's intervention in Afghanistan had been a resounding success. But history has a nasty habit of biting back.

Within a few years of the Russians' withdrawal, the highly ethnocentric warlords of Afghanistan once again began abiding by the Afghan tradition of warring among one another. With no more strategic interest in Afghanistan, the United States, under the direction of President George H. W. Bush, immediately disengaged with the Afghan mujihadeen, leaving reconstruction duties to, among others, Pakistan.

Helped along by Islamist fundamentalists in that country, yet another power emerged in Afghanistan in the early 1990s—the Taliban. Armed with small arms, machine-gun-mounted pickup trucks, and a fiercely fundamentalist Islamist philosophy, these warriors for Mohammed took over the government, established a central authority, and furthered their agenda via coercion and murder. They were subjected to attacks from mountain rebels (in this case, the Northern Alliance) and were then easily overrun when a more powerful nation decided to attack.

The United States and its allies made fast work of the Taliban, who refused to hand over their "guest" Osama bin Laden following the terrorist attacks of September 11, 2001. Within a month, the United States controlled Afghanistan's cities and, later, saw to it that Hamid Karzai, a Western-influenced Pashtun, was elected as its leader. As we write, he remains president, keeping a loose hold on power.

But the Taliban has made a resurgence and now controls much of the south; some military personnel and reporters now refer to that part of the country as "Talibanistan." Control of the country had until recently been in the hands of NATO troops, but President George W. Bush considers the situation dire enough to have recently sent in 3,000 Marines to stem the tide of the Taliban. Time will tell whether the West can break the pattern of history and tame Afghanistan once and for all.

AFGHANISTAN EXISTS IN A PERPETUAL STATE OF WAR. HERE, TALIBAN SOLDIERS FIRE TWELVE-BARREL ROCKETS DURING A BATTLE IN OCTOBER 1996 JUST NORTH OF KABUL. THE TALIBAN SOON TOOK OVER THE CITY AND THE REST OF THE COUNTRY, ONLY TO BE CHASED OUT BY AMERICAN FORCES SOON AFTER 9/11. THE GOVERNMENT PUT IN PLACE, HOWEVER, STRUGGLES TO CONTROL THE NATION—A TESTAMENT TO AFGHANISTAN'S HISTORIC PATTERN OF CATCH-AND-RELEASE.

Soldiers belonging to strict Moslem Taliban photo by SAEED KHAN/ AFP / Getty Images

# ADDITIONAL RESOURCES

# BIBLIOGRAPHY

## CHAPTER 1: DID EMPEROR NERO FIDDLE AS ROME BURNED?

Champlin, Edward. "Nero Reconsidered." *New England Review.* 1998/Vol. 19.

Franzero, Carlo Maria. *The Life and Times of Nero.* Alvin Reedman Limited, 1954.

Tacitus, Cornelius; translated by Michael Grant. *The Annals of Imperial Rome.* New York: Penguin Books, 1956.

Griffin, Miriam T. *Nero: The End of a Dynasty.* New Haven, CT: Yale University Press, 1985.

Hazel, John. *Who's Who in the Roman World.* New York: Routledge, 2001.

Suetonius, *The Twelve Caesars,* New York: Penguin Classics, 2007.

Weigall, Arthur. *Nero: The Singing Emperor of Rome.* New York: Putnam/The Knicker-bocker Press, 1930.


## CHAPTER 2: RAMESSES II: AN ORIGINAL MASTER OF SPIN

Grimal, Nicholas. *A History of Ancient Egypt.* Oxford, UK: Blackwell Publishers, 1994.

Kitchen, K. A. *Pharaoh Triumphant: The Life and Times of Ramesses II.* Warminster, UK: Aris and Phillips, 1982.

Lichtheim, Miriam. *Ancient Egyptian Literature, Volume 2.* Berkeley: University of California Press, 1976.

Menu, Bernadette. *Ramesses the Great: Warrior and Builder.* New York: New Horizons, 1999.

Tyldesley, Joyce. *Ramesses: Egypt's Greatest Pharaoh.* New York: Penguin, 2001.


## CHAPTER 3: THE GOTHS: BARBARIANS IN NAME ONLY?

Artz, Frederick B. *The Mind of the Middle Ages, AD 200-1500.* New York; Alfred A. Knopf, 1954.

Barbero, Alessandro; translated by John Cullen. *The Day of the Barbarians.* New York: Walker & Company, 2007.

Gibbon, Edward. *The Decline and Fall of the Roman Empire: Volume II.* New York: Random House.

Hadas, Moses (editor). *The Complete Works of Tacitus.* New York: The Modern Library, 1942.

Jones, Terry; Ereira, Alan. *Barbarians.* London: BBC Books, 2006.

Williams, Stephen. "Friends, Romans, or Countrymen? Barbarians in the Empire." *History Today,* July 1944.

Wolfram, Herwig; translated by Thomas Dunlap. *The Roman Empire and Its Germanic Peoples.* Berkeley: University of California Press, 1990.


CHAPTER 4: ROBERT THE BRUCE: THE ARACHNID AND THE MONARCH

Gray, D. J. *William Wallace, The King's Enemy.* London: Robert Hale, 1991.

Linklater, Eric. *Robert the Bruce.* New York and London: D. Appleton-Century, 1934.

Prestwich, Michael. *Edward I.* Berkeley: University of California Press, 1988.

Raban, Sandra. *England Under Edward I and Edward II, 1259-1327.* Oxford, UK: Blackwell Publishers, 2000.

Scotland's Kings and Queens. www.nwlink.com/_scotlass.

Scott, Ronald McNair. *Robert the Bruce, King of the Scots.* New York: Carroll and Graf Publishers, 1982.

Scott, Sir Walter. *From Bannockburn to Flodden: Wallace, Bruce and the Heroes of Medieval Scotland.* Volume 1 of Tales of a Scottish Grandfather. Nashville, Tennessee: Cumberland House, 2001.

Stone of Destiny. www.durham.net/_neilmac/stone.htm.

Traquair, Peter. *Freedom's Sword: Scotland's Wars of Independence.* London: HarperCollins, 1998.

William Wallace. www.uni-essen.de/fub3/schoolprojects/movies/braveheart/content/williamwallace.htm.


CHAPTER 5: THE BLOODY RECORD OF HERNÁN CORTÉS

Diamond, Jared. *Guns, Germs and Steel.* New York: Random House, 1998.

Diaz del Castillo, Bernal. *The Discovery and Conquest of Mexico.* Cambridge, MA: DaCapo Press, 2003.

Esquivel, Laura. *Malinche.* New York: Atria, 2006.

Keating, Bern. *Life and Death of the Aztec Nation.* New York: Putnam, 1964.

Levy, Buddy. *Conquistador: Hernan Cortes, King Montezuma, and the Last Stand of the Aztecs.* New York: Bantam, 2008.

Marks, Richard Lee. *Cortes: The Great Adventurer and the Fate of Aztec Mexico.* New York: Alfred Knopf, 1993.

McNeill, William H. *Plagues and Peoples.* New York: Anchor Press/Doubleday, 1976.

Prescott, W.H. *The Conquest of Mexico*. London: Phoenix Press, 2002.

Thomas, Hugh. *Conquest: Montezuma, Cortes and the Fall of Old Mexico*. New York: Simon and Schuster, 1993.

West, Rebecca. *Survivors in Mexico*. New Haven: Yale University Press, 2003.


CHAPTER 6: THE GALILEO AFFAIR: A HISTORIC COLLISION OF SCIENCE, RELIGION, AND EGO

Brodrick, James S. J. *Galileo: The Man, His Work, His Misfortunes*. New York: Harper & Row, 1964.

De Santillana, Giorgio. *The Crime of Galileo*. Time Incorporated, 1955.

Feldhay, Rivka. *Galileo and the Church*. New York: Cambridge University Press, 1995.

Galilei, Galileo; translated by Stillman Drake. *Discoveries and Opinions of Galileo*. New York: Doubleday, 1957.

Rice University, "The Galileo Project." http://galileo.rice.edu/index.html

Schlagel, Richard H. *From Myth to Modern Mind: A Study of the Origins and Growth of Scientific Thought, Volume II*. Peter Lang, 1996.


CHAPTER 7: PAUL REVERE: THE NOT-SO-LONE HORSEMAN

Bakeless, John. *Turncoats, Traitors and Heroes*. Philadelphia: Lippincott, 1959.

Bilias, George Athan. *George Washington's Opponents*. New York: Morrow, 1969.

Birnbaum, *Red Dawn at Lexington*. Boston: Houghton Mifflin, 1986.

Carrington, Henry B. *Battles of the American Revolution*. New York: Promontory Press.

Chidsey, Donald Barr. *The Siege of Boston*. New York: Crown, 1966.

Cumming, William P., and Hugh Rankin. *The Fate of a Nation*. London: Phaidon Press, 1975.

Dupuy, R. Ernest, and N. Trevor. *Compact History of the Revolutionary War*. New York: Hawthorn, 1963.

Fischer, David Hackett. *Paul Revere's Ride*. New York: Oxford University Press, 1994.

Fleming, Thomas. *Now We are Enemies*. New York: St. Martin's, 1960.

Johnson, Curt. *Battles of the American Revolution*. New York: Rand McNally, 1975.

Middlekauff, Robert. *The Glorious Cause*. New York: Oxford University Press, 1982

Pearson, Michael. *Those Damned Rebels*. New York: Putnam's, 1972.

Peterson, Harold L. *Arms and Armor in Colonial America*. New York: Bramhall House, 1956.

Peterson, Harold L. *The Book of the Continental Soldier*. Harrisburg, PA: Stackpole, 1968.

Weir, William. *Fatal Victories*. New York: Avon, 1995.

CHAPTER 8: THE BASTILLE: REPRESSIVE PRISON OR LUXURY HOTEL?

Funck-Bretano, Frantz. *Legends of the Bastille.* London: Downey and Co, 1899.

Godechot, Jacques. *The Taking of the Bastille, July 14th 1789.* London: Faber and Faber, 1970.

Linguet, Simon-Nicholas-Henri. *Memoirs of the Bastille.* Chez Jim Books, 2005.

Lüsebrink, Hans-Jürgen, Rolf Reichardt, and Norbert Schürer. *The Bastille: A History of a Symbol of Despotism and Freedom.* Durham, NC: Duke University Press, 1997.

Pernoud, George, and Sabine Flaissier. *The French Revolution.* London: Secker & Warburg, 1961.


CHAPTER 9: JESSE JAMES: AMERICAN ROBIN HOOD OR SERIAL MURDERER?

Dellinger, Harold (editor). *Jesse James: The Best Writings on the Notorious Outlaw and his Gang.* Guilford, CT: The Globe Pequot Press, 2007.

Steckmesser, Kent L. "Robin Hood and the American Outlaw: A Note on History and Folklore." *The Journal of American Folklore.* April/June 1966.

Stiles, T. J. *Jesse James: Last Rebel of the Civil War.* New York: Alfred A. Knopf, 2002.

Yeatman, Ted P. *Frank and Jesse James: The Story Behind the Legend.* Nashville: Cumberland House Publishing, 2000.


CHAPTER 10: THE EARP GANG: LAWMEN OR LAWLESS?

Constable, George. *The Gunfighters.* New York: Time-Life Books, 1974.

Cunningham, Eugene. *Triggernometry.* Caldwell, ID: Caxron Printers, Ltd. 1941.

Diagram Group, The. *Weapons.* New York: St Martin's. 1990.

Drago, Harry Sinclair. *Wild, Woolly & Wicked.* New York: Bramhall House, 1960.

Horan, James D. *The Authentic Wild West: The Gunfighters.* New York: Crown Publishing, 1977.

Horan, James D. *The Authentic Wild West: The Lawmen.* New York: Crown Publishing, 1980.

Knappman, Edward E. (editor). *Great American Trials.* Farmington Hills, MI: The Gale Group, 2002.

Marks, Paula Mitchell. *And Die in the West.* New York: Simon & Schuster, 1989.

Metz, Leon Claire. *The Shooters.* New York: Berkley Publishing Group, 1996.

Weir, William R. *Written with Lead.* Hamden, CT: Archon Books, 1992

## CHAPTER 11: THE PHILLIPINE INSURRECTION: AGAINST WHAT GOVERNMENT?

Bain, David Haward. *Sitting in Darkness: Americans in the Philippines.* Boston: Houghton Mifflin, 1984.

Bannerman, Francis. *Bannerman Catalogue of Military Goods, 1927.* (Reproduction) Northfield, IL: DBI Books, 1980.

Crouch, Thomas W. *A Leader of Volunteers: Frederick Funston and the 20th Kansas in the Philippines, 1898-1899.* Lawrence, KS: Coronado Press, 1984.

Davis, Richard Harding. *The Notes of a War Correspondent.* New York: Scribner's, 1911.

Esposito, Col. Vincent J. *The West Point Atlas of American Wars.* New York: Praeger, 1960

Ezell, Edward C. *Handguns of the World.* New York: Barnes & Noble, 1981.

Hatcher, Julian S. *Textbook of Pistols and Revolvers.* Plantersville, SC: Small Arms Technical Publishing Co., 1935.

Linn, Brian McAllister. *The U.S. Army and Counterinsurgency Warfare in the Philippines, 1899-1902.* Chapel Hill, NC: University of North Carolina Press, 1989.

O'Toole, G. J. A. *The Spanish War: An American Epic.* New York: W.W. Norton, 1984.

Silbey, David J. *A War of Frontier and Empire: The Philippine–American War, 1899-1902.* New York: Hill and Wang, 2007.

Smith, W. H. B. *Small Arms of the World.* Harrisburg, PA: Stackpole, 1973.

Stone, George Cameron. *A Glossary of the Construction, Decoration and Use of Arms and Armor in All Countries and All Times.* New York, Jack Brussel, 1961.

Trask, David F. *The War with Spain in 1898.* New York: Macmillan, 1981.

Weir, William. *Soldiers in the Shadows.* London: Bounty Books, 2006.

Weir, William. *The Encyclopedia of African American Military History.* Amherst, NY: Prometheus, 2004.

## CHAPTER 12: THE PROTOCOLS OF THE ELDERS OF ZION: A DEADLY KIND OF LIE

Ben-Itto, Hadassa. *The Lie that Wouldn't Die: The Protocols of the Elders of Zion.* London: Vallantine Mitchell, 2005.

De Michelis, Cesare G. *The Non-Existent Manuscript: A Study of the Protocols of the Sages of Zion.* Vidal Sassoon Center for the Study of Anti-Semitism, 2004.

Jacobs, Steve L, and Mark Weitzman. *Dismantling the Big Lie: The Protocols of the Elders of Zion,* KTAV Publishing, 2003.

## CHAPTER 13: HAROLD LASSETER: FINDER OF A REEF OF GOLD?

Bevege, Alison. "I've Found Lasseter's Reef." *The Northern Territory News.* May 11, 2007.

Blakeley, Fred. *Dream Millions: New Light on Lasseter's Lost Reef.* Sydney: Angus & Robertson, 1972.

Hodgetts, Lillian Agnes. "Ruby's Story: The Story of Lewis H. Lasseter." *Simply Australia.* Issue 6, Vol. 3. December 2003.

Lasseteria: The Official Lasseter Encyclopedia. www.lasseteria.com

Seal, Graham. "Whitefella Dreaming: Lasseter's Reef and the Lure of Lost Treasures." *Simply Australia.* Issue 2. December 2001.

Stapleton, Austin. *Lasseter Did Not Lie!* Adelaide: Investigator Press, 1981.


## CHAPTER 14: JOHN DILLINGER: DEAD OR ALIVE?

Gentry, Curt. *J. Edgar Hoover: The Man and the Secrets.* New York: Norton, 1991.

Nash, Jay Robert. *Bloodletters and Badmen.* Philadelphia: M. Evans & Co., 1973.

Nash, Jay Robert. *The Dillinger Dossier.* Highland Park, IL: December Press, 1983.

Powers, Richard Gid. *G-Men: Hoover's FBI in American Popular Culture.* Carbondale and Edwardsville, IL: Southern Illinois University Press, 1983.

Purvis, Melvin. *American Agent.* New York: Doubleday, Duran, 1936.

Sullivan, William C. *The Bureau: My Thirty Years in Hoover's FBI.* New York: Norton, 1979.

Toland, John. *The Dillinger Days.* New York: Random House, 1963.


## CHAPTER 15: THE UNCONQUERABLE AFGHANISTAN?

Ewans, Martin. *Afghanistan: A Short History of Its People and Politics.* New York: Harper Collins, 2002.

Tanner, Stephen. *Afghanistan: A Military History from Alexander the Great to the Fall of the Taliban.* Cambridge: DeCapo Press, 2002.

# ABOUT THE AUTHOR

**W**ILLIAM WEIR is the author of ten military history books, including *Written with Lead* (1992), *Fatal Victories* (1993), *A Well Regulated Militia* (1997), *Soldiers in the Shadows* (2002), *Turning Points in Military History* (2005), *Fifty Weapons that Changed Warfare* (2005), and *Fifty Military Leaders Who Changed the World* (2007). An eleventh book, on guerrilla warfare in the twentieth century, is due to be published by Stackpole.

Weir was a military policeman at Fort Bragg, NC, until he volunteered to serve in the Korean War. He became an Army combat correspondent for the 25th Infantry Division and later public information NCO for the 27th (Wolfhound) Infantry Regiment.

Before serving in the Army, he worked as a reporter for the Kansas City, MO, *Sun Herald*. The *Sun Herald* had died before he returned to civilian life, so he became a reporter-photographer at the Manhattan, KS, *Mercury-Chronicle*. From there he went to the *Topeka State Journal* and the federal beat, including Forbes Air Force Base, as a military editor. The Air Force connection got him a trip to Morocco, embedded for several weeks with the 90th Air Wing.

Weir took advantage of the Korean GI Bill at the last moment and received a master's degree in public relations at Boston University, which led to a job as a public relations specialist at the Southern New England Telephone Co. (now AT&T). He lives in Guilford, Connecticut.

# IMAGE CREDITS

Front cover: The Art Archive / Museo Capitolino Rome / Alfredo Dagli Orti

The pictures in this book are used with permission and through the courtesy of :

AKG Images: p. 57

Alamy: p. 11, 59, 99, 117, 119, 132-133

Associated Press: p. 210, 216, 236, 241

Arizona Historical Society: p. 182, 184

Bridgeman Art Library International:

    Gemaeldegalerie Alte Meister, Kassel, Germany, © Museumslandschaft Hessen Kassel: p. 13

    Musee des Beaux-Arts Andre Malraux, Le Havre, France, Giraudon: p. 16

    Delaware Art Museum, Wilmington, USA, Gift of Mrs Richard C. DuPont: p. 19

    Private Collection, Photo © Bonhams, London, UK: p. 24

    Private Collection, The Stapleton Collection: p. 27

    Egyptian National Museum, Cairo, Egypt: p. 29

    Private Collection, The Stapleton Collection: pp. 32-33

    Louvre, Paris, France: p. 35

    Bibliotheque Nationale, Paris, France, Giraudon: p. 40

    Yale Center for British Art, Paul Mellon Collection, USA: p. 54

    Private Collection: p. 61

    Private Collection, Ken Welsh: p. 65

    © Guildhall Art Gallery, City of London: pp. 68-69

    Private Collection, © Look and Learn: p. 75

    Private Collection, © Look and Learn: pp. 76-77

    Museo Nacional de Historia, Mexico City, Mexico: p. 79

# INDEX

Fremont, John C., 174
Fremont Street, Tombstone, Arizona, 185
French Revolution, 7–8, 136–151, 164
Frigidus, Battle of, 51
Fritigern, 49
Funston, Frederick W., 200–201, *201*, 202–203

G
Gage, Thomas, 121, 122, *123*, 123–125, 130, 134
Galba, General, 25
Galileo Affair, the, 98–115
Galileo Galilei, 9, 98–115, *99*
  *The Assayer*, 113–115
  biography of, 108–110
  *Dialogue on the Two Great World Systems*, 98, 100–101, 104–105, 108
  *Discourses on Two New Sciences*, 108, 115
  family of, 109–110
  legacy of, 115
  *Letters on the Sunspots*, 110
  *Letter to the Grand Duchess*, 110–111
  *Starry Messenger*, 113
  trial of, *102–103*, 104–105, 107, 115
Gallatin, Missouri, 156, 163–164
Gamba, Marina, 109–110
Gaugamela, Battle of, 246, *252–253*, 254–256
Gaul, 25
Gaza, 30
*Geneva Dialogues*, 214

Genghis Khan, 246, *247*, 251, 256–259
genocide, 204
geocentrism, 98
Gepp, Herbert, 226, 227
Germanic tribes, 42–57
Germanicus, 19
Germany, 193, 204, 217–218. *See also* Prussia
Ghazni, Afghanistan, 260
Ghilzais, 261
Gibbon, Edward, 56
Gibson, Mel, 70
Gillis, Lester, 239
globalization, 251
Gnaeus Domitius Ahenobarbus, 19, 21
Goedsche, Herman, 215
gold, 82, 83, 85, 220–231
Golden House, 23, 25
Golden Quest, 228, 230
Golovinski, Mathieu, 217
Gorky, Maxim, 217
Gothic, 52
Goths, 42–57, *46–47*, *54*
  Christianization of, 52
  government of, 52–53, 55
  justice and, 55
  political system of, 52–53, 55
Governor's Foot Guard, 135
*goyim*, 206
Grassi, Horatio, 114
Graves, Phillip, 213–214
Grayfriars monastery, 71
Grayson, William, 199
Great Britain. *See* Britain
"Great Cause", 67, 70
Great Fire of Rome, *11*, 12–25, *13*

Greece, 246, 251
Greeks, 44–45
grenades, 127
grenadiers, 127, *132–133*, 134
Grijalva, Juan de, 82, 83
Guam, 192
guerilla warfare, 201–203, 250, 258
Gustavson, Nicholas, 167

H
Haiti, 85
Hancock, John, 126, 127
Hann, Mark, 192
Hanna, Mark, *194*
Hapsburgs, 81
Harding, 226, 228
Hattusas, 30
Hatusillus III, 38
Hawking, Stephen, 114
Hazaras, 249, 259
Head, Harry, 179, 181, 182
Hearst newspapers, 192
Heath, William, 134
"hedgehog" formation. *See* schiltrons
heliocentrism, 100, 111, 114, 115. *See also* Copernican theory
Helius, 24
Hengist, 55
Henry, Prince of Prussia, 195
Henry the Navigator, Prince, 85
Henry VII, King, 85
Herat, Afghanistan, 254, 259
Hercules, 17
heroes, 8–9
Heywood, Joseph, 167, 169

hieroglyphs, 31

*Hightland Laddie*, 131

Hillel, 23

Himalayas, 248, 249, 259. *See also* Hindu Kush mountain range

Hindu Kush mountain range, 248, 249, 251, 254, 255, 259

Hispaniola, 82, 83, 85, 96

Hitler, Adolf, 7, 204, 211, *216*, 217, 218

Hittites, 6, 28, 30, 31, 32, 33, 34, 36–37, 38

Hoffman, John, 237

Holliday, Doc, 172–173, 176, *177*, 178, 179, 181–187

Holliday, John Henry. *See* Holliday, Doc

Holliday, Melanie, 178

Holocaust, the, 6, 204, 218

Holy Brotherhood, 217

Holy Scriptures, 98, 100, 111, 113, 208

Hong Kong, 194, 195, 196

Honorius, 42

Hoover, J. Edgar, 8, 232, 235, 236, 237, 239, 240, 242, 244, *245*

Horemheb, 30

Horsa, 55

Horus, 28–41

Hotel des Invalides, 138

Houffbauer, Theodor Josef Hubert, *140–141*

House of Canmore, 66

House of Passage, 17

Howard, Robert E., 45

Hubert, Robert, *16*

hubris, 39

Huguenots, 145

Hundred Years War, 139

Huns, 48–49, 51

Hussein, Saddam, 261

## I

Iberia, 85. *See also* Portugal; Spain

Iberians, 51

Illyricum, 51

imperialism, 192–193

Inalchuq, 257, 258

Inca Empire, 85

India, 85, 249, 251, 256, 259, 260, 261

Indiana, 232, 235, 243

Indian Ocean, 85

Indians. *See* Native Americans

Indian Territory, 173

Indonesia, 85

Inquisition, the, 101, 115

Insurrectos, 196, 200, 202, 203. *See also* Philippine Insurrection

Iran, 256

Iraq, 250

I-Reed, 92

Isabella, queen, 81, 85

Islam, 199, 261, 265

Israel, 30

Israelites, 41

## J

Jacobins, 148

Jacobite rebels, 131

Jalalabad, Afghanistan, 260

James, Frank, 154, *155*, 156, 160, 161, 164, 166, 167

James, Jesse, 8–9, 154–172, *155*

as the American Robin Hood, 157–158, 169

biography of, 158

death of, 168–169

in popular culture, 157–158

James, Robert, 158, 160

James, Susan, 160

James, Zerelda, 156, 158–159, *160*, 160

James I, King, 77

James VI, King, 77

Jansenists, 140

"jayhawkers", 158

Jeffers, May, 243

Jefferson, Thomas, 55

Jesuits, 112–115

Jesus, 23, 56

Jews, 6, 204–219. *See also* Israelites

Jhelum River, 256

John I, King of Portugal, 85

John I, King of Scotland, 67, 70

John Paul II, Pope, 114

Johns, Paul, 220, *224–225*

Johnson, Samuel, 120

Joly, Maurice, 214–215, 217

Jordan, 30

Juárez, Catalina, 83

Juaristas, 164

Julia, 21

Julio-Claudian dynasty, 25

## K

Kabul, Afghanistan, 250, 254, 255, 260, *264*

Kadesh, 6, 28–41, *35*

Kadesh, Battle of, 8, 28–41, *35*

Kandahar, Afghanistan, 254

Kansas, 174, 201

Mantua, Italy, 145

Mao Zedong, 41

Marais quarter, Paris, 139

Marblehead, Massachusetts, 121

Marchioly, 145

Marcus, Josie, 174, 179, 187

Marcus, Sadie, 174

Margaret, "the Maid of Norway", 66, 67

Marie Antoinette, 145

Marina, 86–87, 93. *See also* La Malinche

Marjorie, Countess of Carrick, 63

Mark, 23

Marks, Paula Mitchell, 173

Marshall, H.E., *61*

Marxism, 261–262. *See also* Bolshevik Revolution

Massachusetts, 118–135

Masterson, Bat, 176, 179, 181, 187

Matthioli, Antonio Ercole, 145

Maya, 86

Mayans, 83, 86

McBridge, Angus, *76–77*

McGivern, ED, 186

McKellar, Kenneth, 239

McKinley, William, 195–196, 198

McLaury, Frank, 179, 182, 184, 185, 186

McLaury, Tom, 179, 183, 184, 185

McLaury brothers, 174, 178, 179, 182, 183, 184, 185, 186. *See also* Clanton-McLaury Gang

McMasters, Sherman, 187

"mechanic" spies, 121

Medici, Cosimo II de, 113

Medici, Giovanni de, 109

Mediterranean Sea, 85

*Melbourne Press*, 228

Mercer, Wisconsin, 237

Meredith, Victoria, Australia, 224

Merv, Afghanistan, 258

Mesopotamia, 38

Messalina, 21

Mexico, 78–97, *79*, 178, 182

Mexico City. *See* Tenochtitlán

Middle East, 6, 251

Middlesex, Massachusetts, 130, 131

Migration Period, 48

militias, 120, 122, 130, 131, 134–135

Miller, Ed, 169

Mindanao, Philippines, 199

Minutemen, 118, *119*

Missouri, 154, 156, 158, 160, 161, 163–164, 168

Missouri Compromise, 158

Mitchell, Margaret, 178

Mobeetie, Texas, 173

Moliére, 145

Mongols, 256–259

Monmouth, Duke of, 145

Monroe Doctrine, 192

Montesquieu (Charles-Louis de Secondat), 214

Montezuma, Emperor, 81, 87, *89*, 92–96

Mormon Church, 224–225

*Morning Post*, 213

Moroland, 199

Moros, 190, 192, 199

Moro War, 199

Morris, John, 237

Muhammed II, Shah Allah al-Din, 256–257, 258

mujahideen, 248

Muwatalli, 31, 32, 33, 37, 38

## N

Nahuatl, 86

Napolean Bonaparte, 39, 145, 214

Narváez, Pánfilo de, 93, 95, 96

Nash, Jay Robert, 239–240, 242–243

National Assembly (France), 151

Native Americans, 78–97, 122, 127, 134

NATO (North Atlantic Treaty Organization), 265

Naval War College, 193

Nazis, 218

Ne'arin, 36

Nebraska, 160

Negros, Madame, 148

Nelson, Baby-face, 239

Nelson, Josiah, 125

Neo-Nazism, 218

Nero, Emperor, 6–7, 11, 12–25, *13*, *19*

Neropolis, 18

Netherlands, 81, 193

New England, 118–135. *See also specific states*

Newfoundland, 85

New Hampshire, 121, 124

New Haven, Connecticut, 135

Newland, Simpson, 223

Newman, J. C., 239